Wellbeing in Politics

Series Editors
Ian Bache
Department of Politics
University of Sheffield
Sheffield, UK

Karen Scott
Exeter University (Cornwall Campus)
Penryn, UK

Paul Allin
Department of Mathematics
Imperial College London
London, UK

Wellbeing in Politics and Policy will bring new lenses through which to understand the significance of the dramatic rise of interest in wellbeing as a goal of public policy. While a number of academic disciplines have been influential in both shaping and seeking to explain developments, the Politics discipline has been relatively silent, leaving important theoretical and empirical insights largely absent from debates: insights that have increasing significance as political interest grows. This series will provide a distinctive addition to the field that puts politics and policy at the centre, while embracing interdisciplinary contributions. Contributions will be encouraged from various subfields of the discipline (e.g., political theory, comparative politics, governance and public policy, international relations) and from those located in other disciplines that speak to core political themes (e.g., accountability, gender, inequality, legitimacy and power). The series will seek to explore these themes through policy studies in a range of settings—international, national and local. Comparative studies—either of different policy areas and/or across different settings—will be particularly encouraged. The series will incorporate a wide range of perspectives from critical to problem-solving approaches, drawing on a variety of epistemologies and methodologies. The series welcomes Pivots, edited collections and monographs.

More information about this series at
http://www.palgrave.com/gp/series/15247

Charles Seaford

Why Capitalists Need Communists

The Politics of Flourishing

Charles Seaford
London, UK

Wellbeing in Politics and Policy
ISBN 978-3-319-98754-5   ISBN 978-3-319-98755-2   (eBook)
https://doi.org/10.1007/978-3-319-98755-2

Library of Congress Control Number: 2018951562

Cover design by Akihiro Nakayama

This Palgrave Macmillan imprint is published by the registered company Springer Nature
Switzerland AG
The registered company address is: Gewerbestrasse 11, 6330 Cham, Switzerland

Acknowledgements

I have had a great deal of help with this book—I couldn't have written it otherwise and I am enormously grateful. My biggest debts are to Ian Bache, Karen Scott and Paul Allin, who suggested I write the book in the first place, helped me shape the proposal and content of the book, and then provided extremely useful comments on the manuscript. Others who read and commented on the proposal and/or the manuscript and made useful comments include Harry Eyres, Rebecca Gibbs, Helen Goodman, Robin Hardie, Jennifer Holdaway, Tim Jackson, Fergus Lyon, Nicholas Seaford and Richard Seaford. I am also grateful to Helen Goodman, Tony Greenham, Dominic Houlder, Soulla Kyriacou, Neil Lawson, Troy Mortimer, Jonathon Porritt, Richard Rawlinson and Steve Waygood for providing introductions. Former colleagues at the New Economics Foundation, particularly Saamah Abdallah, Juliet Michaelson and Sam Thompson, helped shape my thinking on flourishing through numerous challenging and stimulating conversations and I am very grateful to them for that. Some parts of the book are based on my work for the Centre for Understanding Sustainable Prosperity and I am grateful to Tim Jackson for giving me the opportunity to work with him and others in this area and to Jakob von Uexkull for facilitating this. Finally, Helen was a wonderful source of ideas and encouragement throughout.

I also want to thank all those who agreed to meet me and gave their ideas and time freely while I was writing the book:

- Six politicians: Liam Byrne, Oliver Letwin, Ed Miliband, Jo Swinson, Liz Truss and David Willetts; also one special advisor.
- Two former officials: Nick Macpherson (former Treasury Permanent Secretary) and Gus O'Donnell (former Cabinet Secretary); also five current officials.
- Seven investment managers: David Blood (Senior Partner, Generation Investment Management), Elizabeth Corley (Vice-Chair, Allianz Global Investors), Alex Gilbert (Amber Infrastructure), Peter Michaelis (Lead Manager, Sustainable Investment, Lion Trust), Saker Nusseibeh (Chief Executive, Hermes Investment Management), David Pitt-Watson (formerly head of Hermes Focus Funds) and Steve Waygood (Head of Responsible Investment, Aviva Investors).
- Seven business managers: Mike Barry (Director, Plan A, Marks and Spencer), Chris Brown (Chief Executive, Igloo Regeneration), Nick Butler (formerly Group Vice President for Policy and Strategy Development, BP), Will Day (senior advisor, PricewaterhouseCoopers), Michael Holm Johansen (Chair, Arcus, and formerly President of Central and Southern Europe, Coca-Cola), Thomas Lingard (Global Director, Climate & Environment, Unilever), Mike Rake (at the time Chair, BT).
- Five management consultants: Loughlin Hickey (formerly Head of Tax, KPMG, Trustee of Blueprint), Troy Mortimer (UK Head of Sustainability and Responsible Investment, KPMG), Vincent Neale (Consultant), Richard Rawlinson (Consultant, former Partner, Booz & Co), Joss Tantram (Consultant, formerly at WWF).
- Six business school professors and business commentators: Robert Braun (Lauder Business School, Vienna), Jules Goddard (London Business School), Gay Haskins (formerly Saïd Business School), Andrew Hill (Management Editor, *Financial Times*), Dominic Houlder (London Business School), Colin Mayer (Saïd Business School).
- Twelve civil society leaders: Sarah-Jayne Clifton (Director, Jubilee Debt Campaign), Sarah Corbett (Director, The Craftivist Collective), David Goodhart (Head of Demography, Immigration and Integration, Policy Exchange), Mark Goyder (Founder and Trustee, Tomorrow's Company), Tony Greenham (Director of Economy, Enterprise and Manufacturing, RSA), Michael Jacobs (Director, IPPR Commission on Economic Justice), Gavin Kelly

(Director, Resolution Trust), Neal Lawson (Director, Compass), Nick Molho (Executive Director, Aldersgate Group), Frances O'Grady (General Secretary, TUC), Jonathon Porritt (Chair, Forum for the Future), Alison Tate (Director, Economic and Social Policy, International Trade Union Confederation).

- Four diplomats and international officials: Enrico Giovannini (Member of the Club of Rome, former Italian Minister for Labour and former Director of Statistics, OECD), Anthony Gooch (Director of Public Affairs and Communications, OECD), Ma Hui (Minister, Chinese Embassy), Fidel Narváez (Ecuadorian Embassy).

These individuals represented themselves, not their organisations, and were not intended to be a representative sample of the categories I have divided them into: this was not a qualitative research exercise. I spoke with people whom I thought would have something interesting to say, or who might themselves be members of the counter-elite one day. I should make clear that not all of them think of themselves in that way!

PRAISE FOR *WHY CAPITALISTS NEED COMMUNISTS*

"Charles Seaford clearly and intelligently articulates the challenges that the capitalist system is facing today and manages to thread together the thoughts of those (from both sides of the divide, so to speak) who can see this failure and wish to put the system back on a more sustainable tack. He weaves a plausible road map of how we can help heal our society. This is a must-read for politicians, professional investors and civil society activists who are looking to get a better understanding of the challenge facing us and a glimmer of an idea of how we can tackle it."
—Saker Nusseibeh, *Chief Executive, Hermes Investment Management*

"Speaking as one of what Charles Seaford describes as market liberals, I can say that I see absolutely no need for the new ideology he promotes in this book; but I can say with equal certainty that his thesis deserves to be debated, and that anyone with a serious interest in political ideas will find this book well written and highly stimulating."
—Oliver Letwin, *Conservative MP for West Dorset*

"Big moments, when we face both huge problems and opportunities, require big books about how we make the desirable feasible. *Why Capitalists Need Communists* meets the challenge of the moment by addressing key issues, not just posing the problem but offering answers. Charles Seaford has done the progressive community a great service."
—Neal Lawson, *Director, Compass*

"Free market capitalism is failing and ruling elites are losing their nerve. What better time for progressives to strike back? From workers on boards to resurgent trade unionism, this book signposts the way to a greener, fairer economy."

        —Frances O'Grady, *General Secretary, TUC*

CONTENTS

LIST OF FIGURES

Prologue: Why Capitalists Need Communists

While writing this book I met some capitalists—people responsible for very large sums of money invested in business, or with senior positions within those businesses, and who as a result live very comfortable lives. People like Elizabeth Corley, Vice-Chair of Allianz Global Investors, Mike Rake, at the time Chair of BT, and Saker Nusseibeh, Chief Executive of Hermes Investment Managers. I also met some 'communists'—they don't use that old-fashioned label any more, but that is what they are. People like Sarah-Jayne Clifton, who runs the Jubilee Debt Campaign, or Neal Lawson, who runs left think tank Compass. They are not members of the communist party or even Marxists, but they oppose the system and, like the communists of old, think we need more collective control of the means of production. Members of these two groups have quite different outlooks in predictable ways. But what they have in common is a belief that capitalism as we know it is broken, that things have to change, that things will either get better or worse, and that there are actions we can take to make them better. They also share a desire to make these actions happen, even if they don't quite know, let alone agree on, what they are. (Details of the people I met are listed in the Acknowledgements.)

The capitalists I met are not typical capitalists. I chose to meet some of those who want the system to change, rather than those who are simply trying to preserve the status quo. But what they said reflects a wider mood—so they told me, and so any one reading the press can observe:

they are the vanguard of a discontented class, and while they have opponents, and always will, the 'centre ground' of business has shifted. If they want to, these progressive capitalists can make the running.

And some of them do want to. They want the system they help to run to deliver social justice, prosperity and environmental sustainability. They recognise that it is not doing so now, but they think that it can. They also recognise that the game is almost up: the Brexit vote signalled that voters no longer buy the elite story; if things don't get better, they fear that the initiative may pass to what they think of as the extreme left. They think that the result would then be chaos, rather than constructive reform. Partly because of this, they are beginning to do things.

But what they are doing is not making as much difference as they might have hoped for. The changes are small and technical and will take time to have effect. The problem is large, and political, and is having effect now. The progressive capitalists are stuck. They may not see it like this, but they are trapped in a system that they cannot change on their own: the day job is demanding, the system is complex, and there is no master plan. You can change the system, but you cannot change it from the ground up: there are too many interlocking relationships that hold it in place. A study group here or a quango there cannot set in motion the sequence of changes that will make a significant difference.

The capitalists cannot up the pace on their own. On the other hand, they cannot simply hand over the problem to the politicians. There do need to be changes to the rules of the game, and these do have to be made by government, but politicians on their own simply lack the knowledge and confidence to identify and implement the measures that will make the difference. The two groups have to work together.

But this will not happen as things stand. The capitalists need to recognise the constraints created by their own privilege. Change requires passionate determination, time, energy and a streak of utopianism. These can only be provided by activists, who will act as the capitalists' conscience, push them to go further than they otherwise would, challenge them, organise—and help them accept and indeed ask for the structural changes that will make a better future possible. It is all too easy, when sitting in a plush office, to turn the big problems we face into intellectual puzzles, challenges that justify the existence of the intelligentsia, rather than seeing them as burning human issues, case studies of individual suffering that just *have* to be dealt with. I have worked for a left think tank and know that ideas on their own do not drive change. Only when they connect with the concerns of voters do they do so. It is ideas *and* suffering, linked together, that drives change.

The progressive Establishment's traditional political ally—the 'centre ground'—thought it knew what to do, and for years it managed the system in what appeared to be an effective way. However, it ran out of answers and now it has lost its power. Capitalism's problems mean the initiative is with the left of the Labour Party and the right of the Conservative Party. The trouble is, although the right have a plan of sorts, the left don't know what to do. They have no convincing theory and vision of change of the kind that put Lenin in power in 1917, or even of the kind that gave Attlee power in 1945. Some of them know that power matters, and because they think about power, they have won some small victories. The systemic change that they sometimes talk about remains quite beyond them.

Nonetheless, they have a great strength: they know humbug when they see it, they are happy to challenge the capitalists, and they are fired up to put right the injustices and stupidities of the world as they see them. What if they were to use this strength, and the critical intelligence it gives them, to work with the capitalists? What if they were to help them change the system? What if capitalist knowledge and 'communist' determination were brought together in the same room? What might happen then?

Ah, the reader says, but these two groups are on opposite sides. The capitalists don't really want to change the system, and the 'communists' are incapable of understanding it. Otherwise Momentum and Goldman Sachs would have formed a partnership already. And they haven't. Nice thought to bring them together, but completely absurd.

The argument of this book is that this is not absurd, and indeed it is necessary if we are to put the UK back onto a positive trajectory, and avoid the dystopian future that a projection of current trends suggests. This is not necessary simply because of Brexit, but it is all the more urgent because of Brexit and the debate it has provoked. Progressive capitalists may be a small minority, but in alliance with politicians and activists they can be very powerful. It is always when individuals from different walks of life co-operate that things happen. If they do so, they can form a counter-elite: a group that challenges the assumptions of the incumbent elite and helps bring about real change.

One reason this is possible is there is an emerging alternative to the orthodoxies that have sustained existing power structures for the last 40 years or so, orthodoxies that have prevented capitalists and communists from working together. Remarkably, that alternative has the power to improve the lives of the powerful as well as the powerless, to release them from a narrowness that is currently imposed on them. This alternative forms the subtitle of this book: 'The Politics of Flourishing'.

PART I

Why We Should Change

CHAPTER 1

Introduction

We are at a turning point: the orthodoxies that have dominated political and economic thinking since the 1980s are crumbling, and it is widely recognised that those orthodoxies won't help us solve the big problems we face. I will argue in this book that there is an emerging and coherent alternative, what I have called the 'politics of flourishing', and that members of an emerging counter-elite,[1] upon whom major change normally depends, may be ready to adopt this alternative. It is based on a new set of ideas and ideals that between them can provide the cohesion needed for action and change the terms of political debate.

The biggest of our big problems are climate change and inequality, both of which may worsen as the developing world becomes more prosperous. These and three other related problems—automation, the housing shortage and the rising cost of public services—are the starting point for this book. They are not our only big problems, and inequality in particular is a shorthand for a whole complex of social and economic issues. However, the test of any alternative to the current orthodoxy will be whether it can help solve these problems, and other pressing issues which cluster round them, such as threats to biodiversity, obesity, family breakdown and immigration.[i]

---

[1] See pages 19 and 79 for definition of counter-elite.

© The Author(s) 2019
C. Seaford, *Why Capitalists Need Communists,*
Wellbeing in Politics and Policy,
https://doi.org/10.1007/978-3-319-98755-2_1

MARKET LIBERALISM AND ITS BREAKDOWN

Inequality in particular has led to turbulent politics. The world is getting richer but the lives of many in Europe and the US have been getting worse—and even when they haven't been, people fear that they will. That is one of the reasons UK citizens voted for Brexit in 2016, one of the reasons they gave Labour its biggest vote share increase since 1945 in 2017, and one of the reasons they have become increasingly divided on immigration.[ii] In November 2016, the Americans elected Donald Trump. In France, radicals of the right and left, Marine Le Pen and Jean-Luc Mélenchon, attracted 41% of the vote between them in the first round of the 2017 presidential election. The winner, Emmanuel Macron, was successful because he presented himself as something new, and his party was indeed a new creation. In Germany, the far right AfD (*Alternative für Deutschland*) became the third largest party in the 2017 elections and entered the Bundestag for the first time with 90 seats. In Italy, the anti-establishment Cinque Stelle became the party with the largest number of votes (32%) in the 2018 elections and has formed a government with the right wing Lega.

Turbulence of this kind signals a breakdown, at least a temporary breakdown, of the deal between the elite— those with the most power— and the masses, the deal that is common to most democracies. 'Vote for us' say the politicians, 'accept our wealth' say the business leaders—'and we will deliver steadily improving lives for you and your children.' When the elite does not deliver on its part of the deal, it is hardly surprising that the masses decide the deal is off. As *Financial Times* correspondent Martin Wolf has put it, the "elites have failed" and "the durability of contemporary globalized capitalism cannot be taken for granted."[iii] The root of this failure is in the relationship between the state and capital, or more concretely in the relationships between members of the elite representing the state and members representing capital. It is this failure that leads to blocks of flats burning down, inequality and climate change. Much of this book is about what it will take to reform these relationships.

The orthodoxy that has dominated since the 1980s is *not* 'neoliberalism', the rabid adulation of markets that some extremists adopted and that became fashionable when Thatcher and Reagan were in power: a refusal to recognise market failure and injustice, a rejection of regulation and an insistence on business freedom. Rather it is a much more measured, rational and therefore beguiling system of thought shaped by neoclassical economics, that is the mainstream economic theory taught in universities. It is so much the orthodoxy that it doesn't have a universally agreed name, but I shall call it 'market liberalism.' In this view of the world, markets produce the best possible outcomes but only if their well-understood failures, including environmental externalities and various social injustices, are addressed; crucially, proponents of this view believe that these failures *can* be addressed through a combination of market regulation, tax and subsidy. Economists can advise politicians on the technical failures, and voters can send signals about unacceptable levels of injustice or poor public service. Provided politicians respond with appropriate policies, a virtuous circle should follow: markets will produce economic growth, while political action will ensure its proceeds are fairly shared, softening those social tensions which, for example in the 1970s, have held back growth in the past.

This approach has been shared by all governing parties, with minor modifications, and underpins the Treasury's formal guide to economic policy appraisal and evaluation, the Green Book.[2],[iv] When Tony Blair and Gordon Brown came to power in 1997, it felt for many like a fresh breath of air after the slow decline of John Major's government, and radical new policies were introduced on the constitution and public services. However, there was no significant change from the Major government's economic policy or from its fundamental stance on markets and the working of the economy. The Labour leadership felt that to depart from this was to invite certain political defeat—although the orthodoxy was so strong that they would not have known how to depart from it even had they wanted to.

But, to be fair, there was no reason why they should have wanted to. The traditional market liberal economic programme which they inherited was supremely optimistic and at least partly successful: the combination of free markets, clever economists and wise politicians had produced good outcomes and could be expected to continue to do so. The result

---

[2] It sums up the role of government in two sentences: "The rationale for intervention... can be based on ensuring markets work effectively e.g. ensuring pollution is accounted for by business, or to achieve distributional objectives e.g. to promote fair access to education. Alternatively, this could involve providing goods generally not provided by market mechanisms e.g. defence" (p. 12). The guide allows for "strategic objectives" other than the correction of market failure (p. 20), admits the importance of "health, relationships, security and purpose" to well-being (p. 23), admits the limitations of marginal analysis techniques (p. 28), but still defines economic efficiency as being obtained "when nobody can be made better off without someone else being made worse off" (p. 20).

was a particular style of politics, what I shall call the 'politics of consumption', with politicians' primary role being to raise living standards. For a Labour government this included raising the quality of public services. There were no enemies to threaten these standards, and so, according to the liberal prospectus, the process would ultimately lead to universal liberal democracy and a world where borders were irrelevant: the 'end of history' and a 'flat world', to paraphrase the titles of two books published in 1992 and 2005.[v]

We now know, of course, that this didn't happen. The consensus is that things are more complicated than was previously thought and that the approach to the economy must change. Nonetheless market liberalism remains the orthodoxy, and even its extreme variant, neoliberalism, is alive and well. The European Commission's main economic department, DG ECFIN, for example, continues to argue for less product and labour market regulation in the interests of higher business investment; these arguments depend on entirely tendentious assumptions. In a recent paper presenting the evidence for its recommendation, it did not consider whether there were any trade-offs, whether the costs to workers and consumers that might result from reduced regulation would be justified by the increased investment that would result. It just assumed that they would be. Nor did it assess whether the damaging effect on investment in some countries that it identified would have been less severe had all countries adopted similar tough regulatory standards. Again, it just assumed it would not have been.[vi]

Similarly, in France, Macron won the 2017 general election with a partly neoliberal programme and in September of that year he signed five decrees weakening employee protection under the Code du Travail. He has also promised significant budget and tax cuts, mainly benefiting the richest 10%. Meanwhile, as a *Washington Post* headline put it, "Don't let his trade policy fool you: Trump is a neoliberal."[vii] As the article goes on to explain, he is offering a "messy mix of free market fundamentalism and hyper-nationalistic populism," the latter mainly evident in increased spending on the military and border controls and some "mostly symbolic moves on trade." This similarity between the two men's economic policies (Macron also has his nationalist gestures, such as resisting foreign takeovers of French firms) is striking given the way they are often contrasted, but it is not really surprising: both men's attitudes were formed by successful careers in the more ruthless parts of capitalism. Trump inherited and built up his father's property business in New York.

Macron was employed by Rothschilds, the investment bank, where he worked on big corporate deals.[3]

There is an important difference between them, though. Macron has not abandoned the politics of consumption, the politics where there are no enemies. Trump *has* abandoned it, and has replaced it with what I shall call the 'politics of fear,' the politics where there *are* enemies and politicians' role is to protect citizens from them.[viii] The danger is that Macron's anti-egalitarian policies will strengthen proponents of those politics in France. One of his critics has put it thus: "All in all, it's a program nearly guaranteed to aggravate the problems at the heart of France's political crisis: unemployment, inequality, and poverty. These are the same forces driving growing numbers of French people to withdraw from politics altogether—or worse yet, cast ballots for the National Front."[ix]

For the National Front, like Law and Justice in Poland and Viktor Orbán's Fidesz in Hungary, are also proponents of the politics of fear, and offer their voters community and security. Unlike Trump, though, these European parties are not nationalist neoliberals. Law and Justice has implemented a generous welfare policy, and although Orbán cut taxes and employment protection, he is also attempting to reduce dependence on foreign capital and create jobs for the manual working class. There was a sharp increase in the monthly minimum wage in the second half of 2017.[x] Right-wing governments elected in 2017 in Austria and the Czech Republic are attacking the rights of immigrants, but have no plans to dismantle the generous welfare provisions in those countries. Indeed the appeal of these central European parties is partly as modern guardians of the welfare state, as introduced by social democrats in the West and communists in the East. This is then combined with an appeal similar to that of Trump, that is 'there are enemies out there, normally foreign, and it is the duty of politicians to protect citizens from them.' In a low growth economy, protection from enemies may be a more credible promise than sustained, rising living standards.

Like Trump, those campaigning for the UK to exit from the EU exhibited a mix of neoliberalism and nationalism. One faction, that has

---

[3] These included Nestle's $11.8 billion takeover of Pfizer's baby food business from which he personally made €2.8 million. Investment banking may seem more polite than the New York property market, but as Macron himself put it to *The Wall Street Journal*, the job was a form of prostitution and the skill was seduction.

emerged more strongly since the referendum vote was won, promised radical globalisation: the problem with Europe, they argued, was that it was not international enough, restricting global trade as it did. A rival faction played on nationalism: the problem with Europe, they argued, was that it was *too* international and infringed our national sovereignty. Vote for Leave, they promised, and at least you can belong to something of your own. Although the two factions did not pretend that they had a coherent programme, and even fell out quite seriously, they could well have united around a very traditional political tool: national sentiment as compensation for inequality. Indeed some Leave voters told pollsters that a fall in living standards was a price worth paying for independence, although this certainly wasn't a campaign message.[xi]

It is not, to repeat, that mainstream politics in Britain has been uncompromisingly neoliberal. The right and centre of the Labour Party and the left and centre of the Conservative Party were never neoliberals, but what I have called market liberals: they agreed that markets were almost always the best way of organising economic activity, but also that governments had to intervene in them, and that governments had to invest in public services. It was the failures of this model that created opportunities for stronger programmes on both right and left—the full-blooded neoliberalism of the resurgent Conservative right, and a reinvention of social democracy by Labour.

EXISTING LEFT ALTERNATIVES

Market liberalism has been resilient despite its failures, partly because of the absence of a left alternative until recently. I have already referred to Blair and Brown. Strangely, Macron was appointed Economics Minister in 2014 by his predecessor as president, François Hollande. What better signal of the complete bankruptcy of his socialist economic programme could there be? In 2009, Tony Judt wrote of the left, "we seem unable to conceive of alternatives" and characterised the attitude of the next generation as "'We' know something is wrong and there are many things we don't like. But what can we believe in? What can we do?".[xii]

This hanging question—what can we do?—reflected a damagingly wide gap between the morality and policy of social democracy, at least in the UK and USA. Policy had descended into pragmatism, compromise and a managerial response to inefficiency, and as Judt put it "we find it hard to look past those compromises to recall the qualities that informed progressive thought in the first place"—that is an ethical revolt against the inequity and materialism of the nineteenth century.[xiii] Arguably this failure itself reflected an organisational as well as an intellectual failure. As Jonathan Hopkin wrote in 2012:

> Market liberalism has become locked in precisely because of the weakness of parties, whose organizational decline provides party leaders with an incentive to delegate political power to technocratic institutions and to market actors.[xiv]

A clear-cut example of this delegation was Labour business minister Patricia Hewitt's 2002 reduction of ministers' powers to stop takeovers in the public interest. She argued that such decisions should be 'depoliticised' and left to the Competition Commission. To delegate in this way was precisely to sever the link between morality and policy, to reduce policy to managerialism.

But things have moved on since Hopkin wrote this. In 2018, we can be *a little* more optimistic about the Labour Party's organisational capacity—its membership almost doubled to 570,000 between summer 2015 and November 2017[xv] and this has helped reduce the grip of market liberalism on left policy thinking. As Conservative Chancellor of the Exchequer Philip Hammond lamented, "It's all very sad because for 35 years we had a broad consensus in British politics about our economic model...[whereas now] this model comes under renewed assault."[xvi] Jeremy Corbyn and Theresa May offered voters a real choice in the 2017 general election. Similarly no-one thought that Macron, Mélenchon and Le Pen were versions of the same thing any more than Clinton, Sanders and Trump were. Corbyn in particular has re-injected morality into the Labour Party positioning in a way that none of his predecessors could.

And this morality *is* linked to policy, is more than rhetorical, as an inspection of the economics section of Labour's manifesto at the 2017 general election reveals. While all parties might agree with its preamble that "the creation of wealth is a collective endeavour," the rhetoric was backed up by at least some policies that Conservatives would never contemplate. Labour promised, for example, to set up a national education service to transform adult education, to use public sector procurement and renewed trade union rights as part of a 20-point plan to improve employment security and conditions, to set up a network of regional development banks with a mandate to help deliver industrial strategy, to double the size of the cooperative sector, including setting up locally accountable energy cooperatives, to revive compulsory purchase powers, and to strengthen local rights to shape neighbourhoods in the face of developers. It is true that other parts of the policy package could have been in the Conservative manifesto as well—investment in infrastructure and encouraging innovation for example—and some of it seemed a little dated, even if popular—taking back railways into public ownership. However, anyone who read the manifesto would have felt that the slogan "the creation of wealth is a collective endeavour" did really mean something.[xvii]

At the same time the programme was designed not to appear especially radical—indeed some critics thought it was not radical enough, including former Cabinet Secretary Gus O'Donnell.[xviii] (One of the oddities of British politics is the way the right of the Labour Party seem desperate to have a leftist enemy: you wonder, when they criticise the leadership, whether they ever actually read the manifesto). Its moderation is particularly noticeable when compared with Mélenchon's manifesto produced for the French general election a couple of months earlier. He had promised to raise public spending by 275 billion euros a year over five years and introduce a 90% tax rate on incomes over 400,000 euros. He would have enforced the 35 hour limit on the working week, in effect increasing pay for overtime, and would have increased the minimum wage by 16%. His most radical policy was renegotiating key European Union neoliberal economic policies—failing which he would have called a referendum on membership.[xix]

Indeed, unlike Mélenchon's programme, or some of the rhetoric coming out of the left of the party, the 2017 Labour manifesto reads like a traditional social democratic programme, of the kind John Smith might have proposed had he survived and been leader in 1997. What distinguished it from Blair's manifestos was its emphasis on the active role that organisations other than conventional businesses could play in shaping the economy. These might be state institutions (a national education service, a network of regional banks, a nationalised railway), or worker-led institutions (trade unions and cooperatives), or local entities (responsible for housing and development). It also promised significant, costed increases in public spending.

While the morality and the policies of the manifesto were clear, the trouble was it lacked the bits in between: a vision of a better life based on that morality, and an analysis of contemporary challenges—inequality, climate change, the power of global capital—justifying those policies. It reads like what it was: traditional social democracy, rather than an account of how the contemporary world works and what is needed to change it. Social democracy was a triumph in its day, correcting as it did the defects of mid-twentieth-century capitalism, and massively improving the material conditions of the working class. However life has moved on, and so policy must move on, as even some close to the leadership admit. The 2017 manifesto wasn't radical because it didn't do this. To use the term George Monbiot used in his 2017 book *Out of the Wreckage*, there was no 'story', no picture of the better life and the path towards it which Labour was promising to take us on. (While this book was in production, in September 2018, the independent IPPR Commission on Economic Justice published a report setting out a 21st century version of social democracy, but the work is only just beginning.)

The principal left alternative to Corbyn's version of social democracy has been a form of localism, which *is* both radical and sometimes visionary. In this programme, while the state has to play an enabling or facilitating role, real change is effected when economic and political power is passed down to the lowest possible level.

So, on the economic front, while it is admitted that there are gains from trade, between countries and within countries, there are also gains from local self-sufficiency which traditional economic models fail to take into account, and which are therefore neglected by central decision makers. These include reduced inequality, increased resilience to shocks, lower environmental impact, greater social cohesion, and potentially increased job satisfaction. Given the nature of our economic and social problems, these are real benefits.[xx] This not an argument for local autarchy, just for factoring in these benefits when planning the economy, and for local, bottom–up initiatives such as the Transition Towns, a group of small-to-medium-sized towns where members of the community have taken a series of steps to increase self-sufficiency and quality of life and reduce environmental damage.

George Monbiot also argues in his book for the power of community projects as part of a new 'politics of belonging'.[xxi] Community groups are valuable, not just because they do valuable things, such as improving the local environment, running food banks and so on, and not just because they put pressure on local authorities, companies and governments to do valuable things. They also create a sense of belonging and purpose amongst their members, and in doing so help reverse the sad atomisation described, for the USA, in Robert Putnam's *Bowling Alone*.

It is not just leftists like Monbiot who celebrate localism. David Goodhart, an apostate from metropolitan liberalism, also emphasises the need for a revival of democracy, community and 'voice' for those who feel left behind.[xxii] The coalition government was behind Neighbourhood Planning, a system enabling community groups to stop—and occasionally shape—local development; Laura Sandys, a centrist former Tory MP has talked of 'turbo-charging' localism; and the Liberal Democrats have traditionally made this a central part of their platform. There is even a free market right version: public services run by autonomous organisations that are accountable to their users.

On the other hand, while localism in its various incarnations is fine as far as it goes, it is difficult to see how it amounts to an effective response to automation, rising inequality, the housing shortage, rising pressure on public services or climate change. It will improve some people's lives, but it does not even begin to address the structural drivers of the problems as they affect and will continue to affect most people. It is not clear that it is a credible 'story' in Monbiot's sense.

THE POLITICS OF FLOURISHING

The need for just such a credible political story, one that does describe the structural drivers of these problems and how they are to be overcome, is the reason for this book. In this story, we do indeed face problems which could lead to ever worsening lives. But this deterioration is not inevitable. Men and women of good will can work together, united by a vision of what they are trying to achieve. And if they do so, they will solve the problems and all our lives will get better.

The first of two central ideas in this book is that the vision uniting these men and women will be of a world in which people flourish. This vision underpins the 'politics of flourishing,' a politics where politicians compete to maximise flourishing—rather than competing, as they do now, to maximise consumption or to protect from enemies. This vision is the keystone for a coherent set of ideas that will replace market liberalism, social democracy and radical localism.

What is *Flourishing*? It is a state that has been quite precisely specified—both by moral philosophers and positive psychologists and I will describe it in detail in Chapter 3. At its heart is having a good relationship with the world in which you find yourself, and as a result feeling happy and in control of your own life. This relationship with the world encompasses both close and more distant personal relationships, but also work and non-work activities, how you feel you fit into society, and the self-esteem based on this, and, for want of a better phrase, your aesthetic experience, whether triggered by art, nature or religion. Individuals with good relationships of these kinds tend to feel happy and healthy. In short, it is the good life, as described through the centuries.

It is hardly controversial to say flourishing as just described is a good thing. The more contested issue is whether maximising it should be the ultimate goal of politicians. Should politicians try to ensure citizens have good lives, and if they should, should we equate a good life with a flourishing life?[4] It is possible to answer 'no' to both these questions, and I will return to this in Chapter 3. I won't prove that 'no' is the wrong answer, and instead will have to rely on the reader's intuitions: do the alternatives to good lives and to flourishing appeal more or less?

But even if flourishing is the ultimate objective, does making it an explicit goal help? Is it useful? Why not focus on some well-established routes to better lives, for example maximising consumption and security? Alternatively, why not just work out what is causing our big five problems and develop policies accordingly?

The simplest answer is that if we make flourishing an explicit goal, we will more easily escape the mental constraints that got us into this mess in the first place. A wealthy society such as the UK has the material resources needed for most of its members to flourish in the way just described, but it is not organised to ensure that they do. Therefore, if we want people to flourish and be happy, we should switch some of our attention away from increasing those material resources and towards improving the way society is organised. It is not that increasing material resources is valueless, just that its relative importance can be exaggerated. Making flourishing an explicit goal helps us think about how to reorganise.

We will see later in the book that tackling the big five problems requires us to plan and to redistribute. Planning requires us to have some guiding principles, so that the planners are not simply doing as they please. And redistribution also requires us to have some guiding

---

[4]The term 'well-being' is used in several ways in the literature and in public discourse. In this book I use it in two ways: first, in an entirely abstract sense, to refer to the state produced by living a good life whatever that may be ('good life' is also a neutral term), and in Chapter 3 to refer to the state that is measured in subjective well-being surveys, typically including questions such as 'how satisfied with your life overall are you?' 'Flourishing' refers to a particular form of well-being in both senses.

principles, so that the relevant measures acquire the necessary legitimacy. Making flourishing an explicit objective of policy helps to provide these principles. For example, a central issue raised by automation is what mix of increased free time and increased consumption we should be aiming for. This has to be a collective decision, partly because of the way labour markets work, and partly because the outcome is affected by tax and benefit rules. Any collective decision should be informed by what we know about the kinds of consumption and the kinds of leisure that contribute to flourishing. A central issue raised by inequality is how much inequality to tolerate: this should be informed by what we know about the ways in which income and equality contribute to flourishing. The housing shortage can only be addressed through forms of planning: these should be guided by what we know about the contribution of housing, and the built environment more generally, to flourishing. Decent public services and addressing climate change are going to cost more money than we currently spend on them. Creating the necessary public support for this will require public debate, which is only likely to be effective if it is well informed, including by considerations of what is necessary for flourishing. This, in turn, is only likely if it has become part of the political discourse.

The set of ideas about flourishing that I begin to set out constitute an *ideology*, just as market liberalism, social democracy and localism are ideologies. The term 'ideology' is variously defined, but I am using it here in a descriptive rather than evaluative sense.[xxiii] I mean a view of how society should and does work, shared and propagated by a group, and which cements the power of that group (it may or may not also promote the interests of that group). It performs this role both by facilitating cooperation within the group, and by legitimising its actions more widely. It promotes both values ('free markets are good') and purported facts ('state intervention doesn't work').[xxiv] Amongst subscribers to the ideology, values and facts about the social world are often entwined: facts shape values, and values influence which facts are seen as significant, and how they are interpreted and generalised. This can be dangerous, as when facts are simply denied or made up, or oversimplified generalisations are taken literally (as in the example of state intervention not working). However, it is difficult to know what entirely value-free fact selection would look like.

I will argue that the ideology of flourishing can guide and legitimise the planning and redistribution needed to address the five problems, and give cohesion to those involved. In doing so, it will not just provide objectives, it will also help bring about change. Apart from anything else, it opens up the terms of political debate, from how best to manage a given economic system to how best to deliver good lives, with all the radical implications this may have. It is because it can be effective in this way, as well as attractive, that it can replace the ideologies underpinning the politics of consumption, and help pre-empt the further rise of the politics of fear already adopted by Trump, Le Pen, several Eastern European leaders and some Brexit champions.

CHANGE, ELITES AND COUNTER-ELITES

Change requires more than the capture of power by the leaders of a radical political party. Had Labour won in 2017, Corbyn and his Chancellor John McDonnell would not necessarily have been the 2017 equivalent of Thatcher or Reagan after 1980, both of whom initiated very effective reform programmes. They might well have ended up being the 2017 equivalent of Mitterrand or Hollande, both of whom were forced to abandon their programmes, Mitterrand after 2 years and Hollande after 6 months. For while the modern left may have recovered its moral purpose, it is not at all clear that it yet has a theory of power, of what it takes to make things happen. It is not just that there is no vision of the good life embedded in the manifesto. It is also that there is no clear view of how the world works and therefore what it will take to change it. Some at the heart of the party appear to think that winning the next election will be enough—that there is no real problem with implementation or securing lasting change. Others on the left fantasise that there is a symmetry between the reassertion of free market economics in 1980 and the arrival of a new leftist paradigm now.[xxv] In 1980, Thatcher and Reagan took on and challenged many of their civil servants and their public sectors, but their reforms suited powerful individuals in business and finance. They did not have to take on the capital markets as well, and they had the active support of many industrialists. Corbyn and McDonnell do not have these advantages.

The closest much of the left seems to have to a theory of power is the emphasis that Naomi Klein and others have put on 'bottom–up' movements. "Trump's disaster capitalists," Klein writes in her recent book *No is Not Enough*, "do not control what we do as individuals and in groups around the world," meaning that "we" can take the initiative and ensure the world changes course: "the people's platforms are starting to lead – and the politicians will have to follow."[xxvi] She goes on to argue that this people's leadership depends on a powerful streak of utopianism. Change happens, she suggests, after "crises that unfolded in times when people dared to dream big, out loud, in public – explosions of utopian imagination." Change did not happen after capitalism's 2007–2008 crisis precisely because this capacity for imagination had atrophied. As a result, the "wave of protest and occupations did not produce a fundamental change in the economic model." The task now is to develop this utopian thinking—giving both people and politicians the confidence needed to make big change happen.[xxvii]

Utopian thinking has indeed played an important part in periods of real social change. It has been described as "the education of desire,"[xxviii] with the power to disrupt habit and break down consent, a spur to action. The sense of an unstoppable force driving us towards a better future has motivated revolutionaries in all the major European revolutions.[xxix] This book, too, has a streak of utopianism in it. Klein and others are right to insist that the intellectual development of a new policy framework is hardly enough to bring about real change, to ensure that the turning point we have reached really does lead somewhere. That may be necessary, but it is not sufficient. Power is not exercised in seminar rooms. What is more, while the grassroots Occupy movement may not have delivered policy solutions, it did help create the conditions for Bernie Sanders' presidential bid—and he might have won. It is also true that the grassroots Indignados in Spain foreshadowed the rise of new radical party Podemos, which won 21% of the vote in the 2015 elections. The Greek anti-globalisation and anti-Iraq war movement contributed to the formation of Syriza in the early 2000s.

However if, as she argues, "no is not enough," then utopia is not enough either. Of course we need inspiration, but there is a danger, long identified by progressives and famously by Marx, that dwelling on the vision will divert emotional and intellectual energy from the task in hand, from the 'how' as opposed to the 'what'. Kate Raworth is the author of a successful book on the need to address environmental and social challenges, with the catchy title *Doughnut Economics*. She herself puts at least some of its success down to its silence on the 'how': "It… sets a vision for an equitable and sustainable future" she writes on her website, "but is silent on the possible pathways for getting there, and so the doughnut acts as a convening space for debating alternative pathways forward."ˣˣˣ Similarly, Klein does not say what the fundamental change in the economic model we want to see really amounts to, or how the resulting economy would work, or, more importantly, how the transition will come about once utopians have demanded it. She and a group of social movement leaders prepared a manifesto during the 2015 Canadian general election containing a list of desiderata—more superfast trains, a universal basic income, investment in renewables, a shift of resources to care, teaching, the arts, more localised agriculture and so on—and not surprisingly, perhaps, opinion polls showed many voters warmed to it.ˣˣˣⁱ There is absolutely nothing wrong with this list, and some of the proposals, for example the universal basic income, could have a profound effect. Many of the practicalities are well worked out. However, the question jumps out: what's the idea behind this list? What's the theory of how the world works? It hardly amounts to an alternative to the well-developed orthodoxy based on neoclassical economics that threatens to underpin a shift back to the right. It would not have helped the radical left government formed in 2014 by Syriza in their struggle against the constraints imposed by existing power structures, both within and beyond Greece's borders, that have frustrated its plans. Nor would it have helped the Italian insurgents backed by Cinque Stelle, who won mayoral elections but who have not been able to effect the kind of changes their supporters had hoped for. It is not even as thought through as the Labour Party manifesto. Naomi Klein has argued that capitalism needs fundamental reform if we are to address climate change.ˣˣˣⁱⁱ Does she really think that bottom–up utopianism will defeat Exxon by itself?

Monbiot, in *Out of the Wreckage,* draws on an account of the 2016 American Democratic Party primary campaign by two Sanders staffers, and describes how Sanders's 'story' about the need for and possibility of radical change enthused a mass army of activists.ˣˣˣⁱⁱⁱ They then went on to use 1:1 telephone conversations to convert a large number of voters. This combination of grassroots campaigning and radical political narrative was almost successful. Meanwhile, community projects—in this case his focus is the UK—can both improve people's lives directly, and foster the civic consciousness that underpins this kind of successful mass activism.

Monbiot is convincing so far as he goes, and numerous commentators have pointed out that social media has made it easier for radical narratives to bypass the mainstream press. This is widely thought to explain, at least in part, Labour's relative success in 2017. However, we need to bear in mind that Sanders was leading a presidential campaign with a single very effective message relayed very effectively to the voters through a highly disciplined if voluntary machine. This was effective 'top–down' organisation because it engaged volunteers well.[5] And indeed Monbiot doesn't deny the role of leadership. Perhaps even more important, what Monbiot describes was an exercise in gaining power, not exercising it. Had Sanders won he would have needed more than enthusiastic volunteers and community projects to outwit Exxon.

Nick Srnicek and Alex Williams, in their 2016 book *Inventing the Future*, labelled the reliance on small-scale action favoured by many on the left as "folk-political thinking."[xxxiv] They blame much progressive failure on the preference radical activists seem to have for the tactical rather than strategic, the voluntarist rather than institutional, the inherently local rather than scalable and the ethical rather than political. They characterise this set of attitudes as withdrawal in the face of complexity, rather than an attempt to build a 'counter-hegemony' to neoliberalism. The result is grassroots *resistance*, and as they put it, "we do not resist a new world into being; we resist in the name of an old world."[xxxv] Even when the grassroots are networked, they cannot dislodge the existing hegemony.

Indeed, simply forming social networks of the powerless has never worked, whether to bring about revolution or drive incremental but significant change. Sometimes, the grassroots have helped bring about revolutionary change, for example during the French, Russian and Chinese revolutions, in Eastern Europe in 1989, and arguably in Tunisia in 2011. But in all these cases the role of elite groups was also critical: highly educated professionals who for one reason or another were excluded by the incumbent elite from fulfilling roles within the existing power structure and were ready to step in and take over. In Britain, there has been no revolution, but between the 1860s and 1940s very significant change nonetheless. The Labour Party was originally an entirely working class-led party, but this change came about because of an effective coalition between the working class and members of the progressive middle class who played this elite role. Until the 1920s most of the latter may have been members of the Liberal Party but from the 1920s onwards, the Labour Party itself was the vehicle for this coalition.

[5] The Sanders campaign is often contrasted with the top–down Clinton campaign. The problem with Clinton's campaign was precisely that it wasn't top–*down*: it was just top.

A second central idea of this book is that if the turning point we seem to be at is going to lead anywhere, we will need to see changes within the composition and thus attitudes of the elite, that is amongst those who exercise significant amounts of power over society.[6] Incumbent elites do not change of their own accord, though, so these changes require the emergence of a *'counter-elite.'* In addition, the counter-elite has space to emerge because of the *weakening of incumbent elite morale*; it is only effective because it forms *alliances with the people*; and it actually does something because it is held together by *a strong ideology*. Since we are not in a revolutionary situation, it will be made up of insiders and outsiders: disaffected members of the incumbent elite, and leading opponents of the system. I will argue that the potential for such a group already exists, and that feasible but significant changes to financial and democratic structures can turn potential into reality. Some on the left resist the idea of a counter-elite—I have heard their arguments—but their denial is similar to the modern denial of class: useful to the powerful and comforting to the powerless.

The elite is sometimes referred to as 'the Establishment.' The term was made popular by journalist Henry Fairlie, in an article for the *Spectator* in 1955.[xxxvi] He defined it as a "matrix of official and social relations within which power is exercised." To use the term as he defined it is to highlight this relational source of the elite's power; Fairlie himself did not give it the strongly pejorative connotation it came to have, with its members seen as a self-serving group, resisting all change. The Establishment was important at the time he was writing, he claimed, because "power in Britain…is exercised socially." In fact power everywhere is exercised socially to a greater or lesser extent, making Fairlie's definition still useful now. The counter-elite, as just defined, will, in time, come to form a 'new Establishment,' that is to say a set of individuals with social relations who use these relations to exercise power. They will do this to defend their material interests but also to project their view of the world, to reinforce their shared sense of meaning and purpose.

But it is not just individuals and their connections that bring about an 'Establishment' of this kind. What makes it possible for the individuals to use their connections is a degree of cohesion, traditionally perhaps the result of family and class loyalty, in the 1950s connections formed

---

[6]This is an easy definition, but begs the question where the boundary of the elite lies. This, and the concept of the counter-elite, is explored in Chapter 4.

at school or during the war, but sometimes the result of a more explicit shared ideology, as just defined. Either way, they are effective because their relations establish shared norms, values, and expectations and so make shared projects feasible; they have sufficient sense of what is needed to coordinate, without conscious effort, the myriad actions required for the exercise of power.

Fairlie was writing when the traditional Establishment seemed to be in a state of decay—the dukes and the bankers and the Conservative MPs he described represented an old England that a group of 'new' men who had fought together in the war were displacing. As we will see in Chapter 5, these new men (and a few women), the founders of new universities and new towns, may or may not have originally been part of the old elite, but either way their attitudes and behaviour became consciously 'counter' to those of the old elite. They formed a 'counter-elite' and in due course came to form a new Establishment. Twenty-five years later that generation itself seemed to have lost impetus, and a second group self-consciously distant from the Establishment and this time revolving around international business came to prominence. It then formed a second new Establishment. In other words, on two occasions in recent British history when the country seemed to have reached a dead end (late 50s to early 60s and late 70s to early 80s), a new group emerged with sufficient cohesion to take over from the incumbents, define the terms of public debate and make things happen. In both cases, the incumbents were seen to be failing to address the big social challenges. In both cases, political actors formed alliances with other members of the new elites to challenge the incumbents and introduce a new 'politics', in one case associated with Wilson's 'white hot heat of technology', in the other with Thatcher's return to markets.

Now the current incumbents are failing in the same way, with the underlying economic problems they have created exacerbated by the fiasco of Brexit. Again there is an opportunity for a counter-elite to emerge and take over, and in due course to form a 'new' Establishment unified by an ideology, in this case the ideology of flourishing. From day to day, the distinction between elite and counter-elite will not be clear-cut in this way—and it was not that clear-cut in the late 50s or the late 70s either; but this is the pattern underlying seemingly random events which may be more obvious from a distance. As in the 50s and the 70s, there is almost universal recognition that change is needed.[xxxvii]

Who are these people? Who will form this new Establishment? Their social origins will be more diverse than in the 1950s, or indeed than in the 1980s—not difficult—and they will be prominent in diverse walks of life. To the extent that they are effective, they will form a network, stretching between government, business, the professions, public services, international organisations, the media and academia, trade unions and NGOs. As such, considerable resources will be at their disposal—but of course there is no formal or informal organisation or programme coordinating this. Likewise, their motives will be diverse: the balance between protecting interests and projecting a view of the world varies from individual to individual. They will also need to work with others beyond the elite if they are to achieve change, as counter-elites that have achieved change have done in the past. Everyone agrees that top-down planning, if it is out of touch with the values and concerns of 'ordinary' people, simply won't work, and, as we will see, the counter-elite needs radical outsiders to push the agenda. Capitalists need communists.

**

The rest of the book is structured as follows.

The rest of this part, 'Why We *Should* Change', consists of a single short chapter providing a brief account of the five problems already referred to, of the dystopia that will result if we fail to solve them, and of the utopia that can result if we do solve them.

Part II is about 'Why We *Can* Change'. Chapter 3 describes what the ideology of flourishing is, and why it will help address the problems set out in Chapter 2. It includes the ethical basis for the concept, the way in which the well-being evidence can be used, and the advantages the resulting ideology has over market liberalism, social democracy and radical localism.

Chapters 4 and 5 are about how change has happened in the past. Chapter 4 covers revolutionary and non-revolutionary episodes, how elites sustain their power in normal times, and the role of ideology. In Chapter 5, I look in more detail at two episodes of change in Britain since the Second World War, and at the emergence of two counter-elites, as summarised above. The two chapters suggest four conditions which may be important in bringing about change in Britain now: the existence of a new ideology, however loosely defined; the decay of the incumbent elite's ideology and a resulting loss of confidence; the emergence of a counter-elite; and an alliance between this counter-elite and the wider population.

Chapter 6 describes decay within the incumbent elite: the bankruptcy and loss of belief in its ideology and the disaffection of some of its members. In the final part of the chapter, I assess the extent to which a counter-elite has emerged or is ready to emerge and form alliances. This has not happened, but the door is half open and can be pushed by radicals.

Part III is about '*How* We Can Change.' Chapters 7 and 8 cover policies addressing the five problems that need to be guided by the ideology of flourishing. Chapters 9 and 10 cover the structural changes needed to make the policies feasible, and that will also catalyse the emergence of a counter-elite.

Chapter 7 is about planning and Chapter 8 is about redistribution. Planning is needed to create good jobs, to build decent homes and to deliver the research and infrastructure needed to address climate change. It requires a more active form of government than we are used to, and a closer partnership between government and business than currently exists. Redistribution is needed to address existing inequality and to ensure that the gains from automation are shared fairly, whether in the form of extra consumption or extra leisure. It is also needed to ensure adequate public services and to pay for climate change mitigation. It requires normative changes, which in turn requires skilful design of mechanisms and structures.

Chapter 9 is about why structural change is needed: it describes the limits of the existing system, of what can be done in the absence of structural change. These limits are those of 'ethical capitalism' on the one hand, and of negotiation between different interests on the other. Chapter 10 sets out proposals for the structural change Chapter 9 suggests is needed. These may not have been feasible in the past, but are very feasible now. They include changes to the way the investment industry operates, to corporate governance, and to democracy.

The book concludes with an epilogue in which I summarise the argument of the book, and appeal to readers, whether insider or outsiders, to take part in the change. The insiders, the members of the Establishment, the 'capitalists' who say the system needs changing, cannot themselves change it: they are locked in. They need to work with radicals, the outsiders, the 'communists,' to change the structures and set us on a new path. Apart from anything else, this is in their own self-interest: they will almost certainly retain most of their privileges in a new world (people like them always do); on the other hand if things don't change, life is going to get very stressful. And the communists need to accept the invitation when it is forthcoming, because on their own, from the outside, without the power that comes with inside knowledge of the system, connections, money, position, there is very little they can do.

Notes

i. For the rising salience of inequality, see the World Economic Forum Global Risks Report 2017, https://riskcenter.wharton.upenn.edu/publications/global-risks/. In Britain the two problems that concern most people most are immigration and the state of the National Health Service. https://www.indy100.com/article/these-are-the-biggest-issues-in-the-uk-according-to-the-public--Z1GbiQX4Tx.
ii. UK respondents to the *European Social Survey Wave 1* (2002) and *Wave 7* (2014), quoted in *British Social Attitudes* 34 (2017).
iii. Martin Wolf, *The Shifts and the Shocks* (2015), p. 382.
iv. H.M. Treasury, *The Green Book: Central Government Guidance on Appraisal and Evaluation* (2018).
v. Francis Fukuyama, *The End of History and the Last Man* (1992), and Thomas Friedman, *The World is Flat: A Brief History of the Twenty-First Century* (2005).
vi. European Commission, *Investment in the EU Member States: An Analysis of Drivers and Barriers* (2017), p. 23
vii. https://www.washingtonpost.com/posteverything/wp/2017/03/22/dont-let-his-trade-policy-fool-you-trump-is-a-neoliberal/?utm_term=.10e8f80d0246.
viii. Tony Judt uses the phrase in *Ill Fares the Land* (2010), p. 217, but argues that "if social democracy has a future it will be as a social democracy of fear" (p. 221), a defence against the breakdown of liberal society.
ix. Cole Stangler, 'The Trouble with Macron', *Dissent* (April 2017), https://www.dissentmagazine.org/online_articles/french-election-trouble-with-emmanuel-macron-centrism.
x. https://tradingeconomics.com/hungary/minimum-wages.
xi. https://www.ft.com/content/1b636ba8-76b3-11e7-a3e8-60495fe6ca71.
xii. Tony Judt, *Ill Fares the Land* (2010), pp. 2–4.
xiii. Ibid., p. 151.
xiv. Jonathan Hopkin, 'Cartel Parties and the Crisis: Political Change and Ideological Stasis in Advanced Democracies' (2012), http://personal.lse.ac.uk/hopkin/HopkinCES%202012.pdf.
xv. https://labourlist.org/2017/12/a-snap-election-a-new-leader-in-scotland-and-a-staggering-rise-in-membership-alice-perrys-latest-nec-report/.

xvi. Speech at the Conservative Party Conference (October 2017).

xvii. The Labour Party, *For the Many, Not the Few: The Labour Party Manifesto 2017.*

xviii. Gus O'Donnell, conversation with the author.

xix. https://www.ft.com/content/7fa14c80-fdd1-11e6-96f8-3700c5664d30.

xx. Many of these advantages have been elaborated by the New Economics Foundation (NEF), http://neweconomics.org/.

xxi. George Monbiot, *Out of the Wreckage* (2017).

xxii. David Goodhart, *The Road to Somewhere: The New Tribes Shaping British Politics* (2017).

xxiii. Terry Eagleton, *Ideology* (1991).

xxiv. The *Oxford English Dictionary* defines ideology as "A System of Ideas and Ideals, Especially One Which Forms the Basis of Economic or Political Theory and Policy".

xxv. Conversations between author and Labour Party advisors.

xxvi. Naomi Klein, *No Is Not Enough* (2017).

xxvii. Ibid., pp. 217 and 209.

xxviii. Ruth Levitas, *The Concept of Utopia* (2010).

xxix. Crane Brinton, *The Anatomy of Revolution* (1938, rev. ed. 1965).

xxx. https://www.kateraworth.com.

xxxi. Naomi Klein, *No Is Not Enough* (2017).

xxxii. Naomi Klein, *This Changes Everything: Capitalism vs. the Climate* (2014).

xxxiii. George Monbiot, *Out of the Wreckage* (2017).

xxxiv. Nick Srnicek and Alex Williams, *Inventing the Future: Postcapitalism and a World Without Work* (2015).

xxxv. Ibid., p. 47.

xxxvi. Henry Fairlie, 'Political Commentary,' *The Spectator* (23 September 1955).

xxxvii. The World Economic Forum, *Global Risks Report 2017*, https://risk-center.wharton.upenn.edu/publications/global-risks/.

CHAPTER 2

Dystopia and Utopia

"In the past, everything was worse." So begins best-selling author Rutger Bregman's recent book *Utopia for Realists.* "Welcome," Bregman continues, "to the Land of Plenty. To the Good Life, where almost everyone is rich, safe and healthy." Then he goes on, "The real crisis of our times, of my generation, is not that we don't have it good, or even that we might be worse off later on. No, the real crisis is that we can't come up with anything better."

Bregman is Dutch and perhaps the Netherlands is indeed the Land of Plenty. He should visit a food bank in a poorer part of Britain some time. Or talk to an office cleaner in London, working and travelling between jobs and home all the hours God gives. Or talk to young people who can't find anywhere to live, or to old people suffering the indignities of residential care on the cheap. The problems we face are not abstract, intellectual puzzles that well-meaning radicals pick on in order to give their lives meaning. The crisis is not that we have no reason to get out of bed in the morning. The crisis is that while for some this is a land of plenty, others are living miserable lives. Worse, the reasons they are living miserable lives are going to persist, and even more people may end up living miserable lives in the future unless we do something about them.

Bregman is right, though, that we do need to come up with something better. We do need a utopia to guide and inspire us. In this chapter, I will contrast very briefly a utopia with the dystopia that current trends are leading us towards, and in Chapter 3 I will describe the

C. Seaford, *Why Capitalists Need Communists,*
Wellbeing in Politics and Policy,
https://doi.org/10.1007/978-3-319-98755-2_2

underlying thinking in much more detail. But let us not forget that the problems we face are not problems of ideas and thinking, but problems of individual lives.

In this chapter, I also describe five of these problems: inequality, the housing shortage, automation, the rising cost of public services and climate change. Much of the rest of the book is about how to solve these problems, and the contribution that an ideology based on flourishing will make.

Problems

Rising inequality has several manifestations. First, the gains from growth have been appropriated by those who don't need them, that is by the top 1% and to a lesser extent the top 10%. In the UK, the top 1%'s share of total income after tax and benefits rose from 3% in 1978 to 5.8% in 1990 to 8.6% in 2015.[i] Second, median hourly wages have stagnated despite continuing economic growth: in 2017 they were scarcely higher than they were in 1997, even though the economy grew by 30% in this period. This is not just because of the post-crash recession: they rose by just 12% between 1997 and 2008, during which time the economy grew by 24%.[ii] And finally there is the growth in relative poverty: the proportion of those living on less than 40% of the median income after housing costs rose from 2% in 1978, to 7.5% in 1990 to 9.6% in 2017.[iii]

There is evidence that rising insecurity for all but the most fortunate has had an even more damaging impact on well-being. This insecurity is manifest in wealth inequality, the difficulty young people have in buying a home and the consequent rise in the number of short-term rentals, and most starkly in increasing membership of the precariat, that is those dependent on insecure, badly paid casual work.[iv] The share of wealth owned by the bottom 50% was just 8% in 2017.[v] The proportion of people living in the private rented sector has risen from 11% in 1980 to 20% in 2015/16,[vi] partly because of the decline of social housing, but also because home ownership has been falling since 2005.[vii] Only 2.8% of the workforce were working zero hours contracts for their main job in the summer of 2017, but this was five times the percentage in 2010. Insecure, low-paid jobs, of which these are the tip of the iceberg, produce even more stress and mental ill-health than unemployment.[viii]

One caveat. Despite these statistics, the most widely used measure of income inequality, the Gini coefficient, may appear to tell a different story. This, and various other measures of inequality, rose in the 1980s, stabilised from 1990 and has been falling slowly since 2008. It takes into account differences in income at all levels: there has been less inequality at *middle* levels of income and, as measured by the Gini, this has outweighed the increases in inequality at the extremes.[ix]

One major driver of inequality is *rising house prices* in London and other hot spots such as Oxford, Southampton and Bristol. This was the number one issue in the London mayoral election in 2016 and some commentators think it will be the number one issue at the next general election.[x] The problem is not a physical shortage of land: only 6% of Britain is built on.[xi] Moreover—and perhaps more relevantly given that we do not want to concrete over the green belt or our urban parks—there is plenty of land that could be built on without loss of public amenity: even in central London there are enough undeveloped micro-sites for all the housing currently needed, according to some experts.[xii] However, the market is not converting the abundant physical supply of land into an adequate supply of decent homes at affordable prices.[xiii] Until 1979, rich and poor spent just 15% of their income on housing. By 2016 the poorest 5% were spending 44% of their income on housing, the next poorest 5% were spending 31%, while the richest 5% were spending less than 9% of their income on housing.[xiv] There is also evidence that in hotspots such as London, the size of comparable units has fallen.[xv]

The net effect is that there has been and continues to be a transfer of disposable income from those without assets (whether renting or buying for the first time) to those with assets (existing owner occupiers and private landlords). The injustice involved is sometimes characterised as inter-generational,[xvi] since older people tend to own assets, but given the possibility of inheriting wealth, it is really a matter of old-fashioned class: over time the transfer will be from those whose parents did not own assets to those whose parents did. In the meantime, the cost of housing means that the post-tax and benefits income of the wealthiest 5% after housing costs is almost 11 times that of the least wealthy 5% (it is six times before housing costs).[xvii]

Automation may turn out to be a fantastic advance for human well-being, but it may not be. Academics at the Martin School at Oxford University have estimated that nearly half of US jobs could be automated over the next 20 years, and perhaps 35% of UK jobs.[xviii] The Institute for Public Policy Research has suggested that 44% of UK jobs are vulnerable, and that up to 33% of wages could be lost.[xix] The Bank

of England has suggested 15 million jobs are at risk.[xx] Consulting firm
PricewaterhouseCoopers estimates that 30% of jobs will be lost by the
mid-2030s.[xxi] There may be disagreement about what can be automated
and so what percentage of jobs are at risk, but there is widespread agreement that this percentage is large. Because automation includes automation of thinking ('artificial intelligence') these jobs include many
traditionally middle-class jobs.[1]

Automation is hardly new. It has been going on since the beginning
of the Industrial Revolution, and the complacent response to the challenge is that entrepreneurs will invent new products and services as they
always have done. The resulting new demand for labour will suck up the
excess supply of labour. This is what happened when enclosures threw
people off the land in the early nineteenth century, when power looms
replaced hand looms, when Henry Ford introduced the assembly line
and when computers replaced armies of filing clerks. Marx predicted that
mechanisation would lead to the impoverishment of the proletariat and a
collapse of demand and thus of capitalism, but he was wrong: he simply
had not understood the ingenuity of entrepreneurs and their ability to
create new products and employment. So, according to this complacent
view, at most we need a 'watching brief'.[xxii]

However, this time it is different—it really is. As the World Economic
Forum Global Risk Report says: "evidence suggests that managing technological change is an… important challenge for labour markets. While
innovation has historically created new kinds of job as well as destroying
old kinds, this process may be slowing."[xxiii] These days, new industries
and new companies tend to require fewer employees than they did, or
at any rate fewer employees at the same level, resulting in the phenom-
ena of underemployment and deskilling. In 2015 new enterprises in the
US created 40% fewer jobs than they did in 1995[xxiv] and in 2010 only
0.5% of the workforce worked in industries that did not exist in 2000.[xxv]
We can expect this trend to continue as automation gathers pace: further
underemployment and deskilling is not inevitable, but in the absence of
action there is at the very least a big risk. The problem is that such a
wide variety of tasks can be automated that any new jobs have to be concentrated into a narrower and narrower range of tasks. This is a tall order
in itself, but what is worse, the resulting 'man-made' goods and services

---

[1] Artificial intelligence is a form of automation and raises many policy issues of its own—
but I have not covered them in this book.

will be ever more expensive relative to those produced automatically. While the low cost of automated products will release income to spend on unautomated products, the latter will be increasingly uncompetitive. As a senior government economist explained to me, there is simply no reason to expect sufficient demand for the products that a fully employed workforce could produce. The idea, still popular amongst policy makers, that we can all become computer programmers, that traditional skills training is the answer, is simply incoherent: apart from anything else, code is going to be written by artificially intelligent machines.

Curiously, until about three or four years ago, a kind of technical pessimism had taken hold in some quarters, with the idea that 'the best is over' becoming fashionable. We were, it seemed, reaching a technological plateau and productivity growth in the developed world was coming to an end after a 250-year spree.[xxvi] One sociologist even suggested that "Post-industrial conditions are in important respects the terminus of socioeconomic development", and that this terminus would be associated with a loss of sense of progress and hope, and as a result major political upheavals.[xxvii] In some ways this was prescient: there have been political upheavals over the last few years associated with a loss of hope, and a sense that things are likely to get worse in the future.[xxviii] However the technological foundation for this sense of loss, for this belief in stasis, no longer exists. If we have lost hope it is not because technological advance has stopped, but because we are not confident we can control it.

Society continues to get richer: GDP per capita rose 16% between 2010 and 2017. Despite this, *public services always seem to be under pressure*. The immediate cause is a political decision to hold down tax rates at the expense of service quality. However, behind this political fact lies an economic fact. Productivity gains tend to be concentrated in certain sectors (motor cars, computers, recorded entertainment) and not in others (personal care, education, live theatre).[xxix] Since wages in all sectors are likely to rise at roughly the same rate (and in fact have done so broadly, although it is a complex story), products and services in sectors where there are fewer productivity gains will get relatively more expensive. For the most part the state provides services of this kind, which more expensive relative to the goods provided by the private sector. Social care is a topical example: new, stronger, minimum wage regulations are driving up costs, and this is creating financial crises for the local authorities responsible. More generally, maintaining the same standards in many public services will take up a larger share of GDP.

We are running up a down escalator, with attempts to reduce, or even stabilise, the public sector's share of GDP likely to create serious tension. Automation will accelerate the trend: it is likely that many of the jobs that survive automation will be providing services that we pay for through tax.

The problem is made still worse by the aging population. By 2050 the proportion of the UK population over 65 will have risen by about a third,[xxx] and the Office for Budget Responsibility has suggested that this, and relatively high cost increases, will lead to the health and social care bill increasing by 6% of GDP by 2060.[xxxi] If the state pension bill also rises, in line with the proportion of pensioners and assuming no further changes in pension age, it will cost a further 2% of GDP. These two effects alone would increase government spending from 41% to 49% of GDP, regardless of the rising relative costs of other government services.[2]

The basic facts of *climate change* can be stated briefly. In 2015 the average surface air temperature was c. 1 °C above pre-industrial levels as a result of increased concentration in the atmosphere of 'greenhouse gases.'[xxxii] The most significant of these gases is carbon dioxide (CO_2), with current concentrations of 405 parts per million (ppm) now 40% above pre-industrial levels.[xxxiii] Already this is causing damage to the planet and human well-being, but the consensus is the damage will be very much worse if we do not limit the temperature increase to 1.5 °C above pre-industrial levels.[3] Beyond this point, even a small increase in temperature could lead to a very large increase in damage; worse, there is a danger of positive feedback, with rises in temperatures causing further rises in temperatures, leading to 'runaway' climate change and catastrophe. This temperature limit probably means limiting CO_2 concentrations to current levels—although some argue that safety requires a *reduction* in concentration to c. 350 ppm.[xxxiv] In any case, a 1.5 °C limit probably requires net global emissions to reach zero by 2050, and then to go below zero in the second half of the century ('net' means emissions less CO_2 sucked from the atmosphere as a result of human activity—that is carbon removal technology and reforestation).[xxxv] The difficulty, at root,

---

[2] Of the 41%, 34% is currently funded by taxes, 3% by other government receipts, and 4% by borrowing (Institute for Fiscal Studies Briefing Note 2017). So were this extra 8% to be funded by taxes, it would require, based on current figures, an increase in tax receipts of 22%.

[3] Some scientists argue that a 1 °C limit is needed and some official bodies have accepted a 2 °C rise as the limit.

is that this will cost a great deal of money, and there are no adequate mechanisms for allocating these costs between countries and individuals.

Utopia or Dystopia?

Let us imagine that we do not manage automation effectively or address the existing drivers of inequality, that we do not increase the share of GDP taken in tax, that we do not solve the housing shortage in those parts of the country where it exists, and that we suffer the damaging effects of climate change, here and in other countries. As a result, we find ourselves in dystopia.

Automation has divided society sharply into three classes: the *professionals*, the *servants*, and the *underclass*. Some of the professionals have skills which have been leveraged by technology: for example those with the skills to create and manage the automation process, or entertainers and intellectuals whose work is distributed globally. Others, like doctors, have skills that are not leveraged in this way, but they still command high incomes because their output is valued and they could have chosen a more leveraged career. The servants are those doing work that cannot be automated, or cannot be automated profitably, and who do not have the social connections and intellectual skills to become professionals. Much of their work is personal service, such as cleaning, or working in restaurants, and tends to be for professionals. The underclass consists of those who cannot find work as servants. The professionals spend too much of their income on the output of other professionals (such as good design, or entertainment) to employ sufficient servants to absorb all those displaced by automation. Members of the underclass are dependent on benefits and ostracised accordingly. The high levels of inequality associated with this class system generate a range of social ills, including ill health, crime and strong but unsatisfied materialist aspirations.

In major cities, the professionals, who tend to be the children of professionals, often inherit capital and live in comfortable, spacious homes. The servants, who tend to be the children of servants, don't. They either commute long distances to find work close to where their customers live, or they live in tiny, shared flats. Public services, particularly healthcare, have come under pressure and quality has fallen. Unit costs have risen—hospital porter wages have only risen in line with inflation, but doctors' wages have risen in real terms—and while many professionals have 'gone private', reducing demand, this has not made up for the effects of the aging population; it has also increased pressure for even greater reductions in tax. Meanwhile major climate disruptions in other parts of the world have increased illegal immigration, and the associated social tensions and violence. In addition, the delay in tackling climate change has created more calls on the public purse, and so even more pressure on public services.

Fortunately, it is equally easy to imagine a utopia—a little exercise in fantasy, but as I conceded in Chapter 1, it has its place (the rest of the book is less fantastic). In this version of the future, we do manage automation effectively and address the existing drivers of inequality, we do increase the share of GDP taken in tax, we do solve the housing shortage, and the major countries of the world manage to reduce significantly the damaging effects of climate change. In this utopia, 40% of the tasks now performed by human beings have been automated, and the gains from this have been shared so that the standard working week is four days. Four days rather than three because some of the gains are used to pay for generous parental leave, to eliminate poverty, to incentivise entrepreneurs and technologists and to provide a return to pensioners on the investment in automation they have made. As now, some people work less than the standard working week and some more. Some older people, for example, choose to work less, and some young people without children but who are saving for a deposit on a home choose to work more. Partly because of the emergence of a range of effective social institutions, most people find rewarding, fulfilling activities to fill the other three days, and they have sufficient income to enjoy them.

Cities are planned and designed so that there is room for everyone who needs to work in them to live in them, without long commutes, and with sufficient space for the activities that now occupy three of the seven days of the week. This space is designed amongst other things to foster good human relationships. Everyone has a decent home. There are ever better public services, since automation means we are able to devote more and more of our energies to designing and delivering them. These include not just healthcare, but an education system designed to improve the happiness of children throughout their lives. The measures taken to address climate change have had some spin-off benefits too: reduced traffic noise, clean air, and the survival of otherwise threatened species.

While the details of these two scenarios may be exaggerated, and while the latter clearly *is* rather utopian, what is absolutely clear is that the choice between them is a collective one and the path to whichever we choose has to be managed collectively. We cannot individually choose this or that world, and there is no way that market forces can be relied on to help us arrive in utopia rather than dystopia. And this choice, it is now increasingly recognised, is a moral one.[xxxvi]

NOTES

i. Institute for Fiscal Studies, *Living Standards, Poverty and Inequality in the UK* (2017).

ii. Author's calculations based on Office for National Statistics, *Annual Survey of Hours and Earnings* and on the Retail Price Index and Gross Domestic Product numbers (2017).

iii. Institute for Fiscal Studies, *Living Standards, Poverty and Inequality in the UK* (2017).

iv. On impact of wealth—a bigger driver of well-being than income level— see Bruce Headey, Ruud Muffels, and Mark Wooden, 'Money Does Not Buy Happiness: Or Does It? A Reassessment Based on the Combined Effects of Wealth, Income and Consumption,' *Social Indicators Research* (May 2008, Vol. 87, pp. 65–82). For evidence on the impact of short term rentals, see Laura Stoll, Juliet Michaelson, and Charles Seaford, *Well-Being Evidence for Policy: A Review* (New Economics Foundation, 2012).

v. https://www.equalitytrust.org.uk/about-inequality.

vi. https://www.gov.uk/government/statistical-data-sets/tenure-trends-and-cross-tenure-analysis.

vii. Ibid.

viii. For evidence on insecure employment, see Laura Stoll, Juliet Michaelson, and Charles Seaford, *Well-Being Evidence for Policy: A Review* (NEF, 2012); Saamah Abdallah and Sagar Shah, *Well-Being Patterns Uncovered: An Analysis of UK Data* (NEF, 2012); and Tarani Chandola and Nan Zhang, 'Re-employment, Job Quality, Health and Allostatic Load Biomarkers: Prospective Evidence from the UK Household Longitudinal Study,' *International Journal of Epidemiology* (February 2018, Vol. 47, pp. 47–57).

ix. https://www.ons.gov.uk/peoplepopulationandcommunity/personalandhouseholdfinances/incomeandwealth/bulletins/householddisposableincomeandinequality/financialyearending2017#gradual-decline-in-income-inequality-over-the-last-decade.

x. David Runciman, *Talking Politics: The Fundamentals* (Podcast, 8 February 2018).

xi. https://www.sheffield.ac.uk/news/nr/land-cover-atlas-uk-1.744440.

xii. Anne Power and Laura Lane, *Housing Futures: Our Homes and Communities* (LSE Housing and Communities, 2010).

xiii. There is a government definition of a decent home: Department for Communities and Local Government, *A Decent Home: Definition and Guidance* (2006). Affordability has been judged by the Resolution Foundation to be 35% of disposable household income. Vidhya Alakeson and Giselle Cory, *Home Truths: How Affordable is Housing for Britain's Ordinary Working Families?* (Resolution Foundation, 2013).

xiv. Calculations in Andrew Hindmoor, *What's Left Now?: The History and Future of Social Democracy* (2018) based on Institute For Fiscal Studies, *Incomes in the UK.*

xv. Unpublished analysis carried out at the New Economics Foundation (NEF) in 2014.

xvi. David Willetts, *The Pinch: How the Baby Boomers Took Their Children's Future—And Why They Should Give It Back* (2010).

xvii. Andrew Hindmoor draws attention to this effect in *What's Left Now?: The History and Future of Social Democracy* (2018). The numbers are based on Institute for Fiscal Studies, *Incomes in the UK.*

xviii. Carl Benedikt Frey and Michael Osborne, *The Future of Employment: How Susceptible are Jobs to Computerisation?* (Oxford Martin School, 2013); Carl Benedikt Frey and Michael Osborne, *From Brawn to Brains: The Impact of Technology on Jobs in the UK* (Deloitte, 2015).

xix. Mathew Lawrence, Carys Roberts, and Loren King, *Managing Automation: Employment, Inequality and Ethics in the Digital Age* (IPPR Commission on Economic Justice, 2017).

xx. Andrew Haldane, *Labour's Share* (Speech at Trades Union Congress, 12 November 2015), https://www.bankofengland.co.uk/speech/2015/labours-share.

xxi. https://www.pwc.co.uk/services/economics-policy/insights/the-impact-of-automation-on-jobs.html.

xxii. See for example Matthew Taylor, *Good Work: The Taylor Review of Modern Working Practices* (RSA, 2017).

xxiii. The World Economic Forum, *The Global Risks Report 2017*, p. 12, https://riskcenter.wharton.upenn.edu/publications/global-risks/.

xxiv. Calculated by Nick Srnicek and Alex Williams, *Inventing the Future: Postcapitalism and a World Without Work* (2015), p. 100, based on data from US Bureau of Labor Statistics.

xxv. Thor Berger and Carl Benedikt Frey, 'Industrial Renewal in the 21st Century: Evidence from US Cities,' *Regional Studies* (2015, Vol. 51, pp. 404–413).

xxvi. Robert Gordon, *Is Economic Growth Over? Faltering Innovation Confronts Six Headwinds* (National Bureau of Economic Research, 2012).

xxvii. John Higley, *Elite Theory in Political Sociology*, http://paperroom.ipsa.org/papers/paper_4036.pdf.

xxviii. https://www.ipsosglobaltrends.com/the-optimism-divide/.

xxix. The phenomenon associated with economist William Baumol, who described it in his book, *The Cost Disease: Why Computers Get Cheaper and Health Care Doesn't* (2012).

xxx. United Nations Department for Economic and Social Affairs (UNDESA), https://esa.un.org/unpd/wpp/.

xxxi. Office for Budget Responsibility, *An OBR Guide to Welfare Spending* (2017). State pensions are 4.5% of GDP and other cash benefits paid to pensioners are 1.5% of GDP.

xxxii. https://www.metoffice.gov.uk.

xxxiii. https://royalsociety.org/.

xxxiv. J. Hansen, P. Kharecha, M. Sato, V. Masson-Delmotte, F. Ackerman, D. Beerling, et al. 'Assessing "Dangerous Climate Change": Required Reduction of Carbon Emissions to Protect Young People, Future Generations and Nature,' *PLoS One*, December 2013, https://doi.org/10.1371/journal.pone.0081648.

xxxv. The ADVANCE Project (2016) quoted by Climate Analytics, https://climateanalytics.org/blog/2016/new-research-confirms-feasibility-of-the-15c-limit/. There is no universally agreed precise definition of net zero.

xxxvi. Anthony Gooch put it in these terms (conversation with author).

PART II

Why We Can Change

CHAPTER 3

Flourishing and its Role

In 1942 William Beveridge presented his plans for the post-war welfare state to Parliament, plans that were intended to end the "want… disease, ignorance, squalor and idleness" that afflicted the country, and particularly the working class. As he put it, "A revolutionary moment in the world's history is a time for revolutions, not for patching."[i] 635,000 copies of the report were sold to the public and his proposals got massive support: 73% of employers wanted them adopted, even though just 16% thought they would gain personally (amongst professionals the equivalent figures were 91% and 48%).[ii] When the Labour Party came to power after its 1945 election landslide, its mission was, as it always had been, to improve the material conditions of the working class, and it used the Beveridge report to help it do so.

The most telling criticism of Labour's 2017 programme—its revival of social democracy—was that it lacked a similarly large purpose. What is its diagnosis of Britain's ills? What are its equivalents of Beveridge's "want, disease, ignorance, squalor and idleness"? For the most part, Labour settles for reversing 'Tory austerity,' but reversing the toxic policies of a predecessor government is not a large purpose. In 2016, a visitor from Podemos accused the British left of lacking a narrative. The only stories she could hear belonged to the right: budget cuts and immigration controls.[iii]

© The Author(s) 2019
C. Seaford, *Why Capitalists Need Communists*,
Wellbeing in Politics and Policy,
https://doi.org/10.1007/978-3-319-98755-2_3

The ideology of flourishing would, when developed, provide a large purpose for a left-of-centre government, similar to the purpose that animated the Labour Party in 1945, and enabling it to counter the politics of consumption and the politics of fear, as outlined in Chapter 1.

It could also provide a large purpose for a right-of-centre government. In November 2010, six months after being appointed Prime Minister, David Cameron made the following pronouncement in a speech to an invited audience:

> If your goal in politics is to help make a better life for people – which mine is – and if you know, both in your gut and from a huge body of evidence that prosperity alone can't deliver a better life, then you've got to take practical steps to make sure government is properly focused on our quality of life as well as economic growth....Just as we can create the climate for business to thrive, so we can create a climate in this country that is more family-friendly and more conducive to the good life....To those who say that all this sounds like a distraction from the serious business of government, I would say that finding out what will really improve lives and acting on it is actually the serious business of government.

He had earlier been quite specific about some of the policy shifts this could lead to:

> We had, in Britain, something of an immigration free-for-all justified by the argument that it is supposed to be good for growth, but without enough thought about the impact on public services and social cohesion. We've had something of a cheap booze free-for-all – again, supposed to be good for growth, but were we really thinking about the impact of that on law and order and on well-being? We've had something of an irresponsible media and marketing free-for-all – again, this was meant to be good for growth, but what about the impact on childhood? It's because of this fundamentally flawed approach that for decades Western societies have seen the line of GDP rising steadily upwards, but at the same time, levels of contentment have remained static or have even fallen.[iv]

In the end nothing came of this potentially radical realignment of priorities. Four years later, a senior Cabinet Office official recommended to a group of well-being advocates that they make the case for well-being in terms of its positive impact on growth. But I can't help thinking that if Cameron had had the temperament of Margaret Thatcher, things could have been different. Cameron's version of flourishing would have put less emphasis on redistribution, and more emphasis on traditional social institutions, than the left version. Indeed, some suspected his rhetoric was designed to distract from inequality. But it would have been as opposed to market liberalism as paternalistic Tories have always been.

A larger purpose is needed if we are to address the five problems outlined in the previous chapter, and I will present the role of flourishing in shaping that larger purpose in this chapter. But first I will set out what it is. After all, if we don't know what it is, how can we care about it?

What Flourishing Is

Most people want to lead a 'good life', however they define it, and to flourish is to enjoy a particular kind of good life, a particular kind of well-being. I cannot prove that it is the best kind of good life, I can simply describe it, and contrast it with alternatives, and leave it to the reader to decide whether it appeals.

There is a preliminary distinction to make, though, between a life that is good in itself, for the person living it, and a life that is good according to some external standard. The latter might be a moral code, or it might be success in serving an external objective. So for example, a life might be thought good because the person living it follows Christian principles, or because it successfully advances revolution, national glory or whatever. These versions of the good life were more popular in the past than now, and I will say no more about them: I suspect they don't resonate very strongly with most readers. There is nothing wrong with them, incidentally, provided the morality or objectives are not themselves harmful, and the self-sacrifice involved has been praised through the centuries. It is just that they are not very relevant for most people in this country now.

If we confine ourselves to the good life that is good for the person living it, the main distinction is between a good life as a set of *experiences* and the good life as a set of *relationships*. In the former, well-being characterises a person's experience, and in the latter well-being characterises her relationship to the world around her. These different ways of looking at the good life are long established and continue to divide people.

Jeremy Bentham is the best known advocate of *experience* as the measure of well-being; the pleasure and pain that form the foundation of his ethics developed in the late eighteenth century are varieties of experience. In the nineteenth century, his utilitarianism became the ethical basis of classical and later neoclassical economics and recently, this doctrine has been enthusiastically propagated by Richard Layard and Paul Dolan of the London School of Economics, both progressive advocates of happiness as a policy objective and the so-called 'hedonic' account of well-being. Dolan has developed a subtle variation, in which a sense of purpose is valued alongside happiness.[v] This remains a version of utilitarianism, however, since it is still *a sense of* purpose that is valued rather than the purpose itself. Utilitarianism, incidentally, appears so obvious to its exponents that they sometimes simply cannot grasp that there is an alternative point of view. For example, if you say you value friendship or work for their own sakes, they are inclined to tell you that what you really value is the happiness that these things bring.

Advocates of the *relationship* view sometimes write within religious traditions, in which an individual's relationship with God and creation is paramount. However, secular writers will often refer to Aristotle's ethics, sometimes as restated by Alasdair MacIntyre in the 1980s. Aristotle defined well-being as *eudaimonia*: an elusive concept, sometimes oversimplified by modern writers to mean the state achieved when living a life that is worthwhile (this 'eudaimonic well-being' is then contrasted with the hedonic version). Macintyre built on the concept by emphasising the role of narrative in the good life:

> I can only answer the question 'what am I to do?' if I can answer the prior question 'of what story or stories do I find myself a part?'... What is better or worse for X depends on the character of that intelligible narrative which provides X's life with its unity.[vi]

Two features of such narratives as conceived by MacIntyre are relevant for our purposes. First, they are essentially social, and rooted in the live traditions and 'practices' that make up a society. Practices are activities with internal standards of excellence; so for example dancing has a standard of excellence, as does carpentry, or being a parent, or even being a friend. Second, narratives involve a *telos*, or purpose, just as individual practices do; a 'quest'. This is not for some predefined good. Instead, "The good life for man is the life spent seeking the good life for man"[vii] and involves ordering and balancing the fulfilments available from individual practices. The result should be a coherent, intelligible narrative both for the individual life and the collective life of which it is part. Martha Nussbaum is another contemporary philosopher in the Aristotelian tradition who describes the good life in broadly similar terms. It is the truly human life, and involves humans seeking the human good as they conceive it, and seeking it with others.[viii]

One curious variation on this theme is radical libertarianism. Libertarians believe (or claim to believe) that a good relationship with the world is *entirely* a matter of freedom of choice. It is not just that this freedom is necessary to achieving a good life, it is actually constitutive of it. I suspect this is no more than a debating point: we might concede that freedom of choice is part of any good relationship with the world (and indeed Nussbaum and Amartya Sen have elaborated on what this means in their theories of 'capabilities'), but do libertarians really believe that human relationships, which by their nature restrict freedom of choice, are irrelevant? Or that for many people religion, or satisfying work, which require adherence to a discipline and some restriction on freedom, are also always irrelevant? I doubt it, and if they do, the picture of the isolated individual they paint, without ties or constraints, is terrifying.

So, leaving aside the libertarian variation, the conception of well-being as a good relationship with the world is fundamentally social, in contrast to the utilitarian conception which is fundamentally individual (although in both cases well-being is a property of *individual* lives). This reflects the fact that social entities can be and are described in terms of relationships, whereas they cannot be described in terms of experience (except metaphorically).

Of course it is open to utilitarians to argue that what gives a life story coherence and purpose is the pursuit of pleasure and the avoidance of pain and that all the rest is simply a means to these overarching ends. It is difficult to *prove* this position is wrong. But arguably it reveals the failure of Benthamite utilitiarianism to capture many of our intuitions, and many will shy away from its solipsistic conclusion. Above all, perhaps, relationships, being part of something bigger than oneself, the sense of meaning that is derived from narrative and engagement with the world (through participation in traditions and practices), make mortality less catastrophic: what matters in this conception of a life is not ourselves and our experience, but the universe of which we are part.

Furthermore, this preference for a view of the good life, in which relationships rather than experience are primary, has a sound philosophical basis. Man is by his nature a social animal, and in a quite fundamental way: specifically, *human* consciousness is the result of language (allowing that there may be elements of consciousness shared by humans and dumb animals) and language is by its nature social.[ix] In other words, so the argument goes, relationships are prior to human experience, are in some sense more fundamental than experience.

The modern concept of 'flourishing,' elaborated by Corey Keyes and other members of the positive psychology school, draws on both ethical traditions just described, although it is closer to the Aristotelian conception. Flourishing individuals, in Keyes's words, have positive feelings, an absence of negative feelings, and 'function' well, by which he means they

> like most parts of themselves, have warm and trusting relationships, see themselves developing into better people, have a direction in life, are able to shape their environments to satisfy their needs, and have a degree of self-determination.[x]

They also have a positive relationship with society: they

> see society as meaningful and understandable... as possessing potential for growth... they feel they belong to and are accepted by their communities... they accept most parts of society... they see themselves as contributing to society.[xi]

The focus and unit of analysis remains the individual: this is, after all part of *Western* psychology. However, the description includes *both* experience—positive feelings and an absence of negative feelings—*and* relationship, most obviously in the account of the relationship with society, but also in the more personal aspects of functioning. One might expect that someone living a good life as prescribed by MacIntyre is relatively likely to flourish in the way described by Keyes.

Two other psychologists, Richard Ryan and Edward Deci, have shown that good functioning, broadly as just described, is associated with good feelings; in their scheme, both are grounded in satisfaction of psychological needs.[xii] However, the functioning and the feeling are distinct. It is possible to have positive feelings that are not associated with good functioning.[xiii] Depending on your ethical position, you may then say that the value lies in the functioning, or in the feeling. The philosophical disagreement about what is important continues, even if for practical purposes both sides can converge on the concept of flourishing because, as a matter of empirical fact, those who function well tend to have good feelings.

Because functioning and feeling are distinct concepts, we can question whether someone spending her life watching television game shows in solitude is leading a good life, even if this is the activity she freely chooses, and even if she reports that as a result she feels pleasure and is highly satisfied with her life (the variable often picked up in well-being surveys). Similarly, it is possible to ask if someone taking a happy drug and spending all day content but in bed is leading a good life. For we can examine whether these people demonstrate the characteristics identified by Keyes as signs of flourishing, or whether their psychological needs as identified by Ryan and Deci have been fulfilled: and we might well expect they are not.

Do people value flourishing? I am not aware of any Bentham versus Aristotle poll, but if the features of flourishing can be grouped into successful human relationships and successful human agency (the ability people have 'to shape their environments... and have a degree of self-determination'), then it appears that while relationships are valued everywhere, agency tends to be valued more highly in societies where more basic concerns of security and subsistence have been achieved.[xiv] In line with this, it is arguable that the construct of flourishing 'fits' better those societies demonstrating what Ronald Inglehart and Christian Welzel[xv] in their analysis of World Values Survey findings have called 'secular rational' and 'self-expression' values, that is mainly the English speaking and protestant European countries. However, the central component of it, good relationships with others, is universal.

From here on, I shall assume that flourishing is what we are aiming for. There may be some committed utilitarians reading this book; much of what I say would still apply were I arguing for a politics of pleasure, so perhaps they can make the necessary adjustments.

Why Use What We Know About Flourishing to Guide Policy?

Flourishing may constitute the good life, but should it be the ultimate objective of policy? Or, more simply, should governments try to make people's lives better? To say they should is hardly controversial: in a democracy, voters tend to vote for politicians who do so.

However, perhaps surprisingly, not everyone agrees. Traditionally, some saw the state as fulfilling God's purpose (and some still do), or as the vehicle for conquest, or as a means for supporting an aristocracy. However, even now, genuine alternatives to well-being as an ultimate objective for the state are occasionally advanced. These alternatives are all based on obligations and rights, and they have their own moral force.

The first of these alternative objectives for the state is the upholding of certain rights, and these are deemed to exist prior to the state. Depending on your political position, these rights may include property rights, human rights (including the right not to suffer violence), and rights associated with various conceptions of social justice. They may even include the right to the pursuit of happiness, as set out in the American Declaration of Independence. The resulting role for the state may be extensive—after all the state has to administer parking fines, and social justice requires quite a lot of market intervention—but the idea that it is trying to engineer well-being, directly or indirectly, is alien. In this view, rights and social justice have a moral content that happiness and flourishing lack.

The second alternative objective is the well-being of the community, as distinct from the well-being of the individuals who make up the community. Well-being in this sense might, for example, mean cohesion, or growth, or the working out of some mythical destiny. Traditional nationalists conceive of the community as the nation, but looser and more local (or more international) definitions are possible. An obvious response from individualists is to say that if the well-being of the community is important to the individuals in it, then its well-being will be part of their well-being, as well as vice versa, so there is no need to have a separate objective. However, the real communitarian will respond that community well-being matters even if it is irrelevant to the well-being of individual community members. For there are moral obligations to the community, or the nation, which go beyond those to individuals.

The third alternative is an extension of the second: the role of the state is the well-being of the community and the ecosphere within which it exists. We do not protect the environment just because it is a source of 'environmental services', many of which are vital to our survival, we protect it for its own sake, or, as the Pope has put it, because it is God's creation.[xvi] Indeed it too can be thought of as having rights, as the constitution of Ecuador recognises.[xvii]

These positions all have some force, but this in itself does not mean that individual well-being as an objective should be rejected. A few people may hold this view, but it is a strange and extreme one. For most of us, the positions are a useful corrective to any obsessive idea that individual well-being should be the *only* objective, that, for example, Nature doesn't have value independent of the amenity it provides humans.

So if we agree, then, that individual well-being is *the* (or at least *an*) important, ultimate objective, does that mean that it needs to be an explicit objective of policy making, that we need evidence and ideas and a whole ideology of flourishing? It might be argued, indeed it *is* argued, that we already know all that we need to know about how to make people flourish: grow the economy, help people find jobs, provide a health service and so on. Everyone knows and agrees on what these intermediate objectives are, so the argument goes, and while there are disagreements between the parties, mainly over the level of redistribution and the relative roles of the state and the market, there is a broad consensus on what to do. Discussion of well-being, examination of the increasingly copious evidence as to what increases it and what reduces it, is a distraction from getting on with this.

The political and economic problems I described in Chapters 1 and 2 suggest that this complacent view has had its day, that the conventional answers as to how to make people's lives better are no longer working. It is obvious, given the problems set out in Chapter 2, that simply maximising growth and consumption is bound to be an incomplete answer to our economic problems, and indeed competition from the developing world may make it impossible anyway. Even should it be possible, growth plus automation may lead to mass unemployment; growth may lead to asset price inflation and a shortage of affordable homes; growth may lead to unjust and dysfunctional levels of inequality; growth will not necessarily ensure adequate public services; and growth may exacerbate climate change. We can ask other questions too: is growth helping to create social stability and community cohesion? Is it helping people form good relationships, or, as Cameron asked, is it damaging family life? Is growth causing stress, or even mental illness? None of this shows that growth should not be *an* objective, just that its central place in policy, and its contribution to well-being, need to be examined.

In other words, the traditional standards of success in economic policy are being called into question. In such circumstances, where there are no agreed intermediate objectives, policy makers need to think about the impact of their policies on the ultimate objective, that is to say well-being or flourishing. Most of the time, in most policy areas, traditional standards of success are *not* called into question: lower death rates, better exam results, shorter journey times can normally be accepted as good intermediate objectives en route to a flourishing population without too much argument. For many years growth was an objective of this type, and well-being was indeed a bit of a distraction. Perhaps, in time, new intermediate economic objectives will replace growth, and well-being will again be a distraction. But for now, it needs to be thought about.

At a more theoretical level, the existence of well-being evidence has important implications for the status of market outcomes. Neoclassical welfare economists have traditionally argued that well-being (or 'welfare' as it is called in the theory) cannot be measured directly, and that we are therefore forced to fall back on *that which is chosen* as evidence, with the quantity of well-being identified with how much people are willing to pay. Well-being thus becomes associated with market choices and serves to justify the market as a social institution. Indeed, given this assumption, it can be shown with elegance and rigour that if our original income distribution is optimal and if we take steps to preserve it, then perfect markets will produce optimal outcomes.[1] The questions we should ask, or so the argument goes, are, first: 'Is there a market failure?' and second: 'If there is, what intervention will correct it?' The existence of well-being evidence suggests an alternative set of questions: 'What economic arrangements maximise well-being? Can we move in this direction? If so, what will achieve this?'

It is true of course that the market remains the best mechanism for allocating the results of much (not all) productive effort. No-one is proposing the creation of a well-being based version of Gosplan (the Soviet planning agency) even if some sectors such as healthcare do require central planning. However, the arrival of subjective well-being evidence means we are no longer forced to fall back on *that which is chosen* to tell us what creates well-being. We now have statistical data to supplement or even replace this, and on this basis make decisions about the structure of the economy.

We have these data because the well-being of a population can be measured, at least approximately. This possibility lay behind some of the recommendations of the 2009 *Commission on the Measurement of Economic Performance and Social Progress* set up by President Sarkozy[xviii]

---

[1] The theorem holds when there are no market failures and there are no missing markets; that is, there are markets for everything. There is of course no market for many of the most important contributions to flourishing.

as well as measurement initiatives in the EU, the OECD, and at national, regional and local level. The UK Office for National Statistics now measures flourishing, or rather a very closely related construct, 'mental well-being',[xix] as one of 43 indicators of 'national well-being', alongside four other subjective measures of well-being.[xx] The surveys containing these questions also measure objective conditions that are more directly influenced by policy such as housing, education, employment patterns, benefit entitlements, income and so on. In principle, regression analysis then allows us to assess the association of these conditions with subjective measures of well-being, and thus, to the extent that we know the impact of policies on the conditions, what it takes to increase flourishing and other forms of well-being. This knowledge base is continuing to grow: the World Database of Happiness now has c. 15,000 findings on the conditions associated with well-being.[xxi,2]

These data may be relevant not just in economic policy but in many other areas of policy as well, perhaps because of issues within the field (what are the objectives of education?) or because of interactions between fields (might this regulation improve health but damage employment?) or because priorities at a very high level are being set (should we spend more on early years education or on adult social care?). These questions often arise at local levels where impact on the ground needs to be assessed, or where different policy programmes interact. For example, a local authority (and citizens) might want to know the relative impacts on local well-being of measures to reduce unemployment and measures to preserve the environment. Have interventions to increase community cohesion and increase economic activity improved well-being? Are hospital closures still justified when the well-being of patients and visitors is considered alongside clinical and cost factors? Should there be greater investment in pedestrianisation schemes? Have the public health interventions in one city been more effective at increasing well-being than in another? Can reasons for any differences be identified? What changes to the curriculum would improve children's well-being, and what knock-on effects would this have on their well-being in later life? Would it be more effective to spend more of the social care budget

---

[2] In practice, most studies around the world establish associations between objective conditions and reported life satisfaction, or in some cases feelings of happiness, rather than flourishing; these may be adequate pro-tem proxies at aggregate level, for even if the psychological states referred to are quite different, there are associations between the states.

than we do on ways of reducing loneliness amongst old people? Well-being evidence can, in principle, help answer these questions, and there is now a government-sponsored evidence centre (the 'What Works Centre for Well-being') which local government, devolved government and UK level policy makers can make use of.

FLOURISHING AND THE FIVE PROBLEMS

In Chapters 7 and 8, I will describe the policy approach that I believe is needed to address the big five problems. In the rest of this chapter, I will contrast this approach, grounded as it is in ideas about flourishing, with those of the market liberals, the social democrats and the radical localists. I will also refer to some of the evidence that makes this distinctive approach possible: more details are given in the Appendix.

What is the market liberalism approach to automation? First, that there isn't that much to worry about, because the market will deal with the problem. New technologies have been invented regularly over the last 200 years. Government's role is to ensure there is a well-educated workforce, to de-regulate labour markets so as to minimise unemployment, to attract business from around the world to invest here, and to challenge monopolies. If it does these things, automation will be a tremendous growth opportunity and we can become a world leader in the cutting-edge industries of tomorrow! As for inequality, the living wage should be increased, and chief executives who get paid millions despite bad performance should be ostracised, but inequality is largely a matter of market forces. It may well increase as a result of automation, but this is the price we pay for the increased prosperity automation will bring, and at least we can tax the rich and use it to maintain public services. The housing problem can be dealt with by relaxing planning controls, the cost of public services can be dealt with by introducing charges, and climate change can be dealt with by a mixture of carbon charges and trading, technology subsidy and initiative in the private sector.

What is the social democratic approach? In many respects it is similar to that of market liberalism, but involves trying just that bit harder. To deal with automation and inequality we certainly need to invest in training, but perhaps invest more than the market liberals would like. We also need to attract businesses from around the world, although we should not join the corporate tax arbitrage game, and our foreign policy should be addressing this issue. We need to make a particular effort to attract businesses to less prosperous regions, and we need to make sure that small business gets all the finance it needs, as well as support for training its workforce. Automation is indeed a tremendous growth opportunity, and the social democratic version of what the UK does, what it makes and sells, is not so different from the market liberal version. However, social democracy also tells us that we need to beef up our welfare state to deal with the dislocations that are bound to occur, at least to the extent that this can be afforded given constraints on taxation. These are real, if not as great as those imagined by market liberals. Support for co-ops and start-ups may also help address these dislocations. Trade unions are a vital part of addressing inequality, and labour market reform will also be important to protect the workforce in the new era. Dealing with the housing shortage does not require significant relaxation of planning controls; it does require compulsory purchase of development land, or at least the threat of it, as well as an increase in the social housing budget. Paying for public services will also involve big tax increases. On climate change, the social democrats follow the market liberals, but tend to argue that the industry will need more regulation and the state will need to invest more if we are to move fast enough.

The radical localists have a very different view. They think the answer to just about all these problems is to go local: encourage rapid growth of small business and cooperatives, using technology that is owned by the community; local control of housing policy; local initiatives to reduce carbon emissions; local taxation and funding of the welfare state, with cooperatives and local people playing a major part in designing and delivering the necessary public services. They do not really have anything to say about how to deal with big business, and the major changes it is likely to bring about, except to reduce its significance in people's lives by increasing the importance of small businesses and the local economy.

And what about those who subscribe to the ideology of flourishing? Their approach draws on the social democratic and radical localist approaches but is significantly different. Their fundamental assumption is that we can shape the future. They start by developing a picture of the economy and society that we want to see: what kind of work? what kind of consumption? how much work and how much leisure? how much growth and how much equality? what kind of public services? what kind of housing development? what kind of response to climate change? The answers to these questions are based on evidence about what will encourage human flourishing.[3] Those developing this picture use evidence and do not think 'the gentleman in Whitehall knows best'. They use deliberative democracy to resolve the issues—a way of engaging citizens through structured discussion of specific issues. The resulting plan— and it is very hazy with many options left undetermined—serves four functions: it helps to guide the kind of policies set out in Chapters 7 and 8 (although of course it is only the starting point, in real life everything changes); it sends signals to business and the rest of the world about what the UK is doing, and so encourages behaviour aligned to the plan; it helps provides a degree of stability and security, much needed given the uncertainties that exist; and, to the extent that the deliberative democracy process creates legitimacy, it helps government find politically acceptable ways of paying for public services and mitigating climate change.

A plan of this kind will not be written down in one document: there will be no governmental white paper entitled: 'The Future of the United Kingdom'. It will be contained in a whole array of documents, debates, broadcasts, sermons and speeches: but those who go on to make decisions will see in this array a clear sense of direction.

Importantly, decision makers will believe that the purpose of the economy is to help people flourish, and that it does this through its impact on workers and communities as well as on consumers. They do not believe that these impacts on workers and communities are side-effects, externalities or market failures, to be addressed when specific problems have been identified. Instead they are integral to the economy's purpose.

This is not how they are thought about now. The *official* view, which has been embedded in policy for a long time, is that the interests of consumers are more important than those of producers, and that it is the former that should be prioritised if a choice has to be made. Nick Macpherson was Permanent Secretary to the Treasury until 2016 and made the point thus in 2014: "From the repeal of the corn laws to the present day, [The Treasury] has tended to favour consumers over producers."[xxii] He made a similar point when I met him, emphasising that the Treasury was concerned with the general interests of consumers and citizens, in contrast to the special producer interests that might

---

[3] For a set of feasible, inexpensive policies based on this principle, see Stefano Bartolini, *Manifesto for Happiness: Shifting Society from Money to Well-being* (2011).

sometimes be promoted by other departments. There are understandable reasons for this position: established producer interests are often over-powerful and can lead to inefficiency. However, it is also inefficient to ignore the well-being impacts associated with these producer interests. Consistent with this stance, the Treasury had been "in sceptical mode" about well-being during his time as Permanent Secretary, despite the fact that the agenda was being pushed from the Cabinet Office by the then Cabinet Secretary, Gus O'Donnell, with support from the Prime Minister, David Cameron.

Neoclassical economics cannot provide the theoretical basis for the programme just described, in the way that it has underpinned the politics of consumption, in both its market liberal and social democratic forms. It is a theory of markets, that is to say of how prices are set given our economic structures, but it is not a theory of how those structures come about or what they should be. It does not tell us what kind of society we should be aiming for, and to be fair it does not pretend to, even if market liberals sometimes speak as if it did: it simply assumes welfare is whatever consumers choose in perfect markets.

Free trade is a good example of an issue where a broader approach is needed if we are to consider the impact of the economy on workers and communities. Neoclassical theory holds that free trade is always a good thing, with one or two exceptions, for example when tariffs are needed to protect an infant industry. This is because the theory assumes that the extra output that free trade brings about can be redistributed to compensate those who lose from free trade, for example workers in previously protected industries. In reality, even if that redistribution takes place, a very big *if* indeed, free trade often damages the quality of work of those who are displaced, and often damages the communities they live in. We know from the well-being evidence that simply restoring the income of those displaced will not compensate for the lower quality work or provide better communities. Men moving from factory work to shop work, for example, suffer, not just from a lower income, but from damage to their self-esteem, with a series of knock-on effects on health and community life.[xxiii] This does not mean free trade is always a bad thing, of course. It just means that a different kind of calculation has to be made—and this may be particularly important as we consider how to reduce inequality or create jobs that can survive automation, or ensure communities have the resilience to deal with climate change and other shocks that we simply cannot avoid.

On the face of it, economists should be capable of taking into account the impacts of free trade on quality of work and on communities, and factoring that into their models. There is a potential evolution of neo-classical economics that uses measures of life-satisfaction, happiness and flourishing as outcomes, and models the impact of different economic policies on these. It is not that the techniques of economics are redundant. However, sometimes the calculation is not amenable to quantification: the level of uncertainty is too high for the precision associated with quantification to be useful. In these circumstances, more direct democratic involvement in the decision is the honest response. The economist needs to say to the citizens, we can say so much but no more; it is for you to take the decision, to decide what you think is most likely to help you flourish. We will provide information, point out what is relatively certain and what is less certain, and let you decide. This, as we will see in Chapter 10, does not mean referenda but forms of deliberative democracy, that is structured discussion by citizens who have been provided with the necessary information.

This may sound similar to the way officials are meant to advise politicians: here are the facts Minister, you make the judgement. In reality economists, and the decision-making Establishment that clusters round them, do not like operating in this way, certainly if it involves members of the public. A vivid example of this was the unedifying spectacle in the years before the Brexit referendum of Jonathan Portes, at the time Chief Economist of the National Institute for Economic and Social Research, arguing that those who claimed immigration was damaging their lives were simply wrong. Since the research showed that immigration was good for the British economy, he implied, the largely working-class individuals who maintained that it wasn't good for the economy in their localities, whether because jobs were being 'stolen', homes becoming difficult to find, or public services being put under pressure, should not be taken too seriously by policy makers.[xxiv]

The evidence that Portes cited may well have been correct. But people's felt experience is also a form of evidence, and Portes ignored that.

The Evidence

A plan of the kind described, mapping out how we want to shape the future, is only possible because we have a starting point: the well-being evidence. In the absence of this, it would be random, a fantasy. So, what does the evidence tell us? (For the most part the evidence is about life satisfaction, occasionally about happiness, but rarely about flourishing. Hence, I refer to the well-being evidence, and to impacts on well-being rather than flourishing. However other evidence shows an association between life satisfaction and flourishing.)

Stability, Security and Community

First of all it tells us that stability and security—especially stable and secure employment—is more important than increases in income. The plan needs to make creating stability and security for as many people as possible a top priority. What, after all, is the point of automation if it increases people's standard of living somewhat, but makes them feel hopelessly insecure? This point has been taken on board by parliamentarians: the All-Party Parliamentary Group (APPG) on Well-being Economics recommended in 2014 that "stable and secure employment for all should be the primary objective of economic policy."[xxv] The point here is not just that stability and security are important, which is obvious, but that they are *more* important than income growth once a certain standard of living has been achieved.

The evidence also tells us that work should be brought to existing communities where at all possible, and that we should not rely on population movements and long commutes to address the problem of regional or local underdevelopment. This is partly because close and more distant social relations are, along with health, the most important drivers of well-being, and are often damaged by disruption to communities. It is also because long commutes[xxvi] and having to move home to find work have been shown to damage well-being. So the plan will need to be a series of regional and local plans.

Work Quality

The evidence points to the importance of *good* jobs in ways that go beyond income and security, to the importance of *quality* work in a person's life—its role in flourishing, and in maintaining the physical and mental health needed to flourish. Job quality has a direct impact on life satisfaction, but also an indirect impact, via levels of self-esteem and the health consequences of self-esteem. Well-being at work also has huge economic impacts: both through its effect on productivity,[xxvii] and, through its effect on health and the cost to the NHS.[xxviii]

In Britain, there is some evidence that up to two-thirds of people either like or love their jobs, and a relatively small minority dislike or hate them.[xxix] A survey by the CIPD, the HR managers' professional body, suggests that around half of employees are motivated by the purpose of their work and are enthusiastic much of the time. On the other hand, it also reports that over 20% are often or always exhausted at work, and 30% feel they have too much work to do.[xxx] An American survey, setting a higher bar, concludes that only 8% of British employees are fully engaged with, and 'own' their work.[xxxi]

Concern with work quality is part of a long and live tradition. Karl Marx, for example, wrote that "In creating a *world of objects* by his personal activity, in his *work upon* inorganic nature, man proves himself a conscious species-being" but also that:

> In tearing away from man the object of his production, therefore, estranged labour tears from him his *species-life*, his real objectivity as a member of the species and transforms his advantage over animals into the disadvantage that his inorganic body, nature, is taken from him.[xxxii]

André Gorz, writing in the same tradition, put it thus:

> Working is not just the creation of economic wealth; it is also always a means of self-creation. Therefore we must also ask…whether the work produces the kind of men and women we wish humanity to be made of….can the complex tasks they are allotted fill their life and give it meaning without simultaneously distorting it?[xxxiii]

Pope John Paul II said something broadly similar in his encyclical *Laborem exercens*:

> …as the 'image of God' [a human] is a person, that is to say, a subjective being capable of acting in a planned and rational way, capable of deciding about himself, and with a tendency to self-realization. As *a person, man is therefore the subject of work*….[Work] actions must all serve to realize his humanity, to fulfil the calling to be a person that is his by reason of his very humanity….[Thus] in the final analysis it is always man who is *the purpose of the work*.[xxxiv]

Working Hours

The modern evidence also provides support for giving employees more control over the number of hours they work. Sixty-three percent of people in Britain say they would like to work fewer hours,[xxxv] and in the past a majority of people in Europe have said they would like to work fewer hours even given a corresponding fall in income.[xxxvi] Part-time workers who *choose* to work part-time enjoy higher levels of life satisfaction than full-time workers.[xxxvii] More generally, well-being rises as hours worked rise but only up to a certain point before it starts to drop as hours become excessive.[xxxviii] The evidence also shows that well-being rises with the time spent participating in the community, volunteering,[xxxix] and seeing family and friends.[xl] Given this, it is hardly surprising that long hours are bad for well-being.

Equality and Growth

The evidence shows that we should make reducing inequality a higher priority than increasing GDP, at least for much of the time. This is partly because an extra £1 brings more well-being to a poor person than to a rich person, so other things being equal, the more equality, the more well-being: this is a standard assumption of orthodox economics, which the emphasis on GDP growth, and the business values associated with it, often obscure. The evidence confirms the assumption and makes clear just how little value the £1 creates when wealthy people receive it. It also contradicts claims that when the wealthy don't get the £1, they don't create the jobs, goods and services on which everyone else's well-being depends.

Another reason why reducing inequality can be more valuable than growth is the importance of 'relative income' (i.e. the income a person has relative to the incomes of other people) to well-being. Growth by itself does not increase most people's relative income—indeed, in practice it has been associated with falling relative income for many people, as the better-off enjoy most of its fruits. Redistribution, however, does increase most people's relative income. This is important to well-being, partly because we tend to feel more or less satisfied on the basis of social comparisons, but not only for this reason. There are also goods and services which do not become more plentiful as incomes in general rise, and which therefore tend to get more expensive as more money chases after them. These include houses with large gardens in crowded cities (to some extent all homes in crowded cities), homes in the catchment areas of the top 10% of state schools,[xli] holidays in beautiful and deserted nature reserves, and some goods used as status symbols. How much money you have relative to other people will determine your access to these things.

It is not that absolute as opposed to relative income doesn't do anything for well-being once a certain basic living standard is reached (as is sometimes misclaimed). However, the benefits of any rising absolute income may be reduced or even eliminated by falling relative income. For example, the positive impact of cheaper flights (a source of rising absolute income) may be outweighed by the negative impact of more expensive homes (a result of falling relative income for many).

There is also qualitative evidence that in some unequal societies, material aspirations are particularly strong and cannot all be met. The result is not just a zero-sum game but a negative-sum game: as inequality rises, the extra dissatisfaction of the large number of those with unmet aspirations outweighs the extra satisfaction of the small number with met aspirations.[xlii] Another potential consequence of inequality is insecurity: intuitively, we would expect more equal societies to produce a greater sense of security amongst their members, which we know contributes to well-being. So for example the evidence shows that a higher ratio between unemployment benefit rates and an estimate of the expected wage increases life satisfaction for both the unemployed and the employed.[xliii]

Yet another reason for prioritising inequality is that, *even controlling for income levels*, inequality has a negative impact on both mental and physical health,[xliv] which in turn are strongly correlated with well-being. Inequality is also linked to other social ills, such as crime, which affect everyone's well-being.

Housing and the Public Realm

According to a 2017 report by the UN, the population of the UK is likely to increase by c. 25% to 75 million over the next 30 years.[xlv] To meet the resulting extra demand for housing, and to relieve the existing pressures, will involve a huge programme of development. Of course, having a home is crucial to well-being, but the way homes and the developments of which they are part are designed will also influence significantly levels of well-being. For example, streets can be designed in ways that encourage social interaction, which in turn will increase well-being. Noise and pollution levels are important too. People with homes that have a view of trees suffer lower levels of stress than those living in homes with no such views. Being within walking distance of a park makes a difference to well-being. Access to cultural facilities makes a difference to well-being. Long commutes are very bad for well-being. Insecurity of tenure and poor repair (conditions associated with the private rented sector) are bad for well-being. So decisions made about housing and planning with have a huge effect on whether people flourish or not.

Good and Bad Consumption

The evidence shows that there is 'good' and 'bad' consumption, that is to say consumption that enhances well-being and consumption which fails to do so, or even damages it. In other words, real-life consumption patterns may not be as good as they might be. If equality is to be prioritised over growth (and if measures to address climate change also reduce the rate of consumption growth, which, as we will see, they might), then it will become all the more important to improve consumption, to increase quality rather than quantity. This may be one of the more controversial features of well-being planning, conjuring up images of young pioneer camps, and the restrictions on pub opening hours that persisted until the late 1980s. It is actually a matter of nudging and tilting the market: there is plenty of good consumption, and historically, business has made large amounts of money by producing products and services that enhanced well-being.

So for example, simply having more time to do the things you want to do—time with friends, or volunteering, or pursuing hobbies or whatever—is, not surprisingly, good for well-being. Hassle and stress is bad for well-being. There are an enormous number of products designed to save time and reduce hassle. Many of the best known innovations in the nineteenth and twentieth centuries did this, from the railway and the telephone to the washing machine, the car and the supermarket. In the twenty-first century some internet-based products have also done this.

Having a strong sense of identity, of belonging, of being part of a meaningful world, is also important to well-being. This creates a second positive role for consumption. The role of clothing, furniture and household ornaments in social display and in establishing a 'lifestyle' has long been commented on. This is not simply a matter of keeping up with the Joneses, status competition and showing off. More important is asserting one's individuality and also, paradoxically, one's membership of this or that tribe, one's place in the social world. Anthropologists Mary Douglas and Baron Isherwood argue that consumption is to be seen as satisfying "the social need to relate to other people. And to have mediating materials for relating to them." As such it is "a ritual process whose primary function is to make sense of the inchoate flux of events."[xlvi] Businesses have consistently responded to this need. In the eighteenth century, there was increased demand for well-made items amongst the 'middling sort' as urbanisation disrupted traditional identities and created a complex set of social gradations which could be expressed in different forms of display. In the 1950s, innovation in dye manufacturing made more brightly coloured clothes affordable and fashions changed, both amongst those who had been small children during the war, and those who were keen to put the war and austerity behind them. In the last decade, Apple's designers and smartphone technologists have created new symbols of connection with others.

Controversially, consumption can also increase the sense that one is happy and privileged, and in this way actually make one feel happier and less stressed by the problems of life. André Gorz has drawn attention to this:

> Commodities are always presented as containing an element of luxury, of superfluity, of fantasy, which by designating the purchaser as a 'happy and privileged person' protects him or her from the pressures of a rationalised universe and the obligation to conduct themselves in a functional manner.... [They are] compensatory goods... desired as much for their – if not more for their – uselessness as for their use value; for it is this element of uselessness... which symbolises the buyer's escape from the collective universe in a haven of private sovereignty.[xlvii]

This 'private sovereignty', this escape from 'pressures' and stress, is the opposite of the positive relationship with the world that defines well-being; nonetheless, given the way things are, it can mitigate pressures which reduce well-being.

Relations with others are much the most important source of well-being, and various forms of consumption are valued primarily because they build, and form a vehicle for, these relations (in ways other than those described by Douglas and Isherwood). In the eighteenth century, tea, coffee and sugar merchants became enormously wealthy by providing commodities which became the focus for new forms of sociability, namely the coffee house and, within the home, tea drinking, both partly the result of increased urbanisation. In the twenty-first century, Mark Zuckerberg's Facebook has done something rather similar, partly a technology-led phenomenon, and partly a result of the way people's networks have become physically dispersed and complex. Online dating agencies provide a more niche example, both responding to and creating new norms of social behaviour. In the 1950s and 1960s, the recorded music industry changed the social life of newly prosperous teenagers, while Henry Ford's success in the USA 30 years earlier was at least in part down to his contribution to ending rural isolation and creating opportunities for excursions. Television, which arrived in British homes in the 1950s, contributed to a new form of family life, and, as Roy Thomson famously said, was a 'licence to print money'. More recently, widescreen TV and football broadcasting have provided a new lease of life to some pubs and the sociability associated with them.

All kinds of shared enthusiasms, from motorcycling to ice skating, require products to keep them going and provide the basis for satisfying social encounters for people. The product need not be an object like a football—it could also be a well-designed place, which encourages both sociability and spending. One recent trend is the rise in the number of live events, which have become particularly popular amongst millennials. One study reported 72% of those attending them saying they'd like to increase their spending on experiences relative to physical things in the next year, with 79% saying that going to live events had deepened their relationships, and 69% saying that attending such events helped them connect better with their friends, their community and people around the world.[xlviii]

Activities that require focus or effort by the participant—playing sport or music, cooking, gardening, writing, painting—tend to generate higher levels of well-being than more passive activities.[xlix] This can be manifest in a sense of achievement, self-efficacy, creativity, health and personal fulfilment. Many of these activities involve consumption. Nike provides perhaps the best known example of a commercial brand aligning itself with active consumption of this type, but other brands engage with consumers in a similar way, and perhaps not surprisingly, Google and advertising agency Ogilvy report that "Consumers choose the brands that engage them on their passions and interests 42% more often than they do those that simply urge them to buy the product being advertised."[l]

I have discussed the positive role of consumption at some length, because I want to dispel any suspicion that there is something ascetic about flourishing. There is not. However, the other side of the coin is that people do not always consume well. Why is this?

There are at least four answers: addiction, stress, ignorance and laziness. All four give rise to suboptimal habitual behaviours, in ways that will be familiar to most people.

Addiction is perhaps the paradigmatic form of bad consumption. The product, or even the purchase of the product, gives a hit, but the hit doesn't produce any lasting satisfaction and therefore the consumer craves it, and repeat purchases in order to get it. The hit is pleasurable, but the negative impact on flourishing associated with the craving, the linked sense of futility, and in some cases the health side-effects, is greater than the positive impact of the hit. Not much consumption is addictive in this strong sense, but unhealthy food shares some of the characteristics: it is heavily advertised, may produce an instant kick, but through its effect on health and vitality can have a very damaging effect on flourishing over the medium to long term.[li] What drives profitability is the craving, not any positive impact on well-being.

Advertisers are explicit about the commercial value of craving. A fictional advertising executive put it thus: "I'm an ad-man. My mission is to make you drool. In my line of work, nobody wants you to be happy, because happy people do not consume."[lii] This helps explain the evidence that the more advertising people see, the more materialist and the less happy they are, and the poorer their relationships. The evidence also suggests that much consumption is a reaction to boredom and loneliness and a lack of meaning. It is a search for a hit to alleviate this, at least for a while. The trouble is the effect never lasts: in the end products cannot provide love or purpose.[liii]

Stress also produces suboptimal decisions, whether because we are busy, or bewildered by the choices on offer, or suffering stress for other reasons. An article from management consultants McKinsey describes how a company decided not to improve its product more than marginally, despite research showing that customers significantly preferred rival products—because further research showed that in actual purchase situations, busy customers just bought what they knew (McKinsey recommended other companies do the same).[liv] There is evidence that if you are poor you may make even worse decisions, because worrying about scarcity takes up mental bandwidth,[lv] while excessive choice has been shown to have a similar effect.[lvi]

Ignorance may be prejudice against some products or simply ignorance that they are available and enjoyable. I joined a bridge club recently, and it has enhanced my well-being, but for years I was ignorant that such places existed, and indeed had I known they existed I would have dismissed them as places designed for my parents' generation. Whether the activity requires payment is not really relevant. A woman who had been encouraged by a government-funded project to volunteer at a library, reading stories to children, found it immensely satisfying. She reported that she had not done it before because she had thought that people like her could not do that kind of thing.[lvii]

Laziness—well, we all know about lapsed gym memberships.

Countering these natural failings is not a matter of mass prohibitions or forcing people to learn the piano. But there may be things that can be done: what people consume does change when they learn more about what is available (otherwise new products would not be promoted) or learn about the health implications of different products; there are also a variety of 'nudge' techniques that can be, and have been, used to encourage good habits, from saving for a pension to eating more fresh fruit, and more ambitious advertising could be used to ensure good consumption. There could also be stronger restrictions or additional taxes on advertising (for example banning advertising to children, as it is on Swedish television).

Social Institutions

Work and consumption are not the only or most important sources of well-being for most people, and given the constraints on both that we are likely to see, they should not be. Social relationships and activities outside work are more important, and while, as we have just seen, consumption can facilitate these, the choices people make, whether about what they consume or about other aspects of their lives, may reduce their ability to flourish. Social institutions have a role in helping people make good decisions, that is decisions that help them flourish, and in some cases they will also provide the setting for activities and the sources of meaning that characterise a flourishing life. They are therefore part of any plan for the future.

Institutions such as schools, universities, the Church, the freemasons, guilds, political parties, volunteer-run charities and all kinds of club have always played a role of this kind. Perhaps the critical ingredient that such institutions provide is discipline. At work, you can do well or badly, and to do well you have to bow to the discipline of the organisation or profession or craft, at the same time challenging it when appropriate and making your own original contribution. You take part, in Alasdair MacIntyre's terms, in a 'practice,' activities with internal standards of excellence and with a purpose. For the same reasons, you can do well or badly at school or university, as a member of the Church, or as a freemason, member of a political party, or member of a football team—and again to do well you have to master the internal standards of excellence. It is this discipline that distinguishes active participation from passive consumption. Do-it-Yourself retailer Kingfisher has tried to support this discipline through various community initiatives, but for most consumer goods companies, passive consumption (and craving) is easier to sell. That is why the market is not a substitute for institutions of this kind.

Arguably discipline reduces the need for status symbols, for it addresses some of the same psychological needs. To use Mary Douglas's terms, it creates a social world, and, once mastered, it gives the individual a credible place in that world. It may therefore reduce the pressure to consume. But it is also very different from status-driven consumption. For while you can be a good or bad consumer—by buying the fashionable or unfashionable item, by getting a good price or being cheated—consumption does not generally require submission to a discipline, the adoption of a 'practice' (except perhaps for a small number of devoted fashionistas or connoisseurs). Normally, the place in the world it provides is simply bought—and suffers all the fragility of anything that is simply bought.

The education system, schools, colleges and universities, are amongst the most important social institutions. It follows from this discussion that their role extends beyond developing job-related skills. They also have to develop 'leisure-related' skills—that is the skills needed to master the disciplines of a meaningful and active life outside employment, and thus to flourish. In some ways this echoes nineteenth century objectives for elite education, which have been characterised as to "pass on the moral, intellectual, and religious heritage of Christianity and Greco-Roman high culture"; this was not primarily for the vocational benefits of this heritage but to create "Christian gentlemen."[lviii] The modern version is very different but has a similar high purpose; it was encapsulated in the Robbins report, published by the government in 1963. This set out four aims for higher education: "instruction in skills," the promotion of "general powers of the mind" and production of "cultivated men and women," "the advancement of learning," and finally "the transmission of a common culture and common standards of citizenship... that background of culture and social habit upon which a healthy society depends."[lix] Now we would also place more emphasis on ensuring that the children and students were happy and focused while in the institutions: a good in itself of course, but also the foundation for happiness in adult life.[lx]

Developing leisure-related skills and being concerned with students' happiness is not the same as providing entertainment—a disparaging view of non-vocational coursework that is occasionally voiced. Rather, it is to prepare them to lead 'the good life', and to help those around them do the same. It is to contribute to their personal resources in ways that allow them to feel capable, to pursue meaningful activities, to have aesthetic experiences, to feel a degree of autonomy, to subject themselves to the disciplines of a successful life. There is nothing very remarkable in this list. These are the objectives of many, if not most, educators. There is a well-established practical understanding of how to achieve them. And they are not merely whimsical preferences or luxuries, but the well-researched bases for flourishing.

WHAT MIGHT THIS MEAN?

Table 3.1 is an illustration of the different kinds of policies implied by the four ideologies referred to so far in this book. It is an extreme simplification of course, and focuses on those policies which are especially typical of the ideologies—it is obviously not comprehensive. The flourishing column, while based on the kinds of evidence just described, is especially schematic: any programme will also draw on the social democratic and localist approaches and use their policies; we will explore this in more detail in Chapters 7 and 8.

But who is going to make this happen? How can this possibly come about? Before we start talking about what changes are needed, let us turn to how change has happened in the past.

Table 3.1   Alternative emblematic policies

	Market liberalism	Social democracy	Radical localism	Flourishing
Automation	Deregulate labour markets Challenge monopolies Inward investment Training	Challenge monopolies Inward investment Training Tax and spend	Communities to control the technology	Balance work and leisure Increase work quality and security Link to inequality agenda
Inequality	Limited tax and spend Living wage	Substantial tax and spend Regulate labour markets Strengthen trade union rights	Encourage local economies, smaller business units and co-operatives	Target level and quality of consumption needed for a decent life
Housing	Abolish planning controls	Tax and spend—on subsidised housing Compulsory purchase	Communities to own or control land	Establish standards for homes and the public realm Compulsory purchase
Public services	Introduce markets and charges and so reduce tax and spend	Continue to tax and spend	Use local control to legitimise spend Communities to design and deliver services	Use well-being knowledge and participative democracy to legitimise spend
Climate change	Carbon markets Subsidies for research and infrastructure	Carbon markets and taxes Subsidies for research and infrastructure Regulation	Establish sustainability at a local level and build from there	Use inequality strategy, well-being knowledge and participative democracy to legitimise spend

NOTES

i. William Beveridge, *Social Insurance and Allied Services* (1942), p. 6.

ii. Paul Addison, *The Road to 1945* (1975).

iii. New Economics Foundation (NEF), *Changing Our Economy Today, Not Tomorrow* (event, 11 October 2016), http://neweconomics.org/2016/09/changing-our-economy-today.

iv. David Cameron (speech, 25 November 2010), https://www.gov.uk/government/speeches/pm-speech-on-wellbeing.

v. Paul Dolan, *Happiness by Design: Finding Pleasure and Purpose in Everyday Life* (2014).

vi. Alasdair MacIntyre, *After Virtue: A Study in Moral Theory* (1981), pp. 216–225.

vii. Ibid., p. 219.

viii. Martha Nussbaum, *Women and Human Development: The Capabilities Approach* (2000).

ix. Daniel Dennett, *Kinds of Minds: Towards An Understanding of Consciousness* (1996), p. 17: "Perhaps the kind of mind you get when you add language to it is so different from the kind of mind you can have without language that calling them both minds is a mistake." This has a neuroscientific basis in so far as split-brain research has shown that information is only fully reflected in consciousness if it reaches the language-dominant left-hand side of the brain: Arne Dietrich, *Introduction to Consciousness* (2007).

x. Corey Keyes, 'The Mental Health Continuum: From Languishing to Flourishing in Life,' *Journal of Health and Social Research* (2002, Vol. 43, p. 208).

xi. Ibid., p. 209.

xii. Richard Ryan and Edward Deci, 'Self-Determination Theory and the Facilitation of Intrinsic Motivation, Social Development, and Well-Being,' *American Psychology* (2000, Vol. 55, pp. 68–78).

xiii. Carol Ryff and Bernard Singer, 'The Contours of Positive Human Health,' *Psychological Inquiry* (1998, Vol. 9, pp. 1–2).

xiv. World Values Survey, *Findings and Insights* (2016), http://www.worldvaluessurvey.org/WVSContents.jsp?CMSID=Findings.

xv. Ibid.

xvi. *Encyclical Letter Laudato Si' of the Holy Father Francis on Care for Our Common Home* (2015).

xvii. https://en.wikisource.org/wiki/Constitution_of_Ecuador_2008.

xviii. Joseph Stiglitz, Amartya Sen, and Jean-Paul Fitoussi, *Report by the Commission on the Measurement of Economic Performance and Social Progress* (2009).

xix. Sarah Stewart-Brown and Kulsum Janmohamed, updated by Frances Taggart et al., *Warwick-Edinburgh Mental Well-being Scale: User Guide Version 2* (NHS Scotland, 2016).

xx. https://www.ons.gov.uk/visualisations/dvc364/dashboard/index.html.

xxi. https://worlddatabaseofhappiness.eur.nl/.

xxii. Nick Macpherson, *The Treasury View* (Speech to the Mile End Group, 15 January 2014).

xxiii. Darren Nixon, '"I Can't Put a Smiley Face On": Working-Class Masculinity, Emotional Labour and Service Work in the "New Economy",' *Gender, Work and Organisation* (2009, Vol. 16: 3, pp. 300–322).

xxiv. Jonathan Portes, 'Why You're Wrong If You Think Clamping Down on Immigration from Europe Will Help Low-Paid British Workers,' *The Independent* (18 July 2017).

xxv. Christine Berry, *Well-being in Four Policy Areas: Report by the All-Party Parliamentary Group on Well-being Economics* (NEF, 2014).

xxvi. Paul Dolan, Tessa Peasgood, and Mathew White, *Review of Research on the Influences on Personal Well-being and Application to Policy Making. Final report for Defra* (2006), p. 51.

xxvii. Department for Business Innovation and Skills, *Review of Evidence on Employee Well-being and Its Potential Impact on Workplace Performance* (2014).

xxviii. Department of Health, *Well-being: Why It Matters to Health Policy* (Presentation, 2014).

xxix. YouGov UK, *How Many Brits Like Their Jobs and Their Wages?* (2017), https://yougov.co.uk/topics/politics/articles-reports/2017/08/03/love-wage-balance-how-many-brits-their-job-and-the/. Sixty-two percent of this sample like or love their jobs and 16% dislike or hate their jobs; Qualtrics Pulse, 'The State of UK Job Satisfaction Revealed,' *The HR Director* (14 July 2017), https://www.thehrdirector.com/business-news/hr_in_business/state-uk-job-satisfaction-revealed/. Two thirds of this sample are satisfied with their jobs.

xxx. CIPD, *UK Working Lives: The CIPD Job Quality Index* (2018), https://www.cipd.co.uk/knowledge/work/trends/uk-working-lives.

xxxi. Gallup, *Weak Workplace Cultures Help Explain UK's Productivity Woes* (2017), http://news.gallup.com/opinion/gallup/219947/weak-workplace-cultures-help-explain-productivity-woes.aspx?g_source=EMPLOYEE_ENGAGEMENT&g_medium=topic&g_campaign=tiles.

xxxii. Karl Marx, *Economic and Philosophic Manuscripts of 1844.*

xxxiii. André Gorz, *Critique of Economic Reason* (1989), p. 87, quoted in David Harvey, *Seventeen Contradictions and the End of Capitalism* (2014).

xxxiv. John Paul II, *Laborem Exercens* (1981).

xxxv. CIPD, *UK Working Lives: The CIPD Job Quality Index* (2018), https://www.cipd.co.uk/knowledge/work/trends/uk-working-lives.

xxxvi. European Foundation for Improvement of Living and Working Conditions, *A New Organisation of Time over Working Life* (2003).

xxxvii. Samaah Abdallah and Sagar Shah, *Well-being Patterns Uncovered: An Analysis of UK Data* (NEF, 2012).

xxxviii. Paul Dolan, Tessa Peasgood and Mathew White, *Review of Research on the Influences on Personal Well-being and Application to Policy Making. Final Report for Defra* (2006), p. 51.

xxxix. Ibid., p. 52.

xl. Ibid., p. 59.

xli. Robert Frank, 'Does Money Buy Happiness?', In Felicia Huppert, Nick Baylis and Barry Keverne (eds.), *The Science of Well-being* (2005).

xlii. Oliver James, *Affluenza: How to Be Successful and Stay Sane* (2007); Tim Kasser and Richard Ryan, 'Further Examining the American Dream: Differential Correlates of Intrinsic and Extrinsic Goals,' *Personality and Social Psychology Bulletin* (1996, Vol. 22, pp. 280–287).

xliii. Paul Dolan, Tessa Peasgood, and Mathew White, *Review of Research on the Influences on Personal Well-being and Application to Policy Making. Final Report for Defra* (2006), p. 60.

xliv. Richard Wilkinson and Kate Pickett, *The Spirit Level* (2009).

xlv. United Nations Department for Economic and Social Affairs (UNDESA), https://esa.un.org/unpd/wpp/.

xlvi. Mary Douglas and Baron Isherwood, *The World of Goods: Towards an Anthropology of Consumption* (1979), pp. 4, 65.

xlvii. André Gorz, *Critique of Economic Reason* (1989), pp. 45–46, quoted in David Harvey, *Seventeen Contradictions and the End of Capitalism* (2014).

xlviii. Harris for Eventbrite, *Millennials: Fueling the Experience Economy* (2014).

xlix. For example Matt Killingsworth, *Does Mind-Wandering Make You Unhappy?* (July 2013), https://greatergood.berkeley.edu/article/item/does_mind_wandering_make_you_unhappy.

l. Thinkgoogle, *When the Path to Purchase Becomes the Path to Purpose* (July 2015).

li. On the addictive quality of unhealthy food, see Antoine Hone-Blanchet and Shirley Fecteau, 'Overlap of Food Addiction and Substance Use Disorders Definitions: Analysis of Animal and Human Studies,' *Neuropharmacology* (2014, Vol. 85, October, pp. 81–90). On advertising of unhealthy food to children, see Bridget Kelly, et al. 'Television Food Advertising to Children: A Global Perspective,' *American Journal of Public Health* (2010, Vol. 100: 9, pp. 1730–1736).

lii. Frédéric Beigbeder, quoted by Stefano Bartolini, *Manifesto for Happiness* (2011).

liii. Stefano Bartolini, *Manifesto for Happiness* (2011).

liv. Jon Cummings, Ravi Dhar, and Ned Welch, *Irrational Consumption: How Consumers Really Make Decisions* (McKinsey and Company, April 2015), https://www.mckinsey.com/business-functions/marketing-and-sales/our-insights/irrational-consumption-how-consumers-really-make-decisions.

lv. Rutger Bregman, 'Why Do the Poor Make Such Bad Decisions?' *TheCorrespondent.com* (June 2016).

lvi. Tibor Besedeš, Cary Deck, Sudipta Sarangi and Mikhael Shor, 'Reducing Choice Overload without Reducing Choices,' *Review of Economics and Statistics* (2015, Vol. 97: 4, pp. 793–802).

lvii. Sorcha Mahony, et al. *Understanding the Barriers to Raising Population Well-being* (New Economics Foundation, 2011).

lviii. Russell K. Nieli, *From Christian Gentleman to Bewildered Seeker* (The John William Pope Centre for Higher Education Policy, 2007), p. 2.

lix. British Committee on Higher Education, *Higher Education Report of the Committee Appointed by the Prime Minister under the Chairmanship of Lord Robbins 1961–63* (1963), pp. 6–7.

lx. http://www.cam.ac.uk/research/news/happy-children-make-happy-adults.

CHAPTER 4

Change in the Past (1)

Crane Brinton, in his 1938 classic *The Anatomy of Revolution*, quotes Protopopov, a Tsarist minister, writing shortly after the Bolshevik takeover:

> Even the very highest social classes became frondeurs [political rebels] before the revolution. In grand salons and clubs the policy of the government received harsh and unfriendly criticism.[i]

In this chapter, I draw on the work of a handful of historians and theorists who have described the conditions that have made significant change possible in the past. One of those conditions is the weakening of elite morale, as alluded to by Protopopov.[1] The other three are the emergence of a counter-elite, the formation of an alliance between this counter-elite and the people, and the existence of a strong ideology that unites opponents of the status quo. Students of political science may be reminded of the scheme proposed by Peter Hall in his study of paradigm shifts: weakening of morale is a form of Hall's 'motivation', ideology is

---

[1] Elites have been defined as groups that exercise the most power in a society (John Scott). As with any sociological definition, this has empirical content: it reminds us that power is exercised by groups and that some groups have more power than others.

© The Author(s) 2019
C. Seaford, *Why Capitalists Need Communists*,
Wellbeing in Politics and Policy,
https://doi.org/10.1007/978-3-319-98755-2_4

similar to his 'means', and the counter-elite and its alliances are a version of what he calls 'motor'.[ii]

I am not attempting a 'theory of revolution': sceptics have pointed out that no one has achieved this, and there are far too many historical examples to make any theory convincing.[iii] Nor am I attempting a review of the very large literature on political change—this isn't that kind of book. Instead I am describing some of the conditions for change that others have identified, and asking the reader whether he or she thinks that these or anything similar to them exist in Britain today. To the extent that they don't, I am asking what it would take to bring them about. We are not in a revolutionary situation, but I still believe that the history of revolutions is revealing: the contours are much sharper than in non-revolutionary periods, and this makes it easier to pick out what was critical to change—and, in different form, what may be critical to change now. I cannot prove that the conditions I describe are either necessary or sufficient—they are simply a lens for looking at where we are now.

Later, in Chapter 5, I will use this lens to describe how two counter-elites emerged in Britain between the 1940s and the 1980s, and how these counter-elites were associated with two waves of change. I will then suggest that a third counter-elite needs to take over, and push through a third wave of change.

WHY CHANGE DOES NOT HAPPEN

Before examining what makes change possible, it might make sense to ask why it *doesn't* happen all the time. In other words, what gives elites their power in the first place? How is it that consistently through history, a tiny number of people have been able to appropriate a vast proportion of society's resources, with the majority unable to do anything about it? What is it that is different in periods of revolution?

The uncontroversial part of the answer is that society contains organisations, and organisations are held together by very strong norms of obedience, with severe penalties for breaking them. They generally "require decisions by persons who happen to be strategically located in them," and some of these organisations "are concentrations of power in the wider society." Given this, it is natural that "their top decision-makers have disproportionate societal power and influence." They may then use this to ensure that "they... enjoy disproportionate privileges and protections."[iv]

This only gets us so far, though. Which organisations are "concentrations of power?" Why for example is an investment bank more powerful than a trade union? What gives the leaders of such organisations power outside the organisations they command? Why are they permitted to enjoy disproportionate privileges and protections? It is easy to see that an investment bank controls a mobile form of capital (financial capital) and a union even at its most powerful an immobile form (human capital), giving the bank an advantage. But precisely because it is easy to see this, the question arises: why is this imbalance allowed to continue?

Steven Lukes has pointed out that those exercising power may do so in three ways: they can make decisions, they can set the agenda that determines what decisions are made, and they can influence the perceptions of self-interest that result in support for those decisions and that agenda.[v] It may be that those 'strategically located' in 'concentrations of power' are simply those who are well placed to exercise power in these ways, and it is this that allows them to extend their power beyond the organisations they run, and to secure their privileges. But what is it that makes them well placed in this way? We need to unpick this if we are to avoid a kind of fatalism: the powerful are powerful because they have access to resources, and they have access to resources because they are powerful; therefore they can never be dislodged.

'Social capital' has been defined as the set of "norms and networks that facilitate collective action."[vi] This is useful because it helps us see any group capable of acting collectively as a *network* that has *shared norms*. Depending on the scope of the collective action, those norms may amount to a complete ideology, as defined in Chapter 1. A group merely concerned with running a voluntary cafe needs norms, but these hardly need to add up to an ideology; a group concerned with running or changing society also needs norms, but these *do* need to add up to an ideology. Perhaps the elite is not simply a collection of individuals in powerful positions, but a group of this kind, capable of acting collectively, indeed capable of more wide-ranging and effective collective action than any other group. If this is true, then to understand why it is effective, we need to look at the networks and ideology that define it.

The classic account of an elite conceived in this way was given by C. Wright Mills. The evolution of the economy and of war in mid-century America had meant that "business and government.... cannot now be seen as two separate worlds." The resulting 'power elite' controlling both business and government achieved a degree of homogeneity and effectiveness, not just because of this structural convergence, and not just because the men (sic) involved had come from similar economic and social backgrounds, but above all because of their shared values and codes:

> Even if their recruitment and formal training were more heterogeneous than they are, these men would still be of quite homogeneous social type. For the most important set of facts about a circle of men is the criteria of admission, of praise, of honor, of promotion that prevails among them; if these are similar within a circle, then they will tend as personalities to become similar. The circles that compose the power elite do tend to have such codes and criteria in common....
>
> There is a kind of reciprocal attraction among the fraternity of the successful [and therefore].... members of the several higher circles know one another as personal friends...they mingle with one another on the golf course, in the gentleman's clubs, at resorts, on transcontinental airplanes, and on ocean liners...[they] define one another as among those who count, and who, accordingly, must be taken into account.[vii]

It is not that the power elite is an extension of personal friendships. Nor is it a club with "a permanent membership with fixed and formal boundaries." There are "factions" and "conflicts" within it. However "more powerful than these divisions are the internal discipline and the community of interest that binds the power elite together." As a result, they feel "responsibility to one another.... For nowhere in America is there as great a 'class consciousness' as among the elite." And so, "each of them... comes to incorporate into his own integrity, his own honour, his own conscience, the viewpoint, the expectations, the values of the others." It seems likely that the factions and conflicts that Mills refers to are visible at the level of the individual decisions described by Lukes, but that Mills's internal discipline, the incorporation of others' viewpoints and values, influence the setting of agendas and the influencing of perceptions of self-interest that Lukes also describes.

Does this underlying unity characterise and empower all elites to a greater or lesser extent, or was Mills's account peculiar to 1950s America? As we will see in the next chapter, both Anthony Sampson, writing in 2004, and Owen Jones writing in 2014 felt that a homogeneous elite of the kind Mills described had re-emerged in Britain.[viii] However, in 1962, writing five years after Mills, Sampson had felt that the British elite was more fragmented, and that this was a form of elite failure.[ix] Members of the British Establishment, particularly those representing the old order on the one hand and the new men of modern industry and science on the other, were not sufficiently in touch with each other. Mills in 1956 and Sampson in 2004 were both describing an incumbent elite at the height of its powers; Sampson in 1962 was describing an elite undergoing a form of crisis.

We can also ask whether ideology—"the viewpoint, the expectations, the values of the others" as referred to by Mills—always plays such an important part, if not in a unified elite, then in the separate fragments? Henry Fairlie, as we saw in Chapter 1, appeared to put more emphasis on social connections. Indeed, at the level of explicit political ideology, the 1950s elite was diverse. But Fairlie's connections underpinned a set of social norms that from a distance look like an implicit ideology. It is these norms and codes that Mills too emphasised. Perhaps the stronger the personal social connections within the elite, the less explicit the ideology has to be to perform its function of facilitating collective action. The norms and codes are always there, we might say that an ideology of a kind is always there, but how explicit it is or has to be will vary. This view of ideology, incidentally, has a different emphasis to the Marxist idea that elite cohesion results from its ownership and control of the means of production, but it is not incompatible with it.

Either way, the homogeneity and effectiveness of the elite do not depend on everyone knowing everyone, or on a uniformly dense network. Mills and Sampson both draw attention to the relatively few individuals who straddle different worlds and gain in power as a result. For Mills, the "inner corps" of the power elite consisted of men like "the admiral who is also a banker" or "the general who becomes a statesman" as well as the professional go-betweens—lawyers and investment bankers.[x] In the 1990s, network theorists would formalise these observations, identifying the particular power enjoyed by those who "make connections and act as the key intermediaries between organisations, sectors, and activities that would otherwise be disconnected,"[xi] such as the socialist politician on friendly terms with investment bankers, or the archbishop who understands business.

How does the elite differ from the rest of the population? The critical difference is not so much that those outside the elite lack the resources of those in the elite; if that was what mattered, radical change would never happen because those outside the elite always lack resources. The critical difference is that whereas the elite is normally united, as just described, those outside the elite are normally disunited. John Scott, a student of elites, writes that alliances amongst those leading the opposition may be common, but they rarely fuse into a 'counter-elite' of the kind I have referred to, and capable of taking over the regime.[2],[xii] Michael Moran makes a similar point: organisations challenging business "operate under very serious limits, partly due to the lack of any single ideological agenda or common institutional cohesion."[xiii] Nick Srnicek and Alex Williams lament that leftists "lack a cognitive map of our socio-economic system," that is to say they lack a coherent ideology, and so remain fragmented. This is why all they can do is resist—'save our health service, stop austerity'—rather than bring into being a new world.[xiv]

This disunity, this ideological incoherence, does not come about because those in opposition are temperamentally more argumentative than the elite (although veterans of activism might disagree), but because, unlike the elite, they do not run the system. The elite has an advantage: it has a single ideology because it runs a single system. One system, one ideology that supports and is shaped by that system, one elite. By contrast, the elite's opponents can normally only coalesce around things they are opposed to. In addition, as Mills says, "there is a kind of reciprocal attraction among the fraternity of the successful." There is rarely a comparable basis for mutual attraction amongst insurgents.

In short, the elite enjoys unity based on a shared ideology, more or less explicit, which those outside the elite do not normally enjoy. This is an important source of power. It is also a source of power that exists most of the time, but not all the time.

Loss of Morale Amongst the Elite

Sometimes significant fissures appear within the elite and the "codes and shared values" weaken. This leads to loss of confidence, at least amongst a dissident faction. Brinton, writing about the periods before

---

[2] Scott talks of distinct counter-elites that fail to fuse into a single counter-elite. The distinct counter-elites he refers to are "those that organise the response to the exercise of power." They are not really counter-elites of the kind that took over in France in the 1790s, or Britain in the 1940s and to avoid confusion I will not refer to them as counter-elites.

the English, French and Russian revolutions, describes the elite's loss of self-confidence thus:

> The old ruling class – or rather many individuals of the old ruling class – come to distrust themselves, or lose faith in the traditions and habits of their class, grow intellectual, humanitarian, or go over to the attacking groups.

In the 1780s, a significant minority of the French aristocracy were openly contemptuous of their class and its privileges. William Doyle in his *History of the French Revolution* describes how "the salon-haunting Canon Sieyès of Chartres" was commissioned in 1788 by "The Society of Thirty," an exclusive and mainly aristocratic political club, to write a pamphlet denouncing "privilege as parasitic and socially divisive." Sieyès continued the theme in a subsequent pamphlet, in which he described the nobility as a "caste of idle, burdensome usurpers."[xv]

In Eastern Europe in 1989, there was a collapse of morale within the communist parties, and even within the leaderships, who, for the most part, gave up without a struggle once they realised that Gorbachev would not send troops to support them. The parties had been husks for some time and most members had lost all belief in them. For example, in Hungary, only 50,000 of the 720,000 members rejoined the party after it was dissolved and reconstituted, and in Poland the party simply dissolved itself in January 1990.[xvi]

Paul Addison in his book *The Road to 1945* describes how the wartime ration book had made members of the elite feel they *should* have egalitarian views even if they didn't really.[xvii] 'Fair shares' was the slogan of a publicity campaign run in 1941 to popularise clothes rationing, and it affected what could be said in polite society even if it did not affect underlying attitudes. Unlike the French and Russian aristocracy, the British Establishment had never formed a very isolated sub-culture, and to the extent that it had done, the war put a stop to it. This meant its 'loss of morale,' its acceptance of egalitarianism in this case, did not lead to a collapse. It bent, rather than broke, when confronted with socialism.

In each of these cases the codes and shared values of elite members were weakened. As Mills might have put it, they stopped liking each other quite so much. Their internal discipline and community of interest no longer carried all before it.

This loss of self-confidence was generally justified: it came about because the ruling classes had been unsuccessful in fulfilling their functions. The state had been badly managed, and often this was manifest in debt crises and arguments over tax. In England in the 1630s there was a crisis provoked by the King's attempt to raise 'ship money' in peacetime. In the North American colonies, 'no taxation without representation' was the famous complaint. In France, the government suspended payments on government debt in August 1788, following years of financial mismanagement and massive spending during the American War of Independence. In Russia the cost of World War I led to massive inflation—a loss of 94% of the rouble's value between the outbreak of war and the October revolution. In Britain, the failures of Baldwin's economic management in the 1930s had created a consensus for Keynesian economic policy. The Eastern European regimes too had been facing a mounting economic and debt crisis in the 1980s.

Not surprisingly, it is not just elite members who lose confidence in the elite. Robert Palmer, in his history of seventeenth and eighteenth century 'democratic' revolutions, has described "revolutionary situations":

> By a revolutionary situation is here meant one in which confidence in the justice or reasonableness of existing authority is undermined; where old loyalties fade, obligations are felt as impositions, law seems arbitrary, and respect for superiors is felt as a form of humiliation; where existing sources of prestige seem undeserved, hitherto accepted forms of wealth and income seem ill-gained, and government is sensed as distant, apart from the governed and not really "representing" them.

This, Palmer continues, leads to a crisis:

> In such a situation the sense of community is lost, and the bond between social classes turns to jealousy and frustration. People of a kind formerly integrated begin to feel as outsiders, or those who have never been integrated begin to feel left out....The crisis is a crisis of community itself, political, economic, sociological, personal, psychological, and moral at the same time.

This, however, creates an opportunity:

> ....Something must happen, if continuing deterioration is to be avoided; some new kind or basis of community must be formed.[xviii]

COUNTER-ELITES

Vilfredo Pareto, the Italian sociologist writing in the early twentieth century, described how counter-elites periodically take over—in effect they seize the opportunity described by Palmer. In the normal course of events, particular individuals join or leave the elite, and there are squabbles and fights between different factions. Nonetheless, the elite remains unified by shared attitudes, beliefs and patterns of behaviour, just as Mills later described. Over time, however, it becomes degenerate—that is, it becomes closed to outsiders, mediocre and motivated by mutual back-scratching. This decay creates the opportunity for a previously excluded counter-elite to take over or force its way into the elite. This counter-elite has different shared attitudes and behaviours—it is these attitudes that define it as distinct from the elite. Its rise to power does not necessarily mean revolution: it can take over peacefully. However if the incumbents resist, the situation can escalate into a revolutionary one.[xix]

This is, of course, a schematic account: in all but the most extreme situations the boundary between elite and counter-elite is much less distinct than this summary of Pareto suggests. The counter-elite is not normally sharply defined in the way that an opposition party is, for example, and it does not necessarily take over political power in a clear-cut way after winning an election or mounting a successful insurrection. The counter-elite is an ideal type, and if we look at historical examples, we can identify groups that resemble this ideal type; they acquire influence suddenly, as in a revolution, or more gradually, as in Britain twice since the war. These groups resemble the ideal type more or less closely, but they are all 'elite', in the sense that they have the competence to exercise power and they are all 'counter', to the extent that they can be distinguished from the incumbent elite by their attitudes and behaviours.

A sharply defined counter-elite played a prominent role in the French revolution. The incumbent elite was closed to outsiders and mediocre, and as a result:

> It was the bourgeois, the men of letters, the financiers, in fine all those who were envious of the nobility, who raised against the nobility the petit bourgeois of the towns and the peasants in the country.[xx]

So said the Comte de Rivarol, quoted by Brinton. This group, according to Brinton, was aggrieved precisely because it was close to the ruling class:

> The strongest feelings seem generated in the bosoms of men – and women – who…have enough to live on and who contemplate bitterly the imperfections of a socially privileged aristocracy…. Revolutions seem more likely when social classes are fairly close together.[xxi]

It is natural for able men and women who are excluded from the positions they feel their ability entitles them to resent this. In Paris in the 1780s there were many such men and women, as in late nineteenth century and early twentieth century Russia.

A similar counter-elite formed in the English, American and Russian revolutions. The counter-elite was never entirely made up of outsiders in these examples, however. It always included members of the ruling classes who "have joined the intellectuals, and deserted the established order, have indeed often become leaders in the crusade for a new order."[xxii] These include men like Cromwell in England, Washington in America, and Lafayette and Mirabeau in France. Even Lenin's father was a senior civil servant. Barrington Moore, writing about revolutionary changes in Japan, Germany and England, also describes alliances between 'new' groups and members of the old elite. In Japan and Germany "a relatively weak commercial and industrial class relied on dissident elements in the older and still dominant ruling classes" to drive change. In seventeenth-century England, members of "the landed upper classes… were… an important part of this capitalist and democratic tide."[xxiii]

In short, the counter-elites leading the revolution were made up of dissident insiders, that is dissident members of the elite, and outsiders. Once the tumultuous phase of the revolutions was over, there tended to arise, in Brinton's words:

> a kind of amalgamation in which the enterprising, adaptable, or lucky individuals of the old privileged classes are for most practical purposes tied up with those individuals of the old suppressed classes, who, probably through the same gifts, were able to rise…especially notable in the army and the civil service but it is almost as conspicuous in business and industry and higher politics.[xxiv]

In other words, a new, unified Establishment formed.

In Britain, in the late nineteenth century and early twentieth century, a counter-elite dominated by outsiders rather than dissident members of the elite, emerged—that is to say the Labour Party. Although the party had links with middle-class organisations, notably the Fabian Society, its MPs and its leadership were initially solidly working class. In due course, the party replaced the Liberals as the main progressive party and became the vehicle for the progressive middle class as well as the working class: by 1935 it had a public school-educated leader (Clement Attlee). Thus, by the time it was exercising effective power, the party's leadership had begun to look more like the French revolutionary counter-elite, one with both insider and outsider members.

During the Second World War, this counter-elite became part of government (Attlee was Deputy Prime Minister), and began to take over and change established institutions. This is a common pattern: one study of institutional change suggests that counter-elite members with sufficient energy and commitment can often take over and change the direction of existing institutions, or they can increase the relative importance of what have been secondary institutions, or they can build new functions into existing institutions. They do not need to smash and rebuild.[xxv]

Labour's ideas also became widely accepted. As Paul Addison explains in *The Road to 1945*, by the time Attlee became Prime Minister, many businessmen had accepted the case for nationalisation, and even Conservatives didn't find Labour's programme too hard to stomach:

> By 1945 resistances in Whitehall had been largely overcome, the civil service galvanised… the consent of the Conservative party over much of the field secured in advance, and a team of Labour ministers schooled in office… The effect of war was to confer on Attlee a double mandate: one from the electorate, and one from within the Establishment.[xxvi]

Nonetheless the Labour leadership did still constitute a counter-elite: it may have had a mandate from the Establishment, but it had not simply become the Establishment. Its attitudes and behaviours remained different, largely because it had a solid alliance with the working class. The links with working class organisations—trade unions—meant something, and the party's role—to improve the material conditions of the working class—was universally understood. The 1945 election was hard fought.

The Labour leadership also formed the nucleus for a wider, modernising counter-elite that emerged in the post-war years, as we will see in Chapter 5. This was partly a reaction to what seemed at the time to be an Establishment buried in the past.

THE PEOPLE

The counter-elite does not make revolution on its own. The network has to extend more widely to include those 'petit bourgeois' and 'peasants' that Riverol described. In revolutionary Massachusetts, "network analysis …reveals that Paul Revere was one half of a duo that crossed the class divide in revolutionary Massachusetts between artisans and professionals."[xxvii] He was a crucial link in the network linking those who fought, the artisans, and those who wrote, the professionals. In France, the Jacobin clubs were 68% middle class, 28% working class and 10% peasant.[xxviii] "The peasant movement fused with bourgeois demands" while "another major revolutionary ally was the urban crowd in Paris" writes Barrington Moore. This kind of network and the resulting alliances were essential, for while "by themselves the peasants have never been able to accomplish a revolution [and]… the peasants have to have leadership from other classes," it is also true that "discontented intellectuals can do little politically unless they attach themselves to a massive form of discontent."[xxix] They have to attach to the masses. This does not mean that the masses simply follow the agenda of the counter-elite: they do not.[xxx] It is that an alliance between counter-elite and masses, and thus the networks that make these alliances possible, have been essential to success.

The more moderate the change, the less clear-cut this analysis becomes—but alliances between insiders and outsiders remain important, as we just saw in the case of the Labour Party in 1945. In nineteenth-century Britain just such an alliance—between progressive members of the middle class and the working class—drove forward change, for example strengthening trade unions' position. In the 1860s the law in this area was unclear and the Conservative Prime Minister, the Earl of Derby, set up a Royal Commission to deal with it. This body recommended that unions have immunity from criminal prosecution, but *not* from restraint of trade law, and that the closed shop and secondary action be prohibited. However, three of its members, the Earl of Lichfield, Frederick Harrison and Thomas Hughes, produced a minority report, recommending immunity from criminal *and* restraint of trade laws, and no restriction on the closed shop or secondary action. By this point William Gladstone had become Prime Minister. He was lobbied by the newly formed TUC to accept the minority report, which he did, and which was implemented in the Trade Unions Act of 1871. Harrison and Hughes, who made the minority report happen, were Christian Socialists and sons of a stockbroker and a landowner, respectively. They were dissident members of the elite, insiders who were considered acceptable members of a Royal Commission by government officials despite their socialist views. They were effective because they worked with outsiders—the trade union leadership—as well as with insiders, officials and politicians.[xxxi]

It is not that outsiders *never* have an impact on their own: in modern Britain outsiders have on occasion had a direct influence on events without the help of insiders. They have done this by engendering a sense of crisis which has in turn damaged the ruling party's electoral prospects. The 'poll tax' riots, relating to the introduction of the Community Charge in Scotland in 1989 and in England in April 1990, is a case in point. In March 1990, there were riots across the UK, the most serious being in Trafalgar Square, when buildings were set alight to cheers from the crowd. At the same time public satisfaction with Margaret Thatcher's premiership fell to an all-time low (20% compared to an average of 40% during her premiership) as did satisfaction with her government's performance (16% compared to average of 32%).[xxxii] Labour's lead in the polls reached 20% at this point. Once the tax had been introduced, this lead fell somewhat, but the Conservatives were still well behind in November, when Margaret Thatcher's colleagues decided to remove her as Prime Minister.[xxxiii] John Major, her successor, asked Michael Heseltine, Secretary of State for the Environment, to develop an alternative to the Community Charge, and plans to abolish it were announced in spring 1991. The Conservatives won the 1992 election.

The September 2000 petrol price protest was effective for a similar reason: it too created a sense of crisis which was electorally damaging.[xxxiv] In both these examples street protest worked because it created a crisis, and this crisis magnified the electoral impact of the underlying problem. Protest influences politicians when it influences voters. By contrast, the 2003 Stop the War march did not work: the sense of crisis it created was not sufficiently damaging to Labour's electoral prospects—or at least the party judged that getting rid of Tony Blair (the only way the war could have been stopped) would have been even more damaging.[xxxv]

IDEOLOGY

Networks of intellectuals are another ingredient of successful revolutions. According to Niall Ferguson, "from Boston to Bordeaux, revolution was in large measure the achievement of networks of wordsmiths"[xxxvi]

Importantly they did not just complain or express their alienation from the prevailing system, in Brinton's phrase they *transferred their allegiance*:

> To what did our successfully revolutionary intellectuals transfer allegiance? To another and better world than that of the corrupt and inefficient old regimes. From a thousand pens and voices there is built up in the years before the revolution breaks out... the foundations of the revolutionary myth...the revolutionary ideal.... What differentiates the ideal world of our revolutionaries from the better world as conceived by more pedestrian persons is a flaming sense of the immediacy of the ideal, a feeling that there is something in all men better than their present fate, and a conviction that what is, not only ought not, but need not be.[xxxvii]

He contrasts these zealous propagandists with "the merely alienated intellectuals of the twentieth century." What marked them out was not just their idealism, but also their belief that there was an "abstract, all-powerful force" on their side, a "perfect ally." For the Puritans of the English Civil War this ally was God, for the *philosophes* of the French revolution, it was Nature and Reason, and for the communists of the Russian revolution, it was "The inevitable march of economic forces scientifically understood."[xxxviii]

In 1945, winning the war created the equivalent of Brinton's "all-powerful force." Addison quotes the diary of J. L. Hodson:

> A young Radical friend said yesterday: 'We've shown in this war that we British don't always muddle through: we've shown we can organize superbly – look at those invasions of the Continent which have gone like clockwork; look at the harbours we've built on the beaches. No excuse any more for unemployment and slums and underfeeding. Using even half the vision and energy and invention and pulling together we've done in this war, and what is there we cannot do?'[xxxix]

This is a beautiful distillation of an ideology, shared by the planners in government departments who were "organizing superbly," by young Radicals like the diarist's friend, and by many of those who voted for Labour and who believed in its election slogan 'Now Let's Win the Peace.'

The essence of the ideology was not particular policies or programmes but an attitude: that the world was amenable to planning, that there were no excuses for unemployment, slums or underfeeding. Ideology does not need to be prescriptive in a detailed way to be effective, to fit the grain of society and to help unify the elite around a progressive programme.

Two contemporary examples also illustrate this: the ideologies of the Chinese Communist Party and of the ruling party in Ecuador. Neither of these dictates sets of policies, but they both help to set broad objectives and prescribe an approach to achieving these. This then serves to ensure that members of these groups can communicate with each other and with a wider audience.

Marxism remains the ideology of the elite in China. What does this mean? Ma Hui, a senior Chinese diplomat in London, explains that it is the approach rather than the precise content that matters.[xl] Central to this approach is the idea of dialectic, the idea that events are driven by the resolution of contradiction. The Party defines the contradiction. Until recently it was between the backward level of production and the material and cultural needs of the people, but now it is between unbalanced and inadequate development and the people's needs for a better life, including justice, fairness, a good environment, democracy and freedom.

This might sound vacuous to a Western ear, but it is important, not just because it creates a sense of direction for everyone working in the state or party apparatus, but because it creates a degree of certainty, a sense of inevitability. The Marxist dialectic implies that the direction set by the leadership is more than a choice: it is the result of objective conditions. It is a matter of history, not personal whim—and this contributes to consistent policy. This is not to deny the existence of corruption, the exercise of clan- and family-based power, and personal ambition. But for the last 35 years or so, these have not seriously destabilised the regime. As Ma Hui observes, some Western politicians say privately that they admire China's ability to do long-term planning (this is true—I heard the same) but, he goes on, "It is not just that we have a long-term plan, it is that we stick to it. We are still working out the vision that Deng first articulated in the 1980s, although of course the CPC leadership has adjusted and upgraded the goals." He continues "The implementation is good because we have unity and discipline. If you have 1.3 billion people you have to have unity and discipline. We tried multi-party elections in the 1920s and 1930s and they didn't work." Marxism and the dialectic approach provides the ideological basis, the cohesion and legitimacy that underpin this discipline.

The resulting ideological conviction reinforces executive efficiency. Will there be resistance to the measures needed to address inequality? "In our system that is not a problem" says Ma. What about inequality between the regions? A big problem, but in China, Shenzhen (a prosperous seaboard city), will, for example, twin with a poor city in Tibet and help it—it will provide skilled workers, and investment and so on. "Will a town in Surrey do the same for one in Lincolnshire?" Ma asks. It is possible, but "In China we do it in a systematic way. It is a Party order." Central control of the regions is not all plain sailing of course, but Ma smiles and says, "it is our sales line that the strong leadership of the Party creates our success, but we really do believe it!" It doesn't always get things right of course: Party policies have also increased inequality, and obviously enough it is not Marxism itself that produces bureaucratic energy, *vide* the Soviet Union. The point is a less contentious one: given its fit with other features of Chinese society, belief in Marxist ideology has helped make the bureaucracy more effective.

The Party Schools, and notably the School of the Central Committee, form one channel for this influence. The latter is an important institution and its President is a member of the Politburo. It provides a wide range of courses—Ma for example attended one on the international economy before working in London. "You have to go at least every five years. I went for two months last time. All Ministers have to go on a course every year." There are schools at the centre, in the regions and in cities. The central school mixes people up from all over the country, and "you come to understand the perspectives of people from other regions—a city official has a very different perspective from a central Beijing official. You share challenges and experiences. Compare notes." The networking is useful, "but you mustn't form small groups. You have to eat in the canteen and eating out with a small group of others is punished."

In Ecuador, the ideology of 'Buen Vivir' plays a role a little similar to that of Marxism in China, although it is more aspirational and there is no equivalent of dialectic. It is perhaps more like the 'ecological civilization' rhetoric that the communist leadership has grafted on to its Marxist framework. Like Marxism, it is not a detailed guide for policy makers, but it does provide legitimacy to the regime, it is built into the constitution, and it is a reference point for the broad direction of policy. According to Eduardo Gudynas, a leading scholar in the field, its defining characteristic is harmony, both between human beings, and between human beings and nature.[xli] "It allows us to dream of alternatives," he says. Fidel Narváez of the London embassy agrees that it has little influence on the details of the government's development plan, let alone day-to-day policy making.[xlii] For example, Buen Vivir, if implemented fully, would limit extractive industries, but Ecuador's exports are still dependent on them. However, it does provide a distinctively Ecuadorian legitimacy for the basic goals of that plan: eliminating poverty, reducing inequality and protecting the environment. Importantly, it is partly rooted in indigenous culture, and is not simply a version of European humanism. It also gives legitimacy to those criticising the government for not doing enough to rein in extractive industries and prevent the environmental damage they create: before 2008 this was not even discussed.

Arguably Buen Vivir, like Marxism in China, has contributed to the stability of the regime. Before Rafael Correa was elected president in 2007, there had been eight presidents in the previous ten years, and 20 constitutions since independence. Correa remained president for ten years. While support for the ruling party has gradually eroded in the intervening elections, there has been no return to the instability of the past. Ecuador has a planned economy and there is a significant amount of tax-funded redistribution, but the locally owned private sector has benefited from state investment and the doubling of GDP during Correa's presidency, and the social compact between capital and the state has just about been maintained. That compact is balanced by Buen Vivir, rather as the Chinese Communist Party's compact with capital is balanced by a Marxist framework that continues to make the welfare of the working class a priority. Lenín Moreno, the president who took over in 2017, has criticised Correa for running an excessively top–down planning system, and Correa has in turn criticised Moreno. However, both accept the commitment to Buen Vivir. Their dispute is over who has been the better custodian of the ideal.

The story of revolutions, and even to some extent of 1945, tells us that there can always be a 'restoration.' This happened in France after the French revolution, and in England after the Civil War. The Jacobins may have been able to form a network with the petits bourgeois and the peasants, but they were not able to change the fundamentally hierarchical nature of French rural and small-town society, which reasserted itself and which sat uncomfortably with the idealisation of reason and equality as propagated by the *philosophes*.[xliii] This hierarchy shaped the elite network and its ideology—the latter is always likely to reflect the reality of the society that it runs, for it is precisely this that gives it its unifying power. So it was hardly surprising that the elite abandoned reason and equality once the revolutionary momentum had played out. Similarly in seventeenth-century England, Puritanism never became the creed of the elite that emerged after the Civil War. In America, by contrast, there was no restoration. As De Tocqueville wrote, the "general equality of conditions" predated the American revolution, and the democratic political order of the republic was amongst its "natural consequences."[xliv]

The implication is that not any ideology will do. There has to be a fit with the grain of society. In modern Britain, metropolitan elites have to come to terms with the nature of British provincial society, and those whose feelings of solidarity rest on familiarity rather than openness, as David Goodhart amongst others has argued forcefully.[xlv] Radical leftists can make use of the British belief in fairness, the National Health Service, and the end of class privilege, but they also have to engage with British conservatism and patriotism. If this warning is ignored, even if there is a revolution, there will be a restoration, probably because a government committed to the politics of fear will be elected after a brief and chaotic interlude.

NOTES

i. Crane Brinton, *The Anatomy of Revolution* (1938, rev. ed., 1965), p. 52.
ii. Peter Hall, 'Brother, Can You Paradigm?' *Governance: An International Journal of Policy, Administration and Institutions* (2013, Vol. 26:2, pp. 189–192).
iii. Clifton B. Kroeber, 'Theory and History of Revolution,' *Journal of World History* (1996, Vol. 7:1, pp. 21–40).
iv. John Higley, *Elite Theory in Political Sociology*, http://paperroom.ipsa.org/papers/paper_4036.pdf.
v. Stephen Lukes, *Power: A Radical View* (1974).
vi. Michael Woolcock, 'Social Capital and Economic Development: Toward a Theoretical Synthesis and Policy Framework,' *Theory and Society* (1998, Vol. 27, pp. 151–208).
vii. C. Wright Mills, *The Power Elite* (1956), p. 281.
viii. Anthony Sampson, *Who Runs This Place?* (2004); Owen Jones, *The Establishment: And How They Get Away With It* (2014).
ix. Anthony Sampson, *Anatomy of Britain* (1962).
x. C. Wright Mills, *The Power Elite* (1956), p. 288.

xi. Julie Froud, Mike Savage, Gindo Tampubolon, and Karel Williams, CRESC Working Paper Series, Working Paper No. 12, *Rethinking Elite Research* (2006).

xii. John Scott, 'Modes of Power and the Re-Conceptualisation of Elites,' in Mike Savage and Karel Williams (eds.), *Remembering Elites* (2008).

xiii. Michael Moran, 'Representing the Corporate Elite in Britain: Capitalist Solidarity and Capitalist Legitimacy,' in Mike Savage and Karel Williams (eds.), *Remembering Elites* (2008).

xiv. Nick Srnicek and Alex Williams, *Inventing the Future: Postcapitalism and a World Without Work* (2015).

xv. William Doyle, *The Oxford History of the French Revolution* (1989), pp. 90 and 94.

xvi. Paul G. Lewis, *Central Europe Since 1945* (2014).

xvii. Paul Addison, *The Road to 1945* (1975).

xviii. Robert R. Palmer, *The Age of the Democratic Revolution* (1959), Vol. 1, p. 21.

xix. Pareto's theory is summarised succinctly in John Higley and Jan Pakulski 'Pareto's Theory of Elite Cycles,' in Joseph V. Femia and Alasdair J. Marshall (eds.), *Vilfredo Pareto: Beyond Disciplinary Boundaries* (2012).

xx. Crane Brinton, *The Anatomy of Revolution* (1938, rev. ed., 1965), p. 58

xxi. Ibid., p. 251.

xxii. Ibid., p. 55.

xxiii. Barrington Moore, *The Social Origins of Dictatorship and Democracy* (1967), p. xii.

xxiv. Crane Brinton, *The Anatomy of Revolution* (1938, rev. ed., 1965), p. 243.

xxv. Wolfgang Streeck and Kathleen Thelen, 'Introduction,' in *Beyond Continuity: Institutional Change in Advanced Political Economies* (2005).

xxvi. Paul Addison, *The Road to 1945* (1975), p. 16.

xxvii. Niall Ferguson, *The Square and the Tower* (2017).

xxviii. Crane Brinton, *The Anatomy of Revolution* (1938, rev. ed. 1965).

xxix. Barrington Moore, *The Social Origins of Dictatorship and Democracy* (1967), pp. 479–480.

xxx. Georges Lefebvre, 'Revolutionary Crowds,' In Jeffrey Kaplow (ed.) *New Perspectives on the French Revolution* (1965), pp. 173–190.

xxxi. Mark Curthoys, *Governments, Labour, and the Law in Mid-Victorian Britain: The Trade Union Legislation of the 1870s* (2004).

xxxii. https://www.ipsos.com/ipsos-mori/en-uk/margaret-thatcher-1925-2013.

xxxiii. http://ukpollingreport.co.uk/historical-polls/voting-intention-1987-1992.

xxxiv. https://en.wikipedia.org/wiki/Fuel_protests_in_the_United_Kingdom, *The Guardian* (13 September 2000), *The Independent* (14 September

2000), http://ukpollingreport.co.uk/historical-polls/voting-intention-1997-2001.

xxxv. Alex Doherty and Ian Sinclair, *Reconsidering the Failure of the Anti-Iraq War March* (15 February 2013), https://www.opendemocracy.net/ourkingdom/alex-doherty-ian-sinclair/reconsidering-failure-of-anti-iraq-war-march, James Strong, *Legitimacy and Tony Blair's War in Iraq* (7 July 2017), http://www.democraticaudit.com/2017/07/07/long-read-public-opinion-legitimacy-and-tony-blairs-war-in-iraq/, http://ukpollingreport.co.uk/historical-polls/voting-intention-2001-2005, http://www.electoralcalculus.co.uk.

xxxvi. Niall Ferguson, *The Square and the Tower* (2017).

xxxvii. Crane Brinton, *The Anatomy of Revolution* (1938, rev. ed. 1965), p. 46.

xxxviii. This kind of ideological strength has driven many other revolutions according to Clifton B. Kroeber, 'Theory and History of Revolution,' *Journal of World History* (1996, Vol. 7:1, pp. 21–40).

xxxix. Paul Addison, *The Road to 1945* (1975), p. 19 quoting J. L. Hodson's war diary for September 1944.

xl. All the quotes from Ma Hui are from a conversation with the author.

xli. Eduardo Gudynas in conversation with Oliver Balch, 'Buen Vivir: The Social Philosophy Inspiring Movements in South America,' *The Guardian* (4 February 2013).

xlii. Conversation with author.

xliii. Niall Ferguson, *The Square and the Tower* (2017).

xliv. Alexis De Tocqueville, *Democracy in America* (1839).

xlv. David Goodhart, *The Road to Somewhere: The New Tribes Shaping British Politics* (2017).

CHAPTER 5

Change in the Past (2)

In his 1962 book, *The Anatomy of Britain*, Anthony Sampson described the various elites at the top of the law, academia, government, business, the military and other walks of life—the 'Establishment'.[i] This was a source of much comment and anxiety at the time. As we saw in Chapter 1, the term had been popularised by Henry Fairlie, who argued that there was a powerful group that used its social relations to exercise power and protect its own.[ii] An essay collection on the subject had been published in 1959,[iii] and at the same time a satirical article in *Queen* magazine had set out the rules of a fictitious club, The Establishment, rule number 1 being: "The aim of the Establishment is to run the country." In 1961, a real club with the same name, where satire was performed, was set up in Soho. In time this became thoroughly sleazy, appropriately so, for the widespread anxiety was not just about the power of the elite, but also about the way it seemed to combine power and decay.[iv] The Prime Minister himself, Harold Macmillan, with his drooping moustache, drawling voice and aristocratic wife was its emblem.

Elite and Counter-Elite in Post-War Britain

The widespread anxiety was not entirely without foundation. There was, as Sampson noted:

© The Author(s) 2019
C. Seaford, *Why Capitalists Need Communists*,
Wellbeing in Politics and Policy,
https://doi.org/10.1007/978-3-319-98755-2_5

an hereditary Establishment of interlocking families, which still has an infectious social and political influence on the Conservative party, banking and many industries.[v]

It was family and social links that held this group together: in a family tree at the beginning of his book he showed how descendants of three dukes (Devonshire, Abercorn and Marlborough) and those connected to them by marriage included seven ministers, one ambassador, one governor general, the governor and deputy governor of the Bank of England, four directors of a merchant bank, the proprietors of three newspapers and the owners of a brewer (Guinness). The chairmen of other major businesses—such as BP, Courtaulds, Vickers and AEI—were also part of this network. However, Sampson lamented, this old-fashioned Establishment had "lost touch with the new worlds of science, industrial management and technology." The result was general gloom: a country that had lost its sense of purpose, and that as a result was getting steadily poorer in comparison with its European rivals.

The 20 years following the Second World War was also a period when a whole wave of institutions was set up. These included the National Health Service (NHS), public and independent television, the nationalised industries (coal, gas, electricity, steel, rail, civil aviation, cable and wireless), new universities including the Open University, the London Business School, the new town development corporations, and the National Theatre and the Royal Shakespeare Company. For the most part these institutions were successful and improved the lives of the British people. Britain also played its part in setting up at least partially successful international institutions, including the UN, the IMF, the World Bank, NATO and the OECD, and it got rid of most of its empire.

How, it might be wondered, could such an ossified, even decaying, group be associated with the creation of new institutions, with a broader sense of national life? Sampson exaggerated a bit, writing as he did in the early 1960s when many others were also complaining of decay and stagnation.[vi] However, it is true that the new institutions created in this period were embedded in a society that remained conservative and backward-looking. Post-war Britain saw a revival of many 1930s social patterns, and many traditional institutions remained unreformed: the House of Lords, the public schools, the courts, local government. The empire may have been dismantled but foreign policy was based on outdated imperial memories, National Service alienated the young, and even the 1951 Festival of Britain was partly a celebration of the past.[vii]

However the dukes and the bankers were only one wing of the elite, and unthinking assumptions of continuity and British greatness only one picture of the world. There were other wings that were not rooted in ancient privilege, or at least not in ways that kept them insulated from the 'new worlds.' Sampson himself concluded that a single Establishment with a single set of shared ideas and values was a myth. He did not observe a single group with shared ideas and manners that was running the country. The worlds of the stock market, of the law, of the universities, of big business, of the armed forces, of the civil service—these all felt quite different. As he put it:

> ...the rulers are not at all close knit or united. They are not so much in the centre of the solar system as in a cluster of interlocking circles, each one largely preoccupied with its own professionalism.[viii]

The languages were different, the ideas were different—indeed for the modern reader it sometimes feels as if the centuries inhabited by the various elites were different. Sampson's account of parts of the City, Oxbridge and the law take us back to a pre-bureaucratic era, a style of operation that had been abandoned by the civil service as far back as the late nineteenth century when it adopted the modernising reforms proposed by Stafford Northcote and Charles Trevelyan.

Perhaps more important, we can now see that the elite contained a whole cadre of modernisers, well-connected individuals who straddled the old and new worlds and whose attitudes were often shaped by their wartime experience. They included, but extended well beyond, the Labour leadership that took power in 1945, and they continued to drive change in the 1950s and early 60s. They formed in effect a counter-elite, and it was precisely the contrast between them and members of the old order that gave colour to the accounts of Establishment decay. And it was they, rather than the dukes, that embodied in their different ways the institution building spirit. They included men from outside Britain like Siegmund Warburg, part of a prominent German Jewish banking family, who shook up merchant banking in the 50s and 60s and was contemptuous of the inward-looking "tolerance of mediocrity" he observed elsewhere in the City.[ix] He attended two client lunches every day and believed that "you have to become someone's friend to be their banker."

Committed to excellence, he believed this was manifest in style, and he wanted his bank to display this at all times. Harold Macmillan, despite being the emblem of decay, was in reality also a moderniser, heavily influenced by wartime experience. When Churchill appointed him Minister of Housing in 1951, he recruited Percy Mills, a businessman who had been a temporary civil servant at the Ministry of Supply when Macmillan was Parliamentary Secretary there between 1940 and 1942. He encouraged Mills to set up an independent, regional structure which successfully supervised the construction of over 300,000 homes a year: a "war job," as Macmillan put it, that had to be tackled "in the spirit of 1940."[x]

Oliver Franks was another temporary civil servant at the Ministry of Supply and in 1945 was simultaneously professor of moral philosophy at Glasgow University and permanent secretary. He remained a proponent of planning after the war and embodied the idea that persisted throughout the period that clever people could—and indeed should—get things done. He successfully negotiated Britain's Marshall Aid package and became, amongst other things, Ambassador to Washington, Chairman of Lloyds Bank, one of the first members of the National Economic Development Council ('Neddy'),[1] and, at different times head of two different Oxford colleges. Solly Zuckerman, another academic recruited to the war effort, became Scientific Advisor to the Ministry of Defence, and later to the government as a whole. He exercised an unusual level of influence on government military and strategic policy, in part at least because of his extremely diverse range of contacts in government and beyond, supported by a "glittering social life."[xi] Hugh Gaitskell was another academic turned temporary civil servant, intensely serious about political issues but who also enjoyed wide connections: "His circle is large and surprising: he can be seen at Belgravia lunch-parties, at night clubs, at the celebrations of café society or – more rarely – at trade union socials....Gaitskell dinner parties can include tycoons, Tory peers and American intellectuals."[xii] Other members of the Labour leadership who had been wartime civil servants (and academics) included Douglas Jay and Harold Wilson, while three allies of Gaitskell, the so-called 'revisionists', were contemporaries at Oxford and then the army: Tony Crosland

---

[1] 'Neddy' was set up by the Conservative government in 1962 to bring together management, trade unions and government to help plan the economy.

(also an ex-academic), Roy Jenkins and Denis Healey. Together these men repositioned Labour as the party of modernity.

The civil service itself was a kind of institutional bridge, although imperfect, between the old-fashioned part of the Establishment (some Conservative ministers) and the new worlds of science and business. It had all the failings of a somewhat inward-looking body designed to advise rather than decide, but at least compared to other parts of the Establishment it was meritocratic, not aristocratic: of the 30 permanent secretaries in January 1961, 26 had been to Oxbridge but only 11 to public school.[xiii] Only 4% of senior civil servants had been to Eton, compared with 32% of ministers.[xiv] Its high point may have been the immediate post-war period, when "an ethic of planning and social direction" was "widespread throughout the professions and the mandarin class of administrators."[xv] However, throughout the period everyone continued to believe that bureaucracies were agents of change, and its analytical approach and its organisation was something of a role model for many of Britain's modernising larger companies, the Unilevers and ICIs. As a result of this admiration, there was a steady flow of officials, especially Treasury officials, into jobs at major companies.

While there were obvious differences between the modernisers and the old order, even the modernisers were not as obviously homogeneous as Wright Mills's power elite. There was "a cultural bond…an unmistakable tone of voice," in Noel Annan's phrase, describing his peer group of the time, suggesting something like Mills's code of honour. However, members of this group might equally end up as "revolutionaries or conformists."[xvi] The starkest example of this were the spies: Kim Philby, Donald Maclean, Anthony Blunt. Part of the elite (Blunt even became Keeper of the Queen's Pictures), sharing a "tone of voice" with the rest of the elite, but communists. What bound the group together was not an explicit ideology, but something more deeply rooted.

Even in Westminster politics there was much more ideological diversity than is sometimes supposed. The term 'Butskellism' was coined by the *Economist* in 1954 to refer to a cross-party consensus in favour of the mixed economy, Keynesian economic management and a welfare state, and this consensus did indeed exist in the mid-1950s. In 1960 Daniel Bell wrote a book called *The End of Ideology*, and it was argued then and later that political convergence contributed to the dullness of the times and a declining interest in politics.[xvii] But as historian Kenneth Morgan has written:

> The very concept of Butskellism needs considerable revision. On social and industrial policy, a gulf existed even between the Labour right…and the Tory leadership. On fiscal policy there was a clear distinction in approach. Gaitskell's emphasis still lay on physical planning and heavy state involvement…Butler…favoured financial levers.

While the Conservatives wanted to maintain a social consensus, there was a clear difference between the 'property-owning democracy' they aspired to and Labour's 'socialism'. The destination was different and perhaps more important, the view of how the world worked was different. There was nothing like the consensus in support of market liberalism, with all its purported explanatory power, that has come to dominate politics over the last 30 years.

There were also sharp differences within the parties. It is sometimes suggested that advocates of the free market, monetarism and government spending cuts were considered a lunatic fringe at the time, making their ultimate triumph after 1979 all the more dramatic. But Peter Thorneycroft, who was just such an advocate, was Chancellor of the Exchequer between 1957 and 1958, hardly a fringe position, and at least some of Friedrich von Hayek's views came to be widely accepted in the 1950s. True, Keynesianism was the orthodoxy and Thorneycroft had to resign—but his proposals were taken seriously, including at Cabinet level. The imperialist and decolonising wings of the Conservative Party, led by the Marquess of Salisbury and Iain Macleod, respectively, also fought furiously. The Labour Party was also divided on the perennial questions of nuclear weapons and how far socialism could be taken, and on the extent to which nationalisation was a defining component of the latter.

In short, the elite was diverse—not in terms of class, gender, race or age, but in terms of patterns of behaviour, style, outlook and above all explicit ideology. This created a freedom of manoeuvre for those wanting to change society—there wasn't a lock-in to one point of view, whether on the left or on the right. There was very clearly a counter-elite committed to modernity, but the ideas that held it together, the norms that made it capable of collective action, were far more flexible than those that, at the other extreme, hold the Chinese elite together. Arguably both elite and counter-elite in their different ways were influenced by their wartime experience and in that sense remained committed to public action. *Queen* magazine was right: they formed an 'old' and a 'new' Establishment which, between them, really did want to "run the country."

INSTITUTIONS AND BUSINESS IN POST-WAR BRITAIN

Sociologist Richard Sennett argued in the 1970s that public life had "become a matter of formal obligation. Most citizens approach their dealings with the state in a spirit of resigned acquiescence."[xviii] Public life only took on significance now, he went on, to the extent that it was a projection of private life, and the intimate emotions and relationships found there—hence the over-personalised style of politics. This had not always been the case. In the eighteenth century, public life had more of the qualities of a drama, with its own conventions and significance, independent of those of private life.

Sennett was writing primarily about America and did not consider Britain's experience during the Second World War. Had he done so, he might have considered the drama of war, more intense than almost any other. This for a time reversed the logic of capitalism, which he believed had driven the flight from the public to the personal. Nor did the drama end with the end of the war—it continued to be played out throughout the post-war period. Indeed the ideological and stylistic differences we have observed continued to give it life, whether the matter was the style of merchant banking, the scope of planning, the advance of science or the future of the Empire. For this reason there was, in Tony Judt's words, "a moralized quality to policy debates in those early postwar years" with problems such as unemployment, inflation and low agricultural prices "regarded by everyone from priests to secular intellectuals as tests of the ethical coherence of the community."[xix]

We have already seen something of Labour's ambitions when it took power in 1945, and the way in which the ground had been prepared by work in government during the war, including the Beveridge report on the social ills that a determined government could eradicate, as well as R. A. Butler's 1944 Education Act. Its election-winning slogan in 1945 was 'Now let's win the peace'. In these circumstances it was natural for the people running the country to set up institutions that would help them win the peace, and the creation of which was *dramatic* in Sennett's sense. Nowhere was this more obvious than with the NHS and the nationalisation of the municipal and voluntary hospitals. This was opposed by the doctors, at one point by almost 90% of British Medical Association (BMA) members polled. And yet the resolution of this conflict produced a robust and popular institution, that worked almost from the start and that almost everyone has supported ever since. Aneurin

Bevan, helped in his negotiations by Lord Moran of the Royal College of Physicians, made quite serious concessions to the profession—pay beds for consultants and self-employed status for GPs—but preserved the essential principles of a national service and one that was 'free at the point of use'. He was successful because he accepted that conflict was an essential part of public life and of getting things done. Arguably this attitude is more likely in a world in which there is already significant ideological conflict within the elite, and where diversity of outlook is accepted. Fighting, and fighting again, as Gaitskell put it a decade later, is all part of the drama.

The new town development corporations, set up at about the same time as the NHS, were a response to slum conditions in London, made worse by wartime bombing. They too had to buy off existing interests—the residents of the areas affected and the farmers who owned the land. While Bevan was at one point called a health 'Fuhrer' by a representative of the BMA, Lewis Silkin, the planning minister responsible for new towns, was called 'Gestapo' at a public meeting in Stevenage; the railway station signs there were repainted 'Silkingrad.'[xx] However, the corporations were successful, rarely using their reserve compulsory purchase powers to acquire the land needed but still retaining the vast bulk of the planning gain. The conflict was more contained than in the case of the NHS, but the creation of whole new towns was also a genuinely *dramatic* piece of state action. Not for nothing was it referred to as the 'new town movement'. This, like Macmillan's housing programme, was a continuation of 1940s-style public action.

More generally, most of the institutions set up were intended to be universal, providing a service to the nation—they were public in a way that went beyond their ownership. William Haley, Director General of the BBC from 1944, even believed that the Third Programme, which he launched, could attract a mass audience: combining it with the Light and Home Programmes would "lead the listener on to more serious things."[xxi] This was quickly proven to be somewhat naive. But the BBC as a whole did successfully attract a mass audience, particularly BBC Television and particularly after Hugh Greene became Director General in 1960. The London Business School was founded in 1965 and it too had a broad national purpose: it was originally conceived of as a way of improving the productivity of British industry, even if its direct clients and beneficiaries were a small group of trainee managers.

At least some of the post-war institutions had a very distinct character—what would later be called a strong corporate identity. There was nothing faceless and monolithic about them, any more than the Establishment itself was faceless and monolithic. They were "receptacles of group idealism," in sociologist Philip Selznick's phrase, rather than mere organisations, that is mere "technical instruments judged on engineering premises."[xxii] They were not the dull bureaucracies often associated with universal services. On the other hand, they were not market-driven organisations with brands designed to reflect the preferences and emotional aspirations of their clients. The so-called 'plateglass' universities set up in the early 1960s are a particularly good example: they had very strong and distinctive identities, what their historian called "a university ideology of both learning and living," and most obviously embodied in their architecture.[xxiii] They—and the NHS, the BBC, and the new town corporations of the 1940s—all aimed to lead rather than follow their client groups, in a way that purely commercial organisations rarely find worthwhile.

And in general they worked. Their very different missions and identities were by and large internalised by those working for them, which is to say the institutions were indeed "receptacles of group idealism."

Nonetheless some institutions created during this period failed, notably the National Economic Development Council (see page 94 above) and the Department of Economic Affairs, both set up in the early 1960s to improve productivity in response to Britain's relative economic decline. It is also difficult to argue that The London Business School, set up in 1965, succeeded in its original mission either, with relatively few of its alumni and alumnae ending up as industrial managers. (It became a successful institution on its own terms, helping to staff the international finance and consulting industries—and is now proud of the fact that just 7% of its MBA students are from the UK.)

These three institutional failures were just small parts of Britain's larger economic failure and relative decline. In 1945, Britain was severely damaged by the war and had a capital stock in desperate need of modernisation, but it was still far more prosperous than its neighbours, with strong positions in the most advanced industries, such as aircraft, electronics and vehicles. By the 1970s, while living standards had risen very substantially, it had lost this leading position: all the countries of North Western Europe now had a greater output per head.[xxiv] The standard explanation for this is that British businesses did not *have to* modernise, did not have to invest in more advanced capital, in order to sell goods and remain profitable. Demand was buoyant anyway. This was for a number of reasons: in the 40s and early 50s, it was largely because of a lack of European competition, in the mid- to late-50s it was because of a deliberate policy to stimulate consumer demand,[xxv] and throughout the period it was because of strong demand from the military. At the same time most business leaders were not sufficiently international in background or focus to pre-empt the future threat represented by investment on the Continent. According to some critics they were not sufficiently interested in business either, aspiring as they did to a more gentlemanly lifestyle.[xxvi] Keynes half-joked that Britain's economic prospects would be much enhanced if "the American Air Force...were to destroy every factory on the North East coast and in Lancashire (at an hour when the Directors were sitting there and no-one else)."[xxvii] British motor manufacturers for example, were dismissive of the Volkswagen Beetle and rejected the possibility of taking over the design and plant at the end of the war. During this period UK subsidiaries of US firms tended to have higher profits than UK-owned firms, lending support to criticisms of the prevailing, somewhat insular, management culture. The spirit that drove the institution-building, modernising wing of the elite did not animate post-war British business.

Given these attitudes, a very strong government with a clear perspective on the economy would have been needed to correct the underinvestment. However, even under Labour, the high tide of economic planning ebbed quite quickly and there was little effective supply-side intervention. After a devaluation of the pound in 1949, Stafford Cripps was able to use macro-economic levers to reduce consumption, boost exports and maintain full employment, but there was still inadequate investment in a modern capital stock. Conservative chancellors were if anything worse. Samuel Brittan commented that they were "innocent of economic complexities...[and] did not have the practical financial flair that one might reasonably expect from a party with business links."[xxviii] They relied for advice on the "traditional sections" of the Treasury where there was little economic expertise. In this respect at least, Sampson's view that the Establishment was out of touch was well founded.

To argue that Britain was economically unsuccessful during the 1950s and 60s may seem perverse. This was the era, above all, when a great store of innovation and knowledge built up in the war years was drawn on and spread across the economy as a whole, and managed in a sta-ble Keynesian framework. The result was strong growth and rising living standards. Average weekly wages rose from £6. 8s. to £11. 2s. 6d.,[xxix] while in just three years, between 1955 and 1958, the proportion of households with a washing machine rose from 17.5% to 29%. Advertising spend rose four-fold between 1947 and 1960.[xxx] And the average growth rate between 1949 and 1965 was 3.3%—by comparison, between 1985 and 2012 it was only 2.5%.[xxxi] The anxiety amongst anti-establishment commentators was not occasioned by any absolute economic failure, but by Britain's relative decline, by the perceived persistent influence of an older order, and perhaps by disappointment that the glad confident morning of 1945 had turned into a drizzly afternoon.

BUSINESS AND THE ECONOMY SINCE THE 1980s

By contrast, living standards have not been rising in recent years, and despite the roll-out of information technology, Britain's productivity remains lower than that of its competitors—in 2013 17% lower than the G7 average.[xxxii] The overall growth rate has slowed since the 1960s. What is more, there are some real horror stories, such as the collapse of Marconi (formerly GEC), in 2001, and Carillion in 2017, and plenty of examples of top managers extracting value rather than investing in capac-ity, particularly in manufacturing.[xxxiii]

Nonetheless, Britain's *relative* industrial performance is not quite as bad as it was in the post-war years: relative to European competitors things got worse between 1945 and 1965, whereas at least they have stabilised over the last 30 years, and the manufacturing productivity gap with Germany has narrowed somewhat. We now have world-class sec-tors: motor-cars (after a lot of pain), pharmaceuticals, aerospace, whisky, higher education, creative industries and financial services, and not just because our competitors are still recovering from a war. These sec-tors tend to pay decent wages. Low productivity statistics reflect a tail of unproductive firms paying low wages, and thus the existence of a "two-speed economy." However, at least there is now a high-speed part. And it is this high-speed part that is associated with a second post-war 'new' Establishment, one that emerged in the 1980s. It is this high-speed part of the economy that sustains and is sustained by a newly privi-leged elite, in the same way that the institutions described in the last few pages sustained and were sustained by the original post-war counter-elite.

Some Conservative politicians and journalists have suggested that Britain's relative economic rise, the emergence of this high-speed part of the economy, was down to Margaret Thatcher's tough macro-economic policies and labour market reforms. This is partly true even if, overall, the economy as a whole has *not* been especially successful since the 1980s. Thatcher's negative achievement was using macro-policy to kill off some weaker parts of industry. Simply as a result of arithmetic, the average efficiency of industry went up. More positively, some notoriously inefficient parts of the economy dominated by very conservative producer interests were reformed and eventually prospered—stockbroking, cars and ports for example. The Single European Act of 1987, opening up markets in Europe and competition from Europe, also stimulated and disciplined some sectors of the economy. More generally, it is arguable that Thatcherism prompted a modernisation of British business culture, and that this did contribute to the success of the high-speed parts of the economy,[xxxiv] including some manufacturing. Privatised companies like Rolls Royce, and for a while British Steel, thrived, Japanese inward investment helped double car manufacturing volumes in the 15 years after 1982, and a series of mergers created critical mass in the pharmaceutical industry.

Partly as a result of these changes, and partly because successive governments chose to relax controls that might have prevented it, some of the UK's strongest sectors—investment banking and cars for example—are now dominated by foreign firms. Even outside the financial sector, foreign-controlled firms contributed 29% of gross value added in 2012, and there were more foreign- than UK-owned production and distribution companies.[xxxv]

As for so-called 'British'-controlled firms, they are often just as foreign as foreign-controlled firms, at least in the case of the larger ones. Their ownership may be international: in 2014 54% of the shares of companies quoted on the London Stock Exchange were in foreign hands.[xxxvi] Their management may be international: in 2015 39% of FTSE 100 company chief executives were from outside the UK.[xxxvii] And their operations are largely international: it has been estimated that in 2013 77% of the turnover of FTSE 100 companies came from outside the UK,[xxxviii] while integration into international supply chains has increased apace since the opening up of China and the rest of the Far East in the 1990s.

This has made the most successful sectors more successful. Global best practice is more likely to be adopted by international firms, and if, despite this, costs remain too high, operations will be relocated elsewhere—to Eastern Europe or the Far East. This means that those businesses remaining will be relatively strong. In addition, the kind of national diversity now found in large corporations can lead to better decisions, especially in times of change when different perspectives are needed, and especially if there are strong shared values, which the prevalent market ideology and the rise of the international business school has helped ensure.[xxxix] More controversially, from the 1980s onwards, governments seemed to become ever more attuned to the needs of business, with officials, politicians and business leaders sharing the same market ideology. Business culture seeped into the public sector—and in a reversal of the pattern seen in the 1950s, Whitehall was asked to learn from business practice. At one point in the 1990s, a senior Treasury official even denied the value of the public service ethic. At the same time, the globalisation of business has strengthened the hand of business in its negotiations with government, with the threat of departure from the country much more credible than in the past.

Meanwhile, relatively few new institutions have been created or revived, at least if devolved governments are excluded. While many of the institutions set up in the post-war period continue to thrive, there is nothing to compare with the expansion of national life that took place between 70 and 50 years ago. International institutions—notably the European Union—are somewhere between stagnation and crisis.

The Post-1980s Elite

The variegated Establishment that built the post-war institutions but permitted relative economic decline was very different to the modern equivalent, associated with this high-speed part of the modern economy. Sampson himself makes the comparison: he concluded in his 2004 book that, in contrast to what he had observed 40 years earlier there *was* now a single set of shared ideas and values that predominated throughout the modern Establishment, and that this could be summed up in one word: 'money'. Owen Jones, in his 2014 book on the Establishment, also painted a monochrome picture of a dominant group, all of whom, whatever their walk of life, appeared to share a strong belief in the value of money and markets, and who were able to use markets to maintain their wealth and power.[xxxl]

The result is dull and sometimes seedy when compared with the past. Both Siegmund Warburg and Bob Diamond, chief executive of Barclays in 2011–2012, made their city rivals uncomfortable at times with their aggressive behaviour. But whereas Warburg was committed to excellence and style—a 'prince' as his biographer called him[xli]—Diamond was forced to resign after a scandal involving the manipulation of the LIBOR interest rate. Percy Mills was a businessman who sorted out Britain's housing; in the twenty-first century, business skills are bought by government through wasteful and lucrative sub-contracts to companies such as Capita and G4S, and complex PFI schemes. The best known successor of the intensely serious Gaitskell was Tony Blair; according to one of his speechwriters he was a man who came to power without any clear sense of what he believed,[xlii] and after leaving office he advised dictators for large fees.

On the other hand, the demographics of the modern Establishment are much more diverse than those of the old elite: if the 1962 version was male, white, middle-aged and English, then the modern version is at least a little bit female, non-white and young, and certainly no longer simply English. The business elite in particular has become highly international, and largely educated in a small group of international business schools. The national bases for cohesion—including memories of the War—have been replaced with an ideological one.

The rise of this group in the 1980s and 90s was associated with a successful populist attack on elites and elite values and the continuing rise of the mass market. There was a loss of confidence in the institutions inspired by these values that the previous generation had set up and an identification of the mass market with 'the people'. "Society is dominated by an elite of anti-elitists" said Conservative politician George Walden.[xliii] Labour politician Tessa Jowell provided a nice example. Culture minister, and as clearly a member of the elite as anyone, she remarked that opposition to super-casinos reflected the "elitism and anti-American sentiment" of "snobs who want to deny ordinary people the right to bet."[xliv] Nick Cohen pointed out that "It was essential for the ambitious to swear they were the enemies of elitism."[xlv] Or, as Martin Jacques wrote in 1994, "Society's centre of gravity has shifted from the top to the bottom, from the Establishment to popular culture."[xlvi]

This apparent contradiction led to the rise not just of money but of 'irony' and 'knowingness'—the cultural pattern that masks but also perpetuates social difference, the real difference between elite and non-elite. The effect was that 'everyone' saw through status signifiers, but still subscribed to them: the perfect combination for an elite of anti-elitists. As has been said, we know advertisers and presidents lie, but we still buy their products and still vote for them. Indeed status became associated with being able to see through status, or at least pretending to do so (since the whole exercise remained status driven). At the same time irony contributes to the feeling identified by another commentator "that nothing matters, that nothing should be taken seriously."[xlvii] Public life as a significant drama, in Sennett's terms, became impossible.

This is not the whole story of course. Sports, traditional cultural interests (opera, theatre, visual arts), and personal connections continue to help cement the elite as they have always done, and as Mike Savage has illustrated in his commentary on The Great British Class Survey.[xlviii] A study published in 2008 showed that 25% of the directors of FTSE 100 companies were actively involved in sports or arts institutions, while a prominent French businessman has noted how much more important business social life is in England as compared with France.[xlix] The very top echelon of business and finance remains something of a village, held together by these personal connections—I was very struck by this when I worked on the fringes of this world in a strategy consultancy—even if lower down impersonal trading and mathematics have reduced the importance of relationships, and even if there are fewer dukes and more foreigners.

Equally, there have always been prominent individuals who did not fit the stereotype of the money- and markets-obsessed Establishment, who have criticised markets and who do take the wider world seriously. Whatever Jones says, it is not true that every powerful person subscribed to neoliberalism, even at its zenith. Indeed, as we will begin to see in Chapter 6, the view that something needs to change has become widespread in the last decade, even if not very well developed.

CONCLUSION

In the 1950s and 60s we saw the advance of a counter-elite that was quite demographically homogeneous, very national, and tied together by social networks and memories of the War. Despite this, it did not have a very strong explicit ideology: the views and behaviours reflected diverse professional, social and commercial traditions. This combination of diversity and homogeneity made it good at building institutions but bad at making businesses more efficient. Over time this counter-elite became a new Establishment. In the 1980s, it was challenged by a second counter-elite that was more diverse demographically, much less British, not really interested in running the country, but which shared a belief in the efficiency of the market, indeed which ascribed a kind of moral virtue to it. This group was much more explicitly held together by an ideology than its predecessor. It was very good at making business more efficient and productive—at least those businesses which it controlled, and at least where this was the quickest route to profit. However, it was not very good at building institutions, largely because it didn't really believe in them. In time, it too became the Establishment.

The change in what Britain is good at—in rather sweeping terms, from being relatively good at institutions and relatively bad at industry to being relatively bad at institutions and relatively good at *some* industry— reflects a change in the nature of the elite, the group that controls much of what happens both in institutions and in industry. This may not be a causal relationship; but it is hard to imagine the things that took place between 1945 and 1965 happening had the 1980s elite been in charge, and equally hard to imagine the 1980s with the post-war elite in charge.

In both cases, the very different waves of modernising were associated with an elite group, that had started off as a counter-elite defined in opposition to the 'old' Establishment, but which quite quickly became a 'new' Establishment. If Britain is to undergo a further wave of change of the kind that took place in the post-war years and then again in the 1980s, it is likely that this will also be driven by a counter-elite—a third counter-elite that in due course will become a third new Establishment.

NOTES

i. Anthony Sampson, *Anatomy of Britain* (1962).
ii. Henry Fairlie, 'Political Commentary,' *The Spectator* (23 September 1955).
iii. Hugh Thomas (ed.), *The Establishment: A Symposium* (1959).
iv. A full account of the obsession with the Establishment at this time is given in Dominic Sandbrook, *Never Had It So Good: A History of Britain from Suez to the Beatles* (2005).
v. Anthony Sampson, *Anatomy of Britain* (1962).
vi. For example Michael Shanks, *The Stagnant Society: A Warning* (1961).
vii. Kenneth Morgan, *The People's Peace: British History 1945–1989* (1990).
viii. Anthony Sampson, *Anatomy of Britain* (1962).
ix. From Warburg's private notebooks, quoted in Ron Chernow, *The Warburgs* (1993).

x. http://www.conservativehome.com/thetorydiary/2013/10/how-mac-millan-built-300000-houses-a-year.html.
xi. http://www.independent.co.uk/news/people/obituary-lord-zucker-man-1452840.html; http://archiveshub.ac.uk/features/zuckerman.html.
xii. Anthony Sampson, *Anatomy of Britain* (1962).
xiii. Ibid.
xiv. Tom Lupton, *Tribunal on Bank Rate Leak Report* (1958) quoted in Noel Annan, *Our Age* (1990).
xv. Kenneth Morgan, *The People's Peace: British History 1945–1989* (1990).
xvi. Noel Annan, *Our Age* (1990).
xvii. For example in Vernon Bogdanor and Robert Skidelsky (eds.), *The Age of Affluence* (1970).
xviii. Richard Sennett, *The Fall of Public Man* (1977).
xix. Tony Judt, *Ill Fares the Land* (2010), p. 47.
xx. Peter Hennessy, *Never Again: Britain 1945–51* (1992).
xxi. Asa Briggs, *The BBC: The First 50 Years* (1985) quoted in Peter Hennessy, *Never Again: Britain 1945–51* (1992).
xxii. Philip Selznick, *Leadership in Administration* (1957).
xxiii. Michael Beloff, *The Plateglass Universities* (1970).
xxiv. Sidney Pollard quotes OECD and IMF statistics on p. 5 of *The Wasting of the British Economy* (1984). In 1950 UK GNP per capita was greater than that of Belgium, Denmark, Norway, the Netherlands and France and substantially greater than that of West Germany and Austria. By 1978 it was little more than half of that of Belgium, Denmark. Norway, the Netherlands, France and West Germany.
xxv. Michael Pinto-Duschinsky, 'Bread and Circuses? The Conservatives in Office 1951–1964,' in Vernon Bogdanor and Robert Skidelsky (eds.), *The Age of Affluence* (1970).
xxvi. Martin Wiener, *English Culture and the Decline of the Industrial Spirit, 1850–1980* (1981).
xxvii. J. M. Keynes, 'Overseas Financial Policy in Stage III' (1945) quoted by Peter Hennessy, *Never Again: Britain 1945–51* (1992).
xxviii. Quoted in Peter Oppenheimer, 'Muddling Through: the Economy 1951–64,' in Vernon Bogdanor and Robert Skidelsky (eds.), *The Age of Affluence* (1970).
xxix. Juliet Gardiner, *From the Bomb to the Beatles* (1999).
xxx. John Montgomery, *The Fifties* (1965), p. 288.
xxxi. http://webarchive.nationalarchives.gov.uk/20160105160709/http://www.ons.gov.uk/ons/rel/elmr/explaining-economic-statistics/long-term-profile-of-gdp-in-the-uk/sty-long-term-profile-of-gdp.html.
xxxii. Office for National Statistics, *International Comparisons of Productivity—First Estimates* (2013).

xxxiii. Nicholas Comfort, *The Slow Death of British Industry: A Sixty-Year Suicide, 1952–2012* (2013).

xxxiv. Martin Jacques, 'The Erosion of the Establishment,' *Sunday Times* (16 November 1994).

xxxv. http://webarchive.nationalarchives.gov.uk/20160105160709/http://www.ons.gov.uk/ons/rel/abs/annual-business-survey/business-ownership-in-the-uk--2012/sty-abs-business-ownership.html.

xxxvi. http://www.ons.gov.uk/economy/investmentspensionsandtrusts/bulletins/ownershipofukquotedshares/2015-09-02.

xxxvii. http://www.cityam.com/215983/finance-top-background-ftse-100-bosses.

xxxviii. The Capital Group, https://www.capitalgroup.com/gb/en.

xxxix. For example, Kathleen Eisenhardt, et al., 'How Management Teams Can Have a Good Fight,' *Harvard Business Review* (July 1997); Erika Herb et al., 'Teamwork at the Top,' *McKinsey Quarterly* (2001, Issue 2).

xl. Owen Jones, *The Establishment: And How They Get Away with It* (2014).

xli. Niall Ferguson, *High Financier: The Lives and Time of Siegmund Warburg* (2010).

xlii. Philip Collins, interviewed by Owen Jones in *The Establishment: And How They Get Away With It* (2014).

xliii. George Walden, *The New Elites* (2001).

xliv. *Daily Telegraph* (24 October 2004), quoted in Julie Froud, Mike Savage, Gindo Tampubolon, and Karel Williams, CRESC Working Paper Series, Working Paper No. 12, *Rethinking Elite Research* (2006).

xlv. Cited in Anthony Sampson, *Who Runs This Place?* (2004).

xlvi. Martin Jacques, 'The Erosion of the Establishment,' *Sunday Times* (16 November 1994).

xlvii. Robert McCrum, *The Guardian* (10 July 2000).

xlviii. Mike Savage, *Social Class in the 21st Century* (2015).

xlix. Charles Harvey and Mairi Maclean, 'Capital Theory and the Dynamics of Elite Business Networks in Britain and France,' in Mike Savage and Karel Williams (eds.), *Remembering Elites* (2008).

CHAPTER 6

A Stagnant Society?

In the last chapter, we saw how Anthony Sampson and others writing in the early 1960s expressed anxiety that the country's Establishment, and perhaps the country itself, had run out of steam. Despite the economic successes of the 1950s, there was "a growing obsession with Britain as a kind of museum piece of insular decay,"[i] suffering from relative decline when compared with its European competitors. The title of Michael Shanks's 1961 Penguin Special, *The Stagnant Society: A Warning,* summed up this obsession, while an essay collection published a couple of years later in *Encounter* magazine suggested something even worse: the 'Suicide of a Nation'.[ii] Several of the contributors to this collection claimed to have identified a deep cultural malaise, while the piece by Malcolm Muggeridge summed up the group's mood:

> Each time I return to England from abroad the country seems a little more run down than when I went away; its streets a little shabbier, its railway carriages and restaurants a little dingier; the editorial pretensions of its news-papers a little emptier, and the vainglorious rhetoric of its politicians a little more fatuous. On one such occasion I happened to turn on the television, and there on the screen was Harold Macmillan blowing through his moustache to the effect that 'Britain has been great, is great, and will continue to be great'. A more ludicrous performance could scarcely be imagined. Macmillan seemed, in his very person, to embody the national decay he supposed himself to be confuting. He exuded a flavour of moth balls.[iii]

© The Author(s) 2019
C. Seaford, *Why Capitalists Need Communists,*
Wellbeing in Politics and Policy,
https://doi.org/10.1007/978-3-319-98755-2_6

In 2018, at the time I was writing this, Remainers detected the same ludicrous bombast in the more ardent Brexiteers.

Many of those interviewed for this book (see pages vi and vii) expressed a similar concern that Britain was once again stuck. Of course the specifics of our social and economic problems are different from those of 1961, but once again we can observe—in the press, on social media, in public and private comments—a fear that the incumbent elite has run out of steam. The government's handling of Brexit, static and low productivity levels, housing shortages, executive pay and the gap between words and action in both business and government are the kind of failures cited. It is not just that there are problems—there are always problems; the point is there is a sense that the elite, or the most established parts of it, has lost its grip, has no ideas about how to deal with the problems. Once again there is anxiety about the future, this time not about the post-empire future but the post-European Union future.

Fortunately, we know from experience that this anxiety can be a signal that real change is on the way. Decay creates an opportunity for a counter-elite and for ideological renewal. And fortunately, there are enough individuals with the confidence as well as the anxiety to make that renewal happen. In this chapter I shall first present a somewhat partial, negative account, focusing on the symptoms that fuel the anxiety, then highlight just a few positive signs of hope.

CAPITAL

Before it happened, a failure to apply adequate fire regulations might not have seemed the most obvious manifestation of the big problems facing Britain, but the death of 71 people on 14 June 2017, when fire spread through a tower block in Kensington, quickly became a terrible emblem. Our public institutions had failed to ensure that developers provide the most basic safety, instead permitting the use of flammable cladding in a refurbishment. Both tenants and experts had warned of the danger, but neither group was heard. Safety had become a commodity. This was not just a failure of technology or process: as Justin Welby, Archbishop of Canterbury has said, it was a failure of value.[iv] Those who lived in the tower were treated differently from the more prosperous, and, as he put it, the infinite value of each human being was denied.

But this failure of value reflected a wider failure of system, and members of the Establishment recognise this. It is not just tower blocks which are going wrong. Nick Macpherson, who left the Treasury in 2016 and is now Chairman of Hoare's, Britain's oldest private bank, told me when I met him that "to the extent I am concerned about capitalism" it is because "wealth will become more and more concentrated, capital will be ever more difficult to tax, redistributing the fruits of progress will be ever more difficult, social cohesion will break down and willingness in general to pay taxes will fall." More and more jobs will be "miserable and low paid" and, he added with mandarin understatement, "this is troubling." In similar vein, Jeremy Hayward, the former Cabinet Secretary, is reliably reported to have told a meeting of the CBI that capitalism as we know it is finished. Jo Swinson, currently deputy leader of the Liberal Democrats, also told me, when I met her, that "capitalism is in a crisis… is not the right model." Will Day, a senior advisor at PricewaterhouseCoopers agreed that "shareholder capitalism is a real problem" and revealed that his colleagues "know that shareholder capitalism is broken." The head of another consulting firm said that his clients realise that "the current model is not working," that they worried about inequalities and the NHS not being properly funded, and they feared that their country was falling behind. Paul Polman, the recently retired former Chief Executive of Unilever, has written that capitalism is like an equation that does not "solve" for "equity or prosperity" and "does not address the values that really matter in life—well-being, shared prosperity, community, trust, and perhaps greatest of all, purpose." As a result it "imposes a tremendous cost on our planet and on its most vulnerable people."[v] Another close observer of Britain's largest companies confirmed to me that many of the business leaders he knew were concerned about the future of capitalism and lack of trust in business.

Excessive pay at the top, rewards for failure, absurdly comfortable pension arrangements, generous payments to departing executives that are not contractually required and aggressive tax avoidance—these are familiar abuses and the most obvious reasons for this lack of trust. Increasingly, though, the lack of trust and associated impatience with amorality extend into the business world itself. In October 2017, the *Financial Times* reported the views of 50 business leaders on the subject: "The underlying promise of western capitalist economies—that a rising tide lifts all boats—has been broken," and "a better model" is needed, according to Shriti Vadera, Chair of Santander UK. Capitalism had "lost its way" according to Robert Swannell, former Marks and Spencer Chair.

Carolyn Fairbairn, Director General of the CBI, said that capitalism had taken a number of "wrong turnings," and, she went on, "the toxic issues of [...] payment of tax and executive pay stand in the way of redemption." Nigel Rudd, long-time FTSE 100 Chair, said capitalism had been "hijacked by the management class."[vi]

Chris Brown, a successful property developer whom I spoke with put it most bluntly: "the system as we have it is genuinely corrupt" and he lamented the "fawning around rich people," too evident in the business world. Saker Nusseibeh, Chief Executive of one of London's leading investment firms, Hermes, made a similar point. Part of our problem, he said, is that top managers are allowed to behave as if they owned the businesses they run. They also feel entitled to minimise the taxes they and the business pay, and since for the most part they are sufficiently wealthy not to depend on public services (unlike most of the pensioners in whose name they say they operate), they feel no concern for the impact on public funds that this might have. Andrew Hill, the FT's Management Editor, believed many such people "behave as if they are above government." David Blood, Senior Partner with former US vice-president Al Gore at Generation Investment Management, another relatively progressive asset management company, agreed that most companies need to be put under pressure to do the right thing, including paying their taxes, taking into account environmental limits, and treating workers in the company and in the supply chain decently.[vii]

Troy Mortimer, a partner at KPMG, thinks that the average manager, if challenged by investors to scale back tax avoidance activities, is likely to respond along the following lines: "my objective is to maximise the bottom line and share price." If pressed, he or she might ask "so what am I being measured against? Perhaps I should work elsewhere." As for investment managers, he says, they are perfectly happy with the status quo, even when the status quo is not in the long-run interest of their clients, because their margins, and therefore their personal incomes, are so high. (Mortimer's former colleague Loughlin Hickey, who was KPMG Head of Tax, adds that it is not just well-paid CEOs who would lose out were the system to change, but well-paid consultants as well.) There is a responsible minority in the investment industry, but Steve Waygood, Head of Responsible Investment at Aviva, one of Britain's largest fund managers, puts this at about 10%; the rest pay "lip service." As David Pitt-Watson, formerly at Hermes, and an Executive Fellow of Finance at London Business School, puts it: "there are 100 institutional investors who own a significant proportion of the means of production. And who treat their role with utter indifference." They are not just greedy, they are suffering from a kind of anomie, a refusal to take their role in society—their very responsible role—seriously.

None of the criticisms quoted here come from outside the system—they come from within the system itself. In a survey conducted in 2017 by Aviva Investors, 42% of mainstream investment bank equity analysts said that "sell-side research" (the reports they write, designed to improve investment decisions) had a "detrimental short term focus" and 48% said it produced "too much noise instead of in-depth analysis."[viii] In other words, nearly half this influential and highly paid group think there are fundamental problems with what they do. Peter Michaelis, a fund manager, reveals his even stronger feeling about the industry: "the story most people [in the City] have in the back of their mind is that you have to lie, steal or cheat to be successful. The idea that you can be [financially] successful by serving the world well does not fit this story." Another City figure, disgusted with the system he was helping to run, told a friend "the only thing I can do is go sick." Which he did. Still others go and join the Alpha Movement, an evangelical Christian movement in west London which seems to specialise in alleviating capitalist guilt. More generally, according to Hickey, there is a "burden of guilt" in business. Jo Swinson sums up the situation succinctly: "we have an elite problem."

This burden of guilt may not have changed the system but it has produced a lot of talk about changing the system. In the words of Vincent Neale, also formerly at KPMG, "what is worrying is how much bullshit there is." He gives an example:

> The carbon disclosure project has been signed up to by just about every big company in the world and has been going for 20 years. It has cost a fortune, but in terms of real change it has achieved zero. Everyone gets praised, there is a table and a ranking, investors love it. It has actually achieved absolutely sweet f--- all, and as such is really dangerous.

Some might dispute his conclusion that the carbon disclosure project has produced nothing at all, but Neale is clearly right that initiatives of this kind easily drift into the sand, with endless discussions about how to measure and how to harmonise, putting off the day when transparency leads to action.

On the face of it, Forum for the Future is a counterexample. It is an NGO that works with business to help stimulate the kind of innovation needed for a sustainable economy. But its Chair, Jonathon Porritt, admits that "the work of Forum is mainly to persuade business leaders not to resist change, that is the best we can hope for. A very small number will be pro-active." He is dismissive of the idea that they can or will change anything. Another person close to well-meaning business leaders describes a meeting at which they discussed the need to do good things. One of them had pointed out "if we were sitting here with Fred Goodwin [who led RBS to collapse, and who combined personal extravagance with aggressive cost cutting] and others like him, they would all have said exactly the same thing as us."

Talk without action is particularly evident at the Davos World Economic Forum, the annual meeting of the largest global companies, also attended by NGOs and politicians. The Forum makes pronouncements about public policy issues such as inequality and climate change, but few business leaders think that *doing* something about these issues is part of their job. There are too many other things to do and worrying about public policy that does not have a direct and immediate impact on profits is never going to be very high up the agenda. The public communiqués may be about societal issues, but the private meetings are about company issues. As Michael Holm Johansen, who was formerly head of Coca-Cola for central and southern Europe, told me, "when my Chief Executive met with [José] Barroso [formerly President of the European Commission] at Davos, his [the Chief Executive's] agenda was Coca-Cola's agenda."

Talk without action is also common when it comes to top pay. Hickey is now a trustee of The Blueprint Trust, an organisation dedicated to instilling greater morality and purpose into business, and he describes this phenomenon.

We had a CEO dinner specifically on high pay. The overall conclusion of that was that the whole pay system has become distorted, not least by the emphasis on so called long-term incentive plans with little actual performance measurement. It also was a signal of a command and control culture, as it assumes a hard driving leadership motivated by extrinsic factors (money, status, power) which then permeated throughout the organisation. The end result is that the CEO is seen to be out of touch, both inside and outside the company.

[However]...everyone blames everyone else. The CEO says that they don't set the pay, the remuneration committee use consultants to benchmark and no-one wants to say they have a second-rate CEO, the board feel they have to align interests with shareholders, and the shareholders say they want senior leadership to concentrate on total shareholder return, which is what they feel they are judged by. And CEOs sometimes justify it around the perilousness of their position, their marketability and past track record. So, in short, yes there is a lack of leadership from all in the chain.

POLITICS

If business seems stuck, then at the time of writing (April 2018) Theresa May's government seemed even more stuck. It too displayed a lack of leadership, and seemed to have lost its grip to a degree most of us had never seen before in a British government. Leading members of the business world, lifelong Conservatives, could not bring themselves to vote for the Conservative party at the 2017 election.[ix] The party was paralysed by internal conflicts, and to some extent by conflict between different groups of voters. One commentator even suggested that the Conservative right *wanted* the country to suffer the economic pain that Brexit would bring, seeing it as a way of injecting some discipline into the country and of reinforcing privilege.[x] This was not true of the Conservative mainstream, or of the Prime Minister, but her position was even worse in some ways. She was like the driver of a car with a satnav that is telling her to drive over a cliff, and she was doing exactly what she was told. When asked by a foreign journalist whether Brexit was worth it, she simply couldn't answer. Thinking had been put on hold.[xi]

Labour too has been paralysed, although less by conflicts within the party and more by conflict with some of its traditional working-class voters: a long-standing rift between its more liberal and less liberal supporters, only now brought to the surface as Remain versus Leave. Its response has been strategic ambiguity, designed to retain appeal on both sides. To date this has worked—Remainers tend to think Labour is more opposed to Brexit than it actually is. By the time this book is published, it will have had to make its position clearer, although it could be saved by a bad exit deal from the government and a successful campaign for a referendum that would make party positioning less important.

The troubles of both parties over Brexit reflect more fundamental failures in a quite different area of policy: industrial strategy. A successful, sustained industrial strategy would have reduced the extent to which regions of England felt left behind. It would have defused the anger with the metropolitan elite and the European Union that those who did feel left behind expressed when they voted Leave. Neither party developed a strategy that succeeded in dealing with the problem. Indeed, neither party really tried.

There has been relatively little difference between the Conservatives and Labour in this most crucial of policy areas, as politicians from both parties, as well as officials, admit—although the Conservatives remain more ambivalent about it. The more interventionist approach to microeconomic management associated with the phrase 'industrial strategy' was revived by Peter Mandelson when Gordon Brown was Prime Minister, and though Vince Cable and David Willetts were initially sceptical when they took over as business department ministers in 2010,[xii] they were persuaded, and pushed the policy forward. Sajid Javid, on the Conservatives' free market wing, pressed the pause button when he was Secretary of State for Business, Innovation and Skills, and his actions damaged the institutional memory, according to Willetts; this may have limited what *his* successor, Greg Clark, an enthusiast, has been able to do. There are also continuing doubts in the Cabinet: Clark has been coming under attack for being too left wing, and an official in his department said the government was deliberately ambiguous on how much economic change it wanted to see.

But even without this ambivalence, industrial strategy as conceived by both parties would not have addressed the problems that led to Brexit. It wasn't designed to. The business department's rhetoric has been about creating advanced, world-beating industries, and there has been much less emphasis on what it would take to improve the productivity of less-advanced industries, or of services that are delivered locally, or on how to rescue left behind communities of the kind that voted Leave. There are policy programmes targeted at regional development, like the Regional Growth Fund, and the 'Northern Powerhouse' centred on Manchester, but they are not designed to achieve these broader objectives. The Blair-Brown governments ran more ambitious Regional Development Agencies (RDAs), but their impact was limited—they did not reduce inequality between regions,[1,xiii] and they were closed down in 2012. Raising the productivity of small businesses, the 'slow-speed' part of the two-speed economy, has now been delegated to a future Commission.

---

[1] Household incomes in the North-East as a proportion of the national average fell from 87.3% in 1997 to 85.7% in 2012. One North East was regarded as one of the more effective agencies.

The left behind were simply not on the Department's radar. Shortly after the referendum, I met its former chief economist, who expressed amazement at the economic illiteracy that led people in deprived areas to vote Leave. Willetts, when talking about industrial strategy to me, chose to emphasise the importance of removing barriers to industrial growth in Oxford and Cambridge—not, perhaps, the communities that need most help. In economists' jargon, the role of industrial strategy has been to generate the information, coordination and public goods needed to maximise the growth of industries in which we have potential comparative advantage. More simply, it has been designed to make the successful even more successful, to contribute to dynamism rather than to community. It was never designed to reduce the tension between these two goods and was never meant to address the now widely acknowledged problems of globalisation.

For that we still have to rely on 'trickle down'. This is one of those ideas that has been completely debunked, but still attracts support because people can't think of anything better. The theory is that if industrial strategy fosters a dynamic economy and some good new jobs in an area, perhaps at the cutting edge of technology, then this will generate other jobs, mainly providing services to those working in the jobs that the strategy creates directly. Even if it doesn't do this, it will create tax revenue which can be used to pay benefits. Willetts, who now heads a progressive think tank, the Resolution Foundation, and who is normally full of constructive ideas, was somewhat stumped when asked how industrial strategy could go beyond this. He acknowledged the research published by his own think tank, which shows how limited the trickle-down effect is, but didn't really have an alternative.[xiv] Nick Macpherson, too, was sceptical that anything much other than improving education can be done to shape the economy so as to avoid the troubling problems he identified. The sense of an ideological cupboard that is bare is overwhelming. The Labour Party certainly wants to deal with the problem, but it too offered quite traditional policies in its 2017 manifesto—the flagships being more adult education, investment in infrastructure and research and development, and ensuring small business gets the finance it needs through a network of regional banks. These seem sensible policies, but there is no sense of why they should be transformative.

The predictable result is precisely what we have: a two-speed economy, with those businesses that are competing directly in global markets forced to innovate and deploy high-level skills, while other businesses that are not competing in this way remain stuck in a low-productivity, low-skill, low-wage equilibrium. A London-based commentator, Andrew Marr, wrote an article in the *Evening Standard* in February 2018 about how wonderful life is in the UK,[xv] as indeed it is for many of those in the high-speed economy. Meanwhile elsewhere, people 'just about manage,' or don't manage at all and are forced to turn to food banks in increasing numbers. For many companies, whether in personal services or parts of unavoidably local supply chains, a low-productivity, low-cost, low-wage strategy appears more profitable and certainly less risky than investing in productivity and skills. Combine this with increasing numbers of immigrants from Eastern Europe and it is hardly surprising that the latter become scapegoats.

Hence the Labour Party's troubles over Brexit. The failures of industrial strategy have contributed to anti-immigration and anti-European sentiment in the working class. But this is toxic to the party's liberal middle-class supporters. Hence the dilemma: how to combine the solidarity that underpins the welfare state, a solidarity which immigration can strain, with an open and liberal society.[xvi] It is not that there has to be a dilemma—in good times it need not exist and combining solidarity and openness may be easy—but industrial strategy failures created a choice. Many voters chose solidarity.

There is a Conservative version of this dilemma as well: how to combine an appeal to traditional values with the market forces that erode them.[xvii] Like the left's dilemma, this too is made sharper by immigration and globalisation—but it is different in that there is a resolution. This is a nostalgic fantasy about Britain as a great trading nation, a vision of a glorious past in which want, disease, ignorance, squalor and idleness are simply airbrushed out. The hold this fantasy has on activists may explain some of the Prime Minister's paralysis in the face of Brexit, just as the Labour Party's dilemma explains its paralysis.

In both cases, to resolve the dilemmas in a constructive way requires a creative leap, a new synthesis, a compelling vision, but, as we have seen, neither the market liberals nor the social democrats have provided this. Hence the sense of drift.

CIVIL SERVICE AND ACADEMIA

What of the civil service? Is it, too, stuck? Some observers report a demoralised service, partly because of Brexit and partly because of radical manpower cuts, both of which have reduced its capacity to make decisions.

A new government might put this right, and ministers and officials I spoke with agreed that officials can respond to skilful leadership by ministers and help drive change—a view confirmed by history. It is good news that the Labour frontbench team is being trained on how to provide this leadership by Bob Kerslake, the former head of the service. On the other hand, a new government will not change the service's long-standing faults: placidity, isolation from reality, caution, and a tendency to support established rather than emerging interests. These reflect the official's role: to *serve* ministers, *warn* of dangers and *minimise* disruption.

More than one official told me that civil servants were very willing to discuss the kind of issues raised in this book, and indeed were even writing papers on some of them. Macpherson reported that "some [Treasury officials] will be questioning whether capitalism is the most efficient way of allocating resources, influenced by Piketty." There is also an active dialogue between some officials and some academics, both formal and informal. Nonetheless, it is all rather theoretical: despite the intellectual interest, civil servants "do not have a keen sense of impending crisis," I was told by one of them. Macpherson himself exemplified this by pointing out that "we have been talking about where jobs are going to come from for 200 years." Ken Clarke, Chancellor of the Exchequer from 1993 to 1997 said of the Treasury after he left it in 1997 that it was "brilliant intellectually," like "high table at an Oxbridge college," but "slightly unworldly" as no one had any "practical experience of running anything."[xviii] Francis Maude, who was Minister with responsibility for the Civil Service under David Cameron, observed after he retired that isolation from the practical world was fiercely defended: "outsiders are treated as 'country members' of the club" while a "premium" was placed "on blandness."[xix] In the late 70s there *was* a sense amongst officials that change was needed, according to Gus O'Donnell, who joined the Treasury then, but he did not feel there was a similar urgency now.

A similar passivity infects much of academic life as well. One might have expected the international research community to be working hard to address the systemic nature of the problems we face, to be in overdrive, forming the foundations for the kind of coherent framework that animated the institution builders of the 1940s and the neoliberals of the 1980s. However, the structures of modern academic life do not encourage the kind of synthetic imagination allied to practical and diplomatic action that characterised, for example, Keynes's career. It is not that there isn't plenty of potentially valuable social, economic and environmental research taking place. Of course there is. There are also heterodox economists working on new approaches to our established economic problems. The problem is the lack of synthesis and translation into action.

At one level this is the result of organisational failures: until recently, at least, the Economic and Social Research Council (ESRC), one of the main funders of research in the UK, actively discouraged secondary work, and some argue that academic evaluation systems have discouraged blue-sky thinking. These are the foundations of any action-oriented synthesis. However these failures themselves reflect a broader absence: an absence of the kind of *institutions* described in Chapter 5, and of the collective purpose associated with them—and indeed with the Robbins report that mapped out the 1960s and 70s expansion of higher education (see page 65 above). The ESRC has lacked any real mission of its own, being in essence a layer of insulation put in place to protect academics from interference by the government. In the absence of its own mission, it has followed the agenda of the academics who advise it, and for whom specialisation is everything. The universities themselves are no longer "receptacles of group idealism" as Philip Selznick put it in his definition of institutions (see page 99 above); a kind of individualist specialisation has taken hold.

CONDITIONS FOR CHANGE MET?

Let us not exaggerate how bad things are, though. It is true that business, politics, the civil service and academia seem stuck, and talk is not translating into action at sufficient scale. It is this that echoes the early 1960s 'stagnant society'. However the whole argument of this book is that the potential for radical change exists, and that would be difficult to sustain if there were no signs of life. And fortunately, there is some light in the gloom. Consider the conditions for change described in Chapter 4.

First, the dissatisfaction described in this chapter shows that at least some members of the elite have lost confidence in the official 'market liberal' ideology and indeed in other members of the elite. It is consultants and investment managers who are criticising business and the City, not just left politicians and activists. It is lifelong Conservative voters and leading business people who are abandoning their party, not ordinary swing voters. This is good news because it foreshadows change. This is what happened in 1780s France and early twentieth-century Russia.

It is true that market liberalism remains the official creed. And it is true that even an ideology with few genuine believers can help preserve elite unity and put off change. A dead ideology has an afterlife, and will continue to influence events long after it has become an object of cynicism. The *Ancien Régime* in France in the 1780s and communism in Eastern Europe in the 1980s did not inspire very many people and much the same is true of the free market now. Despite this, the dominant public discourse, the dominant way of thinking about public life and institutions, was influenced by traditional ideas in France and Eastern Europe for quite a long time, just as it is now.

Why is this? It is not because people are stupidly conventional (although some are), or because vested interests have power over the media (although some do). It is rather because people whose support is needed for things to happen assume, correctly, first that orthodoxy prevails, second that this means unorthodox proposals will not get the support they need, and third that such proposals are therefore not worth supporting. We might call this self-reinforcing pattern 'ideological *fashion*'. It can survive a long time, even when the underlying ideas have failed, and been seen to fail, for it sustains and is in turn sustained by organisations and other structures.[xx] It can trap individuals who would otherwise think more freely. Jesse Norman is the Conservative minister responsible for the switch to electric cars. When he says he wants a 'market approach' to this challenge, it seems unlikely that this is based on some deep conviction based on careful thought that this is the right way to tackle this challenge. Norman is too intelligent a man for this to be true. It is rather the last gasp of a dying set of ideas, automatically exhaled because that is what he thinks Conservative ministers do and what he thinks his colleagues expect him to do. Perhaps he has also persuaded himself that it is true, but if he has, this will not be a deepseated belief. I got the feeling, when I met her, that this is even true for Liz Truss, Chief Secretary to the Treasury and a leading free-market Conservative. Her deep-seated belief is in personal independence, the freedom to be an independent person, but her views on the market are more like a suit of clothes, a way of expressing these beliefs—and expressing her difference from her socialist, public-sector parents. She would, of course, deny this if asked.

It is when ideology has degenerated in this way that the opportunity for a counter-elite arises. It is difficult to get people to change their fundamental beliefs—after all, ideology has been described as "a world image convincing enough to support the collective and individual sense of identity"[xxi] and a sense of identity is the last thing people are inclined to change. However, it is not so difficult to get people to change a suit of clothes, at least if something new and attractive is sold with conviction. If a counter-elite with some convictions appears alongside an incumbent elite, many of whom are only following fashion, then ideological change is likely.

Has any group of this kind emerged, comparable to the modernisers of the 1950s or the business leaders of the 1980s? Not yet, but the conditions for this to happen exist. Some of the disaffected members of the elite are thinking about what to do about their disaffection, and are open to ideas from outside their traditional worlds—we will hear more of this in Chapter 10. Business people know that they have to change, and several of those I spoke with, in business and politics, wanted to improve the quality of the dialogue. On the other hand, there is no homogeneity, no shared codes of honour, to use Wright Mills's terms, to bind progressive individuals in the City and business with progressive civil servants, politicians, trade unionists and leaders of activist NGOs. Changes to capitalism's structures are needed to bring this about (described in Chapter 10).[xxii] The point is that, amongst those I spoke with, there is at least recognition that it would be a good idea.

What of the mobilisation of those outside the elite, whether passively, when addressed as an electorate, or actively, when they engage in direct protest? Brexit, and the binary choice that it has forced on us, has mobilised people, both as voters and as protestors. Millions of people voted for Brexit because they wanted change. Paradoxically, many of those campaigning to stop Brexit are motivated by the same desire for change. One young voter said he would never have forgiven himself had he not taken the opportunity Corbyn offered to vote for change—not any particular change, just change. However, as, again, we will see in Chapter 10, conventional representative democracy is not the only channel for popular pressure on events, and the counter-elite can form alliances using the investment system, deliberative democracy and social movements.

Finally, what of a new set of ideas and ideals that can unify a new counter-elite and help forge this alliance? I have suggested in this chapter that both the market liberal and the social democratic ideological cupboards seem bare. It is not that the Labour Party did not have a convincing array of policies at the 2017 general election: it did. It is not that these policies were not linked to a moral position: they were, and

Jeremy Corbyn stood for that moral position very effectively. It is rather that they are not linked, to quote Crane Brinton again, to "a feeling that there is something in all men better than their present fate." Because of this, they do not cut through traditional and stale left–right arguments, arguments which serve to divide rather than unify the counter-elite. The good news is that despite the failures of academia, work is advancing on a 'new economics,' and as we saw in Chapter 3, we are closer than some may think to articulating the "something in all men" that is "better than their present fate."

Notes

i. Kenneth Morgan, *The People's Peace: British History 1945–1989* (1990), p. 199.

ii. The various books and the way they have been interpreted or misinterpreted by historians is summarised in Matthew Grant, 'Historians, the Penguin Specials and the "State-of-the-Nation" Literature, 1958–64,' *Contemporary British History* (2003, Vol. 17:3, pp. 29–54).

iii. Malcolm Muggeridge, 'England, Whose England?' in Arthur Koestler (ed.), *Suicide of a Nation?* (*Encounter*, July 1963), p. 14.

iv. Radio 4 Today programme (January 2018).

v. Paul Polman, 'Re-establishing Trust,' in Dominic Barton, Dezsö Horváth, and Matthias Kipping (eds.), *Re-imagining Capitalism* (2016), p. 18.

vi. Patrick Jenkins, 'Top UK Business Leaders Decry Current State of Capitalism,' *Financial Times* (22 October 2017).

vii. Unless otherwise stated, all the quotes in this chapter are from conversations with the author.

viii. Aviva Investors, *Investment Research: Time for a Brave New World?* (2017), p. 9.

ix. FTSE 100 Chairman, conversation with author.

x. Will Davies, 'What Are They After?' *London Review of Books* (8 March 2018).

xi. Polly Toynbee, 'The Same Conundrum, No New Answers,' *The Guardian* (2 March 2018); Stephen Moss, *The Guardian—Tweet* (7.19 a.m., 2 March 2018).

xii. David Willetts, conversation with author.

xiii. http://www.centreforcities.org/wp-content/uploads/2014/09/09-12-08-RDAS-The-facts.pdf; https://www.ons.gov.uk/economy/regionalaccounts/grossdisposablehouseholdincome/bulletins/regionalgrossdisposablehouseholdincomegdhi/2014-06-04.

xiv. Neil Lee and Stephen Clarke, *A Rising Tide Lifts All Boats? Advanced Industries and Their Impact Upon Living Standards* (Resolution Foundation, 2017).

xv. Andrew Marr, 'Cheer Up—The Apocalypse Isn't Coming and Life's Getting Better,' *Evening Standard* (16 February 2018).

xvi. David Goodhart, 'Too Diverse,' *Prospect* (February 2004).

xvii. David Willetts, conversation with author.

xviii. Ken Clarke, *Kind of Blue: A Political Memoir* (2016), p. 328.

xix. Oliver Wright, 'Woeful Mandarins Can't Handle Brexit, Warns Ex-minister Francis Maude,' *The Times* (13 September 2017).

xx. For a discussion of this point as it applies to flourishing, see Ian Bache and Louise Reardon, *The Politics and Policy of Wellbeing* (2016), p. 121 et seq.

xxi. Eric Erikson, quoted by Alvin Gouldner, 'Ideological Discourse as Rationality and False Consciousness,' in Terry Eagleton (ed.), *Ideology* (1991).

xxii. In other words, the change will not just happen because of incremental changes within the system: it is 'exogenous' rather than 'endogenous', to use the distinction made by in Ian Bache and Louise Reardon, *The Politics and Policy of Wellbeing* (2016).

PART III

How We Can Change

CHAPTER 7

Planning

We can plan our lives and our world to make them better than they otherwise would be. That was the assumption set out in Chapter 3. Well-being science identifies the conditions that make it more likely that we will flourish, whether these are personal or social. Either way we can often shape these conditions—indeed it is only worth bothering to identify them because we can. To say this is not to deny chance, complexity and chaos: sophisticated planning takes account of these things. It *is* to deny that we collectively are powerless, or that there is nothing that can be done in a globalised world to counter economic 'forces'.

We have to assume we can change things if we are going to tackle the big five problems outlined in Chapter 2. To avoid dystopia, to reach utopia, we have to set out consciously to shape the world in which we are going to live. In particular, we have to plan if we are to address three of these problems: automation, the housing shortage and climate change. In this chapter I describe what this means.

JOBS

The dystopian three-class division of society described in Chapter 2 is a simplifying fiction of course. There will never just be wealthy software salesmen, struggling cleaners and an excluded, semi-criminal underclass. In particular, some personal service workers can be valued and well paid: not all 'servants' will be on the minimum wage, and there will never be

© The Author(s) 2019
C. Seaford, *Why Capitalists Need Communists,*
Wellbeing in Politics and Policy,
https://doi.org/10.1007/978-3-319-98755-2_7

such a sharp division between professionals and servants. For example, a dance teacher or a tour guide can both be experts and earn reasonable incomes, even though they are not among the elect whose skills are fully leveraged by technology. They may even supplement their income by selling videos online, taking advantage of opportunities created by information technology, and in this way their skills may be partly leveraged: there isn't a watertight barrier between leveraged and unleveraged skills. One of the challenges of automation is to ensure that more people than would otherwise be the case find jobs like these: jobs that cannot be automated, that can command decent wages and that can be sources of fulfilment. If this challenge is met, we can increase substantially the levels of flourishing in society.

This will not be possible if 'professionals' as defined in Chapter 2 only buy the output of other professionals and forms of personal service that do not command much premium to the minimum wage—the scenario imagined in the dystopia. To put the point schematically, if all I ever buy is beautifully designed but automatically produced objects, music downloads, dry-cleaning and pizza, and if everyone with a middle-class income is a bit like me, then things are not looking good. If, however, I take up various evening classes, buy handmade furniture and go on holiday in family-run hotels, then I am doing my bit for utopia. The whole craft buying, slow-food eating tendency is easy to deride: it is irritating when it elevates a particular form of taste into a particular form of morality. However, to the extent that it creates demand for unleveraged skills that cannot be automated, it is showing the way.

I am not going to estimate how much of this we need—how many jobs will be lost to automation, how many jobs entrepreneurs will create anyway, or what reduction in working time we should be aiming for. Perhaps the four-day week of our utopia is too pessimistic: perhaps technology will advance faster, we can be even more redistributive and people can find even more fulfilling unpaid things to do, and we can aim for a three-day week, or even a two-day week. I am not making a value judgement as between work and leisure or attempting to predict which will help people flourish the more, and nor do I have anything against music downloads. I am simply observing that what people buy will affect the level of demand for those skills that large numbers of people can acquire, that command a premium, and that cannot be automated. This will in turn affect the level of inequality before redistributive measures, and—on the assumption that these more skilful jobs and the incomes they provide help people flourish—the overall level of flourishing. One of government's challenges will be to work with business to ensure that there is both sufficient demand for and sufficient supply of these skills. If the resulting products are the kind that tend to encourage flourishing, as discussed in Chapter 3, then this will be doubly beneficial.

It is, I hope, obvious that there is absolutely no reason to suppose market forces will deliver this. Even in the free-market fantasy in which markets for products, capital, labour and training all work perfectly (a considerably more far-fetched fantasy than our utopia, by the way), there is no reason to think this. For in this fantasy, consumer taste is always decisive. If consumers choose to spend their income on beautifully designed, mechanically produced objects, music downloads, dry-cleaning and pizza, then so be it. It is true that if workers prefer to engage in handicrafts than to work in mechanised factories, handicraft wages may fall relative to factory wages. Handmade tables will then be slightly cheaper than they would have been, and demand for such tables will be slightly higher—worker preferences do have some impact on consumer choices. But in the world we have conjured up, handicraft wages would have to fall to intolerably low levels, perhaps zero or even less than zero, to rekindle demand for its outputs. Since the whole object is to foster skills that command a decent wage, this doesn't represent success. In reality, consumer taste and technology would have made certain skills redundant.

Is this inevitable? After all, if consumers want music downloads and so on, this may be unfortunate but what can we do about it? Tastes are fixed, so it is argued. The world might be a better place if consumers wanted handmade tables, but they don't.

Tastes, however, are not fixed. Consumers sometimes discover new activities, products and services, and then repeat purchase them, particularly if they enhance their well-being. Business influences taste through advertising and other techniques—so perhaps we can influence taste in a way that increases demand for skills that cannot be automated. Perhaps business can use its skills in this way. I do not know if it can or it cannot, but it is worth exploring. It would make our dystopia much less likely.

Even if business can do this, that doesn't mean it will, of course. Why should it bother? The answer is it won't, unless this is part of a plan agreed with government. And it almost certainly won't form such a joint plan with government given existing business structures and incentives. Fortunately, these structures and incentives can be changed—I return to this in Chapters 9 and 10. In other words, changing business structures and influencing taste are all parts of the same plan.

So let us imagine that tastes do change, whether of their own accord or as a result of a joint government–business programme. Can we ensure a supply of skills to match the resulting demand? While there is no reason to expect perfectly operating markets to deliver taste changes of the kind just described, perfectly operating markets should, in theory, deliver the necessary skills: the demand for products should create demand for skills, the demand for skills should create demand for the necessary training, and the demand for training should stimulate the necessary supply. In practice it doesn't work like this, largely because a whole series of uncertainties make people less responsive to changes in demand than they otherwise would be (this is a market failure as described by neoclassical economics, and, unlike changing taste, addressing it can be thought of as addressing market failure).

To illustrate this, imagine that consumption is moving towards the more benign pattern just described. Consumers of the future want to spend a lot more than they now do on evening classes, handmade furniture and holidays in family-run hotels. A free-market system has responded, and the result has been investment by business in schools, craft workshops and small hotels. Unfortunately, there is now a shortage of qualified evening class teachers, craftsmen and competent hotel staff. Employers do not want to spend money on training because they expect the trainees to be poached, and while some individuals have bought training for themselves, too few have done so. This is either because they don't have access to the necessary finance, or are unsure as to whether the cost will be justified, or because of a traditional prejudice against teaching, handicrafts and service jobs. In any case, there is a shortage of college places to meet even this inadequate demand: it takes time to train the trainers, and the increased consumption of handmade furniture is a new phenomenon; for the colleges, investing in such a new phenomenon is a risky matter and takes time. The long and the short of it is that after an initial surge of activity, business has become cautious—workshops without workers are a waste of money—and capital investment has fallen off.

The last paragraph reflects how skills development was conducted in the UK until recently. The policy was to allow student choices to drive decisions about which courses and skills the further education sector should provide—a 'market' approach which in effect delegated decisions about the future of the British economy to 16-year-olds. In 2009 I was told by the most senior official responsible for skills policy that this was fine because if 'the market' was involved, then everything would work out in the end. Unfortunately it didn't work out. For years, skills development did not match current employer needs, let alone future needs, and this led to much frustration amongst both employers and would-be employees.

We are moving away from this approach, at last, with employers now having a more significant say in further education priorities, and this has become the orthodoxy. Management consultancies like McKinsey, for example, argue that business and government need to "work together" and "consider bold new approaches" to provide the skills needed to address our underemployment and deskilling problems.[i] There is still a tendency to focus on current needs rather than on likely future needs, though, and this means, obviously enough, that the system is not preparing us for the future. What skills businesses say they need are based on current commercial considerations and inevitably these are shaped by what is likely to be profitable given how things are at the moment. As Richard Rawlinson, a consultant to several major multinationals points out, most companies simply do not know what skills they are going to need over the longer term; worse, because they assume mobility of employment, they are less willing than they were to invest in this longer term. Because government follows rather than leads industry, this business uncertainty infects government decisions as well.

The answer is not for government to ignore business and decide unilaterally what skills business should be using in 15 years' time, but an effective government–business partnership embodied in one or more institutions that also involve academics and trade unions. This would have the best chance of coming up with an approximately right long-term plan—and would also help create policy stability, which would in turn encourage associated business investment.

We saw in the last chapter that industrial strategy is not designed to rescue left-behind communities. But nor is it based on the kind of long-term analysis just suggested either. Its proponents often identify innovation as their most important intermediate objective, as it is the main source of long-term growth in GDP per capita, and Britain happens to be rather good at it. This does not mean it will lead to better paid, secure and fulfilling jobs that will survive automation, however. If we want this, our planning has to include decisions on the *direction* of innovation.

We need to get on and make these decisions now, and not just accept the 'watching brief' of the complacent.[ii] Automation is already contributing to inequality. It, along with competition from the developing world workforce, explains the fall in demand for so-called 'mid-level' skills in the UK, a long-standing trend that has been exacerbated recently by complex global supply chains. This fall in demand has led to the median wage being paid at a lower level of skill than it had been, in turn creating downward pressure on that wage[1]—as we saw on page 26, median hourly wages in 2016 were not much more than they had been in 1997 in real terms, despite 30% growth in GDP. It is true that there are some pockets of good news: some manufacturing, for example cars, employs workers at least as skilled as in the past and continues to pay good wages.[iii] However, much manufacturing, ceramics for example, pays low wages for low productivity jobs[iv] and automation could well have a similar but more extreme impact in the future.

Housing

Some on the right think there isn't really a housing problem. Housing, they argue, is like any other commodity, and if you cannot afford to live in inner London, then go and live in the outer eastern suburbs. Alternatively, just abolish planning controls. However, these prescriptions do not reflect the moral intuitions of most people, who think that you have a right to a decent home reasonably close to where you work, and perhaps reasonably close to where you have always lived. They tend to believe that there should be planning controls on where houses are built. What is more, these moral intuitions are consistent with the economics. Housing is *not* a commodity like any other: its price depends on collective decisions (planning, investment in infrastructure) and on

---

[1] Note that the impact of this 'hollowing-out' of the workforce is on the level of the median wage and not on the shape of the wage distribution: the proportion of workers paid within 25% of the median wage has not changed significantly since 2001 (*Good Work: The Taylor Review of Modern Working Practices*, 2017). Reference is sometimes made to the 'hourglass' shape of the labour market, with the numbers of those with mid-level skills reduced relative to those at the top and the bottom—but it is the skills curve not the incomes curve that has become hourglass-shaped.

value created by economic actors other than the landowner or builder (proximity to desirable neighbourhoods). Land and therefore houses are different.

Much of the affordability problem stems from our failure to capture the value created when collective decisions are made on our behalf. When our agents in this process, that is local authorities, grant planning permission they generally allow the landowners to keep almost all the increase in value that results. For the most part, this is not because they are stupid or corrupt but because they are in a weak negotiating position. Landowners have the right to do nothing, to withdraw from the deal, if they don't like the terms of the planning permission an authority grants them.[2,v] Since many landowners take a long-term view (much land continues to be owned by very old institutions such as the Church, Oxbridge colleges, and the aristocracy), they tend to think that no deal is better than a bad deal and prefer to wait for a more compliant authority to be elected. This is why any authority that attempts to insist on too many affordable homes may find itself with no homes at all, and this is why there is a shortage of affordable housing. The public sector has had to pay the 'market' price for land and because this price is high, at least in much of the country, it has had to use taxpayers' money to subsidise social housing. And there is a limited amount of taxpayers' money. This has become such standard practice that most people fail to see how bizarre it is: taxpayers are paying landowners for value that public authorities have themselves created through the planning system. And it means that constraints on public spending have turned into a constraint on housebuilding.

There are two ways of dealing with the resulting undersupply: 'unblocking' the flow of development land, in other words making the market for land work better; and allowing the state to act as the entrepreneur, in effect side-stepping the market altogether. Housing is a case study of how a state entrepreneurial approach is sometimes needed— how we need to plan, rather than just attempt to make the market work better.

---

[2]The situation was made even worse by a rule which prohibited planning conditions threatening the 'viability' of a development. Viability was assessed using the price paid for the land, but since this normally assumed minimal conditions, the rule was circular and made it difficult for councils to increase the share of affordable housing. A classic example of legislation in the interests of vested interests and no one else.

For such attempts over the last 35 years have been entirely unsuccessful. The number of private sector completions in 2016–2017 was almost exactly the same as the number in 1974–1975 (145,310 vs. 145,180) and in the intervening period, the number has only gone above or below a relatively limited range (140,000–165,000) during recessions in the early 80s and from 2009, and during booms in the late 80s and early 2000s.[vi] Supply has remained static in this way because the housing market consists of numerous, small local markets. The decisions of a single producer affect the price and it is often rational for individual developers to restrict supply and raise prices. As a government-commissioned report puts it, and as any developer will tell you, "Where the supply of housing land is more restricted, developers who obtain land will seek to maximise profits by controlling the rate at which the site gets built out."[vii] This helps explain a long-term under-supply, with prices higher than they otherwise would be. It is very difficult to create incentives to counter this economic reality.[viii]

Proposals for streamlining or liberalising the planning system continue to be made. However, no one has been able to show why an approach with such limited impact in the past would have more impact now, or why the relatively small increases in supply these measures would bring about would reduce prices significantly in those hot spots where prices are least affordable.[ix] It is true that if planning controls were abolished altogether, land prices, particularly around the edge of cities, might fall sharply. However few people think the resulting anarchic ribbon development would be desirable. There have also been proposals to lower capital costs for the private rented sector, which are higher than they need be,[x] and this too could increase supply but the impact on rents is uncertain. How much would the cost of capital fall? To what extent would the resulting increased demand for land lead to higher land prices cancelling out the lower cost of capital? And so on. The point is, it is very difficult to tinker with a highly complex market, and no one has succeeded in doing so.

A more radical and popular proposal is a Land Value Tax, to be imposed on land with planning permission that has not yet been developed, what are sometimes called 'current land banks'. It would certainly create a strong incentive to develop but it would not make that much difference: the current land banks are not that big, and in any case running them down would only have a one-off effect.[xi] As with any tax designed as an incentive, its impact would be unpredictable, and its impact on prices would be particularly unpredictable.

A more pro-active, state-entrepreneurial approach would be to grant planning permissions in the absence of applications from developers and *then* to force builders to build, either by applying a Land Value Tax or by threatening compulsory purchase if they failed to do so. This could have much more impact: 'strategic' land banks—developers' holdings of or options over land which does *not* have planning permission—are around ten times the size, of 'current' land banks.[xii] In addition, there is plenty of other land that could be developed that has not been earmarked in this way. It is in effect side-stepping the market altogether, with the state using planning and compulsory purchase or similar powers to influence both the quantity and price of at least some new housing.

This is more akin to the work of the new town development corporations of the 1940s and 50s described in Chapter 5—a building programme that housed two million people—and recently there have been several proposals for a revival of this approach. These include full-scale new towns as well as smaller projects. British planners point to the more active role that local authorities sometimes play to good effect in the Netherlands and in Germany,[xiii] and there are successful examples in the UK of local authorities forming partnerships with the private sector, shaping developments, capturing planning gain and taking the lead on city extensions.[xiv] Labour has recently announced its intention to reinstigate compulsory purchase at prices close to current use value.

This entrepreneurial role does *not* depend on a massive increase in public spending or subsidy, or on state borrowing. Construction, financing and land ownership can remain with the private sector. It does require the government to plan, and it means that land ownership rights are not treated as sacrosanct: addressing the housing shortage requires more than tinkering with market mechanisms, an incentive here and a regulation there.

Some argue that the political climate is not favourable for state activity of this kind in the way that it was in the 1940s and 50s.[xv] It is true that there will be fierce opposition. There have already been threats from landowners to use human rights legislation to sue a Labour government should it implement its new compulsory purchase policy. However, there was fierce opposition to the new towns too, and indeed to the National Health Service. Progress often requires conflict. Experience in the housing industry, and indeed the health industry, shows that once the private sector understands there is no point fighting, it will collaborate constructively. At the same time, state entrepreneurs do have to accept that the modern pro-active state needs to be more democratic and allow for greater local participation than the 1940s version. In the end, though, a pro-active role is justified because a decent home is an essential condition of a flourishing life, and we share norms as to what constitutes a decent home, what constitutes a reasonable amount to pay for it and where we should be entitled to live. These norms are not set by the market, hence there is no reason why the market price for a decent home in our home city should conform to them.[xvi]

CLIMATE CHANGE

Participants at the 2015 United Nations Climate Change Conference in Paris in December 2015 agreed that they would do their best to limit the average global temperature rise to 1.5 °C above pre-industrial levels, although the formal target remained simply "well below" 2 °C. Emissions targets and strategies remain a matter for nation states. While the conference did not solve the problem or even set us on a path to a solution, it did set in motion a process that could lead us to that path. In this it was strikingly more successful than the 2009 conference in Copenhagen.

This success, and the massive fall in solar and wind power generation costs, might suggest we are over the hump, but we are not. This is partly because there is no obvious substitute for oil when it comes to powering lorries and planes, or for many petrochemical products.[xvii] In addition, some governments simply haven't got a grip on the kind of transition planning and investment in infrastructure that is going to be needed to make the most of the technologies we do have. The British programme to encourage use of electric cars is a painful example of this. I will return to a third problem—costs—in the next chapter. There are other problems—for example people's desire to eat meat—which I have not addressed in this book, but which require the same kind of approach described in the section on jobs: an attempt to influence taste, combined with a skills and industrial policy that ensures that jobs are sustained.

Much of the technology needed for the shift from carbon-emitting energy is still in the "speculative stage," according to Nick Butler, formerly Group Vice President for Policy and Strategy Development at BP. As a result, most oil companies "are waiting to see which technologies make the big breakthrough and then they will move." Carbon pricing can increase the incentives, but business is risk averse in a way no incentives can overcome. That is why Butler, along with most commentators, believes that state investment remains essential. Only governments, they say, will invest to the extent needed in high potential new technologies such as batteries and grid technology. This is the stuff of the green growth policies that contributed to progress in Paris.

Students of the subject largely agree that these policies cannot just rely on traditional tools: tax breaks, subsidies, regulations and so on, that will prompt a little more investment in wind farms and insulation, a little more research into battery technology and hydrogen cells, and so on.[xviii] Such tools work at the margin, to provide the final push to businesses who are contemplating investing anyway. They are quite inadequate given the scale of the changes needed: almost 80% of the world's power is still generated using fossil fuels,[xix] and there are just 2 million electric vehicles but nearly 1 billion internal combustion vehicles. The changes will have to be coordinated across sectors and nations, and will require provision of public infrastructure. This is different in kind from the marginal change that traditional tools are designed to deliver and it requires governments to take the initiative.

As with automation and housing, this means the state has to collaborate effectively with the private sector. In other countries there are institutions designed to facilitate this, at least to a limited extent, and these institutions could be scaled. For example, in Germany the government-owned KfW's mandate is to "sustainably improve the economic, social and ecological condition of people's lives." The Nordic Investment Bank's mandate includes following principles which "enhance the environment," while the European Investment Bank supports projects which contribute to "social cohesion and environmental sustainability."[xx] There are British initiatives too, but they are limited. So in London, for example, the Greater London Authority (GLA) has set up a small (£400 million) investment fund to encourage investment in energy saving, decarbonisation and job creation, using 'soft' EU money to leverage in private investors. These techniques are often designed to reduce private-sector risk until the industry or technology reaches a commercially viable scale. Governments may also fund early-stage research in universities, normally most effectively when companies are also involved.[xxi]

Risk reduction and direct funding at sufficient scale can also signal government commitment to a sector and to the policies needed to make investment in it worthwhile. Combined with regulations and fiscal measures, they can set a convincing direction of travel for the economy. For example, a government may introduce a carbon tax that produces a short-term response from firms, but governments can change their mind or be replaced by governments with different policies; if firms think this is likely they may not change their investment plans. If government 'puts its money where its mouth is' and itself invests substantial sums, they may have more confidence in the permanence of the tax and be more inclined to invest accordingly. As yet, this has not yet had any effect in the UK, and the scale of public–private collaboration is not at a level to match the challenge.

What about government's lack of grip on the planning needed? At this point we confront the sheer boneheadedness of politicians and the timidity of officials. Consider the switch over to electric cars. The issue is really not that complicated. Hybrids are already commercially viable: Volvo will only make electric and hybrid engine cars from 2019 and Jaguar Land Rover will follow suit in 2020.[3] The current generation of pure electric cars have range problems, but these are likely to be cracked. Mass-market cars with ranges of 300 miles plus and charging times of under an hour are likely to be available by the early-to-mid 2020s. By that point there needs to be a comprehensive, easy-to-use network of charging points, located in places where people park their cars (car parks and streets). And from then on, it needs to be much cheaper to buy and use an electric car than a petrol car. A mix of carrot and stick can also ensure that old petrol cars are scrapped reasonably quickly. All government has to do is signal that this is going to happen (which will accelerate the development process), start to invest in the charging point network (putting its money where its mouth is), and continue to provide a small amount of symbolic support to the development programme. Is it doing so? No.

In December 2017 my wife bought an electric car and at the beginning of 2018 it 'conked out,' as she put it. She was left stranded in the middle of nowhere late at night. The range indicator had malfunctioned—the manufacturer later explained that you should never rely on it, which is rather bad news—and there had been no charging points anywhere en route. On another trip, we spent hours looking for a charging point that was working, trying to understand how to use the inordinately complicated payment system (different networks use different systems),

---

[3]Admittedly, both companies make premium products. It may also be significant that both are owned by Asian holding companies: Zhejiang Geely Holding Group and Tata Motors respectively.

and then, before coming home, waiting for a phone to charge sufficiently to make the call needed to release the car. She had an even worse time on a third trip. If electric cars are going to be part of our utopia, we have a long way to go yet.

As it happened, the Automated and Electric Vehicles Bill was passing through Parliament at the time. Ministers admitted that they were 'disappointed' that local authorities were installing charging points so slowly, that different charging points used different kinds of plug, and that some require special pre-pay arrangements. The Bill, now an Act passed with all-party support, gives the Secretary of State the power to require a standard method of connection and payment across different operators' networks. It does nothing, however, to ensure that these will add up to a comprehensive national network in five years' time, when electric cars will really start to become competitive. Laughably, it gives the Secretary of State the power to direct fuel retailers to install charging points—as if drivers are going to hang around petrol stations for the hour or so it takes to fully charge a car. There is nothing about car parks or streets with parking meters, which a child of six could tell you are rather more convenient places to charge up. This incompetence matches a lack of ambition: England is not planning to phase out petrol cars until 2040 (Scotland will do so in 2032). Is it surprising, as Butler says, that "The [oil] industry does not expect demand for oil to fall anytime soon"?

Picking on fuel retailers may be stupid, but the principle of directing industry is a welcome innovation—or rather a welcome return to an old approach. As one official approaching retirement put it to me a few years ago, "In the old days, if we wanted something, we would have just rung up the CEGB [Central Electricity Generating Board] and told them what to do. Now we have to devise complex and expensive incentive schemes which may or may not work." He felt it had been much simpler and more effective to decide what was wanted and then to do what was needed; in short, to plan. This is what any competent business would have done—and as we have seen, what Harold Macmillan did when he led the UK's largest ever housebuilding programme in the 1950s.

Macmillan himself summed up the necessary approach when he was prime minister:

> Do we, or do we not, set out to control the basic pattern of events, to direct development, to plan growth, to use the instruments of Government to influence or determine private decisions? Believe that this

is inevitable. Forces at work now too complicated, risks of setback too great to leave to market forces and laisser faire. Dirigisme. But it must be creative dirigisme.[xxii]

CREATIVE DIRIGISME

Neal Lawson runs Compass, a radical left-wing think tank, and has been advocating progressive policy for years. When I described some of the argument of this chapter, his first response was "there was a reason the Soviet Union collapsed you know, Charles." To hark back to the good old days of Harold Macmillan, or the indicative planning that guided the French economy from 1947, is to invite ridicule.

There is a trivial criticism of planning which we can dispose of quickly, based as it is on the failures of traditional industrial policy. No one is suggesting that governments should decide that there is going to be a surge in demand for, say, supersonic flights and peanuts (two notorious industrial policy failures of the past) and direct investment accordingly, or that it should prop up defunct firms. Everyone agrees that it is for business to decide what will be profitable to make. I am not proposing, for example, that government should predict how many evening class teachers in different subjects the country will need in ten years' time and issue production norms and pay bonuses for achieving this. But government and business together might still predict that teaching and communication skills are going to become increasingly valuable. They might even go further and consider the following facts: physical fitness, dancing and singing in choirs are good for well-being; it is possible to nudge people into habits and consumption patterns that increase their well-being; once these habits are established, people will pay a reasonable amount for these services; and machines can't for the most part replace teachers of these things. They might then conclude that it would be a good idea to invest in the marketing to promote these services, and to invest in the skills to deliver them. A direction of travel is agreed, it is given a fair wind, but if it doesn't work the plan is changed.

This requires partnership. If government makes the massive investment in adult education likely to be needed to create skills that can survive automation, but does not do this in partnership with business, we could well end up with a supply of skills for which there is no demand, and demand for skills for which there is no supply. On the other hand, if government simply takes its orders from business, there is the opposite danger, that we will end up with skills for some well-paid jobs in world leading industries, plus lower-grade skills equipping workers for badly-paid jobs that generate zero job satisfaction—and that before too long have been made redundant. The coordination of the supply of and demand for skills, such that human potential and flourishing are optimised, requires real collaboration and a shared set of goals. Negotiation is not enough.

Is this partnership possible? Leave aside motivation for now (I return to this in Chapters 9 and 10), and consider whether governments can influence business decisions on what will be profitable to provide. The answer is: perhaps. There isn't only one answer to the question 'what will be profitable in ten years' time?' and perhaps governments can persuade business to answer it in a way that helps bring about a low-carbon economy where people flourish. Perhaps government and business can take a view on the *kind* of products likely to create demand for skills that UK citizens either have or can acquire, and that will still be in demand given automation. Perhaps they can identify which of these can also help, or at least not obstruct, the shift to a low-carbon economy. Perhaps government can then direct public investment in skills, research and infrastructure in a way that is consistent with this view and work with business to coordinate this with private investment.

Sceptics say that this kind of planning and partnership might be desirable but is not possible, and so should not be tried. When proponents point to successful examples, typically in Asia, sceptics concede that fast-developing economies that are 'catching up', such as Japan in the 1960s, Korea in the 1980s and China in the 2000s, may have benefited from the kind of coordination that only governments can provide. But this was because planners knew where their countries were going, and they knew this because more advanced economies had already got there. Economies that are already at the technical frontier are more complex and uncertain.

Planning is not simply a response to likely future conditions, however. It also shapes those conditions. One of the functions of indicative planning as practiced in France after the war was to *reduce* uncertainty. Opponents of planning might as well oppose building bridges on the grounds that rivers make building difficult. Plenty of business people recognise this. Mike Barry, in charge of sustainability at Marks and Spencer, said to me, if we want to deal with the consequences of automation and avoid a loss of jobs, we have to have business and government "sat together in the same room." This is how progress has already been made on sustainability issues, such as advancing the 'circular economy' (which encourages the re-use of raw materials and components). Loughlin Hickey, the former KPMG partner we met in Chapter 6, and Michael Holm Johansen, formerly of Coca-Cola, agreed that there needed to be a shift to a more collaborative and open approach.

Planning would not be as useful as it is if our only objective were to maximise GDP. As we saw in Chapter 3, there is an elegant argument available to traditionalists proving that if we define welfare in terms of consumption, then markets do optimise welfare under certain conditions. Planning is only useful in this scheme because of coordination failures that tend to afflict economies when they are 'catching up' the most advanced economies, a process which requires big structural changes. However, maximising GDP is not our only objective. We face big problems and these require structural changes just as big as those faced by developing economies. The fact that markets may be the best way of allocating consumption goods and maximising the value of output under certain conditions is simply irrelevant.

But why is planning and collaboration between government and business needed to make these big structural changes? Why aren't the more traditional tools—tax, subsidy and regulation—adequate to the task? The answer, in a nutshell, is that these traditional tools rely on modifying price signals, and price signals are generally about what is happening now.[4] They optimise action within a given set of structures rather than indicating how those structures should change.

So, markets work well when relatively narrow and short-term decisions are being made, for all the standard reasons economists have elaborated since Adam Smith: the 'invisible hand' ensures that selfish producers generate socially useful outcomes. They work by providing signals to economic actors about what people are prepared to buy and sell at what price. For example, customers are buying plenty of product *x* at the current price so make more of it, they are not buying product *y* so make less of it, lower the price, or change it in some way. The reasons why markets sometimes do not work well in this way even in the

---

[4]The prices of certain items that buyers can expect to re-sell—items bought and sold in capital markets and some liquid commodity markets—will reflect expectations of future prices, but typically these expectations are distillations of calculations about future prices of items whose current prices do not reflect the future in this way. These calculations are not simply based on current price signals but on the kind of planning described below.

short term—the 'market failures' that justify interventions—are also well understood. It is generally agreed there should be taxes to discourage smoking, regulations to prevent the use of dangerous chemicals in foods or the formation of monopolies, and provision by the state of goods that it is difficult to charge for, like security or democracy.

However, markets are less effective at optimising big decisions about the long term.[xxiii] The price signals they provide become less relevant over time. This is why well-run companies do more than respond to these signals when making long-term decisions: they combine them with other sources of knowledge about likely future consumer, supplier and competitor behaviour, and *plan*: a new product perhaps, an investment in a new plant, or a gradual reduction in the output of another one. Long-term decisions are not strictly 'market' decisions, even when made by profit-seeking firms. They are influenced by price signals sent by product, capital and employment markets, as well as by a host of other forms of knowledge, and the social patterns that shape and filter that knowledge. It follows that if we want to change decisions about the long term, we cannot rely on levers that influence price signals alone. A whole host of other factors are relevant.

Governments could of course simply try to influence the short-term decisions, on the grounds that lots of short terms add up to the long term. But this would make it very difficult to predict the impact of policies over the long term. The whole market process is too complex and the number of potential interactions between market participants and between market participants and government is too great to make even approximately accurate predictions about the impacts of a short-term intervention over the long term.

If government is to steer us away from the dystopia and towards the utopia described in Chapter 2, it will need to go beyond traditional tools—tax, subsidy and regulation, the kind of tools that it has confined itself to over the last 35–40 years. These are designed to make markets work better and are useful in their place. However they are too inflexible, too short term in their impact and too tentative when it comes to mobilising the very significant action needed to address the slide towards dystopia. The world is too unpredictable, the time-frame for any plausible solution too long and the scale of the problems too large for these tools to be effective. Indeed it is this lack of fit between tools and problems that explains the paralysis of liberal politicians in Europe and the United States, and the resulting rise to prominence of right-wing populists and populist causes.

This does not mean we need 'central planning' in the old sense. It *does* mean a refusal to leave vital issues to chance; we need new forms of planning with a family resemblance to the indicative planning that sets expectations and influences decisions, and that was used with some success in France between the 1940s and the 1970s. The modern version will involve a much more flexible and therefore fine-grained coordination and alignment of public and private interests, and one that takes into account popular concerns and desires beyond the 'economic.' It will have as its objective flourishing, not simply economic growth.

NOTES

i. The McKinsey Global Institute, *An Economy that Works: Job Creation and America's Future* (2011).
ii. Matthew Taylor, *Good Work: The Taylor Review of Modern Working Practices* (RSA, 2017).
iii. The average weekly wage in motor manufacturing in 2016 was £424 ('Table 21,' *Annual Survey of Hours and Earnings* [Office for National Statistics, 2017]). https://www.ons.gov.uk/releases/annualsurveyofhoursandearningsintheukprovisional2017andrevised2016. Production operator salaries in UK car factories in that year were up to £39,800 and average salaries around £31,000. http://www.auto-express.co.uk/car-news/98986/the-global-car-manufacturing-wage-gap-what-do-car-factory-workers-earn. In the United States "Manufactured imports, even those from developing countries such as China and Mexico, are concentrated in US manufacturing sectors that pay significantly higher than average wages." Robert Lawrence, *Blue Collar Blues: Is Trade to Blame for Rising US Income Inequality?* (2008).
iv. The average weekly wage in manufacturing of 'other non-metallic mineral products' in 2016 was £303, and in 'other manufacturing' £275. ('Table 21,' *Annual Survey of Hours and Earnings* [Office for National Statistics, 2017]).
v. Kate Barker, *Review of Housing Supply. Delivering Stability: Securing Our Future Housing Needs—Final Report* (2004).
vi. Department for Communities and Local Government, *Permanent Dwellings Completed, by Tenure and Country*, https://www.gov.uk/government/uploads/system/uploads/attachment_data/file/669003/LiveTable209.xlsx.
vii. Kate Barker, *Review of Housing Supply. Delivering Stability: Securing our Future Housing Needs—Final Report* (2004).

viii. Ibid. and Matt Griffith and Pete Jefferys, *Solutions for the Housing Shortage: How to Build the 250,000 Homes We Need Each Year* (Shelter, 2013).

ix. For example: Erika Morton, *Making Housing Affordable: A New Vision for Housing Policy* (London: Policy Exchange, 2010); The Housing Forum, *Everyone Needs a Home: Report of Working Groups* (2011).

x. By reducing real and perceived risk. Vidhya Alakeson, *Making a Rented House a Home: Housing Solutions for 'Generation Rent'* (Resolution Foundation, 2011).

xi. Local Government Association, *An Analysis of Unimplemented Planning Permissions for Residential Dwellings* (2012); Savills World Research, *Market in Minutes: UK Residential Development Land* (2013); and Andy Hull and Graeme Cooke, *Together at Home: A New Strategy for Housing* (IPPR, 2012).

xii. Office of Fair Trading, *Homebuilding in the UK: A Market Study* (2008).

xiii. Sarah Monk, Christine Whitehead, Gemma Burgess, and Connie Tang, *International Review of Land Supply and Planning Systems* (Joseph Rowntree Foundation, 2013).

xiv. Town and Country Planning Association, *Best Practice in Urban Extensions and New Settlements: A Report on Emerging Good Practice* (2007); Underwoods, *Compulsory Purchase*.

xv. Tony Dolphin and Matt Griffith, *Forever Blowing Bubbles? Housing's Role in the UK Economy* (IPPR, 2011).

xvi. For a similar point see FTI Consulting, *Understanding Supply Constraints in the Housing Market* (2012).

xvii. Nick Butler, correspondence with author.

xviii. Michael Jacobs and Mariana Mazzucato (eds.), *Rethinking Capitalism: Economics and Policy for Sustainable and Inclusive Growth* (2016).

xix. Dimitri Zenghilis, 'Decarbonisation, Innovation and the Economics of Climate Change,' in Ibid.; Nick Butler, correspondence with author.

xx. Charles Seaford, Lydia Prieg, Sagar Shah, and Tony Greenham, *The British Business Bank: Creating Good Sustainable Jobs* (NEF, 2013).

xxi. Nick Butler, correspondence with author.

xxii. Quoted in Peter Hennessy, *Prime Minister: The Office and Its Holders Since 1945* (1998), p. 261.

xxiii. Saul Estrin and David Winter in Julian Le Grand and Saul Estrin (eds.), *Market Socialism* (1988): 'Markets may not be good at stimulating large, non-marginal changes in the structure of the economy'.

CHAPTER 8

Redistribution

American economist Jeffrey Sachs has condemned the immorality that underlies inequality in the United States:

> America today presents the paradox of a rich country falling apart because of the collapse of its core values. American productivity is among the highest in the world. Average national income per person is about $46,000 – enough not only to live on, but to prosper. Yet the country is in the throes of an ugly moral crisis. Income inequality is at historic highs, but the rich claim they have no responsibility to the rest of society. They refuse to come to the aid of the destitute, and defend tax cuts at every opportunity. Almost everybody complains, almost everybody aggressively defends their own narrow, short-term interests, and almost everybody abandons any pretense of looking ahead or addressing the needs of others.[i]

The causes of rising inequality can appear complex, but the complexities all stem from three underlying drivers: the industrialisation of the developing world, advances in information technology, and a change in public morality rooted in the crises of the 1970s. These led to the decline in demand for mid-level skills referred to in the last chapter, and three other proximate causes of inequality: structural changes in business, a range of political decisions, including those that led to the decline of the trade unions, and immorality in the business world.

This chapter is about how to address this. It is also about how we can pay for the "needs of others," that is for decent public services and

© The Author(s) 2019
C. Seaford, *Why Capitalists Need Communists,*
Wellbeing in Politics and Policy,
https://doi.org/10.1007/978-3-319-98755-2_8

for addressing climate change. It is about what we have to do if Britain, too, is to avoid "falling apart." It is partly a matter of mechanisms—regulations, taxes and so on—but it is more, as Sachs observes, a matter of legitimacy, morality and social solidarity.

We need to be precise, though, about how mechanism and morality interact. A generalised rebooting of morality will not cut through specific and damaging behavioural norms that have led us to where we are now, while the design of intricate mechanisms is pointless if the principles on which they are based cannot command electoral support. It is not that everyone has to be happy about tax rises—they never will be—but they do have to be accepted by most people as part of a reasonable and legitimate response to our problems.

STRUCTURAL CHANGES IN BUSINESS

Two structural changes have occurred in business since the late 1970s, when equality peaked: companies have got bigger and intellectual property has got more important. Automation means that the latter, at least, is likely to continue.

The prosperity brought about by developing world industrialisation—especially prosperity amongst the middle class—has increased the demand for goods and services produced by Western companies. Firms have responded to this increased demand through the use of ever more efficient information technology, resulting in their becoming ever larger and more profitable. These firms have in turn helped developing countries integrate into the world economy, further boosting the prosperity on which the firms depend. Some of these firms—notably the big US tech companies—have also been able to expand very, very fast indeed because of the almost zero marginal cost of their product (once you have built a piece of software it costs nothing to make copies), and in some cases because the customer gains when there is a dominant supplier in the industry (as in social media). For these reasons, in 2016 the total turnover of firms in the US Fortune 500 was 2.9 times the equivalent for 1980 taking into account inflation, and the profits were 3.7 times the equivalent.[ii] This increase in size and profitability has leveraged the contribution of those running the firms, or advising them as lawyers, bankers and consultants: they can add value to bigger chunks of economic activity, creating greater scope for them to negotiate increases in their income.

The increase in company size has resulted in part from advances in software, but it has also increased the value of that software and sometimes of other forms of intellectual property—know-how, brands, patents and so on. Just like managers and advisors, these too can now add value to bigger chunks of economic activity. For example, the Starbucks brand is worth a lot, not because of some intrinsic quality it has but because the company that owns it is very big. Companies owning this kind of property can be very, very profitable indeed and this has had two effects: often, employees of such companies are better paid than employees of other companies, simply because there is more money to go around; at the same time there is fierce competition for those who are best at creating and exploiting this form of property, pushing up their salaries.[iii] An extreme form of the latter effect is the so-called 'winner-takes-all' market. In the IT, Internet age, if you have even marginally the best product in your category, you may dominate, so it can be worth paying very high salaries indeed for the best talent.

Structural explanations of this kind have to be consistent with international variations in inequality levels, and they are. Very large firms are less economically important in France and Germany than in the UK or United States. In 2013 the profits of the largest German and French firms (those on *Forbes* Magazine's list of the 2000 largest companies in the world) were equal to 2.6% of German GDP and French GDP respectively, whereas in the UK the equivalent figure was 4.3% and in the United States it was 5.2%.[iv] The United States is relatively strong in software design and the UK in the creative industries, with a high proportion of investment in intellectual property. Germany by contrast is relatively strong in vehicle manufacturing, with a low proportion of investment going into intellectual property. Germany and France also have smaller financial sectors than either the United States or the UK, where they have boomed. These facts help explain why the share of income enjoyed by the top 1% in France and Germany has not increased to the extent it has in the UK: in the UK its share rose from 7% to 13% of total income between 1981 and 2012, whereas in France it only rose from 8% to 9% and in Germany from 11% to 13%.[v]

What is to be done? There is little that can be done about the increase in firm size, and indeed it is not clear that we should want to do anything about it. If large firms are the most efficient organisations, then so be it (sometimes they are not, and there is a case for breaking up some inefficient or monopolistic firms, but that is a whole different argument).

We probably do want to do something about intellectual property and its tendency to increase inequality, however—just as we want to do something about land (page 135). This is particularly important given that software and the design of processes and machines will create so much value in a world of automation—a far higher proportion of the cost of a good than now will go towards paying for these. Because they generally have zero marginal cost, these forms of intellectual property are also inherently monopolistic, meaning that much of the value will be captured by those who create, sell and manage them.

Fortunately, there are several things we can do. For example, we could insist that the software has to be open source, if not initially then after an initial protected period, in the same way that drugs come off-patent after an initial period. Alternatively, the state or some other collective agency, for example a national pension fund or a democratically controlled sovereign wealth fund, could be given an option to buy software copyrights at a low price after this initial period. A variation on this, particularly appropriate if economies of scale do not lead to software monopolies and the economic rent earned by software is relatively low, would be an automation software sales tax. A third, more conventional, approach would be to tax profits on software, or on wealth more generally, at a very much higher rate than we have seen for many years.

I am not making detailed policy proposals in this book—but the choice between these options does involve some broader principles. Conventional economists are likely to argue that the best option is to reduce copyright terms, while at the same time taxing and redistributing incomes and wealth in the standard way. The thinking is that this will reduce the cost, and therefore increase the use and value, of the software—provided of course that the copyright terms are long enough to incentivise the development in the first place. The distribution of the value created is then a separate issue, or so it is argued. The trouble is the distribution of the value is *not* a separate issue. If reducing copyright terms had the desired effect, and as a result the gains from automation were spread widely among consumers rather than among a few software owners, it would be difficult to create public support for significant redistribution of these gains to those who had lost their jobs as a result of automation. This is a pattern that we have already seen in this country, with resistance to higher basic tax rates, and contempt for those on unemployment benefit. Repeat this pattern many times, and you are in danger of significantly increasing inequality. So, rather unusually, it follows that we do not want the gains from innovation to be enjoyed widely—for if they are, it will be more difficult to redistribute those gains in a way that is equitable.

It is also worth noting that limiting copyright terms may not even work in this way. Open source software has not, in practice, seriously undermined the monopoly profits of major software owners—look at Google, Facebook, Amazon and Microsoft. Nor has conventional competition policy. There are huge economies of scale and in many cases network effects in the software industry, and it is these as well as copyright law that have led to monopoly profits and have confounded competition authorities.[1] In practice, for both these reasons, it is likely that some form of appropriation of monopoly profits (whether through taxation or copyright transfer) would be needed.

If the intellectual property royalties, or taxation on these royalties, were appropriated by a sovereign wealth fund, then the fund could pay a dividend to all citizens, and thus help fund a universal basic income (UBI) paid to all working age adults—perhaps equal to one day a week on the average wage (i.e. about £100 a week). This would add up to a very large sum—approaching £130 billion a year in the UK if the income was itself taxed and if it partially replaced some benefits—so the royalties would have to be very big or taxes would have to go up substantially (given the other claims on tax revenue the latter could be a stretch too far). On the other hand, if we are saying that the intellectual property on which these royalties are paid has enabled us to produce the same output with 40% fewer people, the hypothesis set out on page 27, then even if much of the gain goes to consumers, the royalties funding this universal income could be very high indeed.

This fits into a family of proposals for a UBI. In most versions, this replaces some but not all benefits and national insurance allowances.[2] The idea has started to attract much attention and has been hailed as a panacea by some left-wing writers.[vi] Finland, the Netherlands, Canada, California, Uganda, Brazil and Scotland are all running pilots or

---

[1] Once you have written the software, an extra copy costs nothing to make. The value of much software is greater the more people use it.

[2] The proposal made here is designed to make the average person as well off working a four-day week in the future as they are working a five-day week now. It could therefore replace benefits of up to £100 a week, but not tax allowances. It could do the latter if increased by £40 a week.

feasibility studies and the OECD has conducted an analysis of its potential fiscal impacts in a range of countries.[vii] The useful but unsurprising conclusion of this work is that for UBI to be more than a streamlining of the current benefits and tax allowance system, there will have to be major increases in tax rates. The more limited streamlining has its merits—UBI set at a modest level would help eliminate poverty traps and some of the inequities of modern means-testing—but it is not radical redistribution.[3] The difference between these proposals and what is proposed here is the source of funding for the income: royalties on the software that is making work redundant. The beauty of this is that the more jobs are made redundant the greater the royalties are likely to be, and therefore the greater the compensating minimum income can be.

A SHORTER WORKING WEEK

A universal income would make reduction of the working week feasible, but it would still be difficult to achieve. The five-day week has been remarkably persistent, despite the dramatic productivity improvements of the last 70 years.

Does this matter? Should we try and change this norm? There are three reasons why perhaps we should: if everyone continues to work a five-day week, this might create unemployment given automation; the extra consumption that the extra day finances might exacerbate climate change and other threats to sustainability; and a five-day week might reduce people's chances of flourishing.

The standard economic theory is that whether people work a four- or five-day week should not affect levels of unemployment—the extra money earned on the fifth day is extra money spent, which in turn creates employment. However, the whole automation story is that a rising proportion of expenditure will fail to produce jobs, or at least decent ones. Setting out some illustrative numbers may make this point clearer. Imagine that before automation there are one million workers working a five-day week. Now, after automation the same output can be produced by the 600,000 workers who were working, and continue to work, in non-automated sectors. They still work a five-day week. The other

---

[3]In the UK an income of £371 per month for every working age adult and £261 per child, and keeping housing benefit, would cost a net £44 billion after savings on benefits and tax and NIC allowances (OECD).

400,000 workers, displaced from sectors that have been automated, seek to join them in these non-automated sectors—but they can only find jobs if demand in these sectors increases by 66% (400,000/600,000). This may be possible in theory—automation will have increased the economy's capacity and thus the population's wealth—but it seems quite unlikely in practice. If, however, everyone now works a four-day week, demand for the output of the non-automated sector only has to increase by 33%. This seems more feasible—although of course there still needs to be a matching of skills supplied and demanded.

The climate-change argument for a four-day week is more nuanced. There are reasons why in the long term it may help if consumption is reduced and individuals work shorter hours, but in the short to medium term we may need to increase output to pay for mitigation in other parts of the world: we return to this on page 159.

As for the well-being argument, there is a clear-cut case for giving people the option of working less if they choose to: the evidence is that working longer hours than you want to damages well-being. There may also be a case for encouraging (not forcing) people to choose to work shorter hours: there is evidence of a vicious circle, in which longer working hours reduces the time and energy people have for a rewarding social life and other non-work activity, which in turn makes people want to consume and work more to compensate for this—although it never does.[viii] If this vicious circle exists, then at least some people are making a mistake about what will maximise their well-being.

What can be done to reduce working hours? The first step is to change labour market regulation and/or national insurance rules so as to make it easier for individuals to choose a shorter working week should they want to. The second step is to introduce the UBI in the way already described, so as to reduce the incentive to work the fifth day. The third step might be a range of nudges and other actions by government that help shift norms. For example, in the 1980s the Dutch government stipulated that all new government jobs should be 80% full-time equivalent.[ix] By 2016, average annual hours worked in the Netherlands were 14% fewer than in the UK and 19% fewer than in the United States,[x] and the Dutch reported the best work–life balance in the OECD.[xi]

Obviously, some people will continue to work five or more days a week whatever the opportunities and norms, and this may be the right thing for them to do: some people get deep satisfaction from their work, and one analysis of UK well-being data found that those men who work very long hours tend to find what they do in life (not just work) more worthwhile than those men who work shorter hours (the association was not statistically significant for women).[xii] Others may value the income that the extra day provides, and the things that it allows them to do in their spare time, and they may value this more highly than an extra day's leisure. There is probably nothing we could or should do about the former group, but are there things that we could and should do to increase the relative appeal of free time as compared with income?

Yes, there are two things, both of which are also valuable in their own right. The first is reducing inequality. There is a positive correlation between the Gini coefficient and the average number of hours worked in a year in the 20 OECD countries with GDP per capita of more than $30,000 (i.e. the more unequal the society, the longer hours people work),[xiii] and there are reasons for thinking there is a causal connection. Firstly, unequal societies tend to have more very poor people in them than equal societies, and for poor people every penny counts. They often work very long hours indeed to make ends meet. Secondly, well-being is particularly sensitive to relative income, i.e. whether you have more or less than others (as we saw in Chapter 3). It follows that the more unequal a society, the greater the value of income and thus the greater the value of income relative to leisure. For slightly different reasons, goods used as status symbols tend to become more important in a relatively unequal society, and working to pay for these becomes more worthwhile. In a rigidly stratified, traditional society, many people may 'accept their place' and the associated lack of freedom and status. However, in more modern societies, self-esteem starts to require the possession and display of status goods, to reassure oneself and perhaps others that one is not subordinate. In the words of one consumer goods company CEO: "The brand defines the consumer. We are what we wear, what we eat, what we drive."[xiv] The greater the inequality, that is the greater the gap between the 'successful' and the 'normal', the greater the need for this reassurance.

The other thing that can be done to increase the relative appeal of free time is to support the social institutions which enable people to engage in disciplined, purposive and sociable activity outside of work, again as discussed in Chapter 3. There is a nagging worry as to whether people will find enough to do in their extra time in ways that do not involve more spending, so sending them back to work. At least some people may be deterred from working and consuming less for fear of boredom and lack of meaning in their leisure time. Will they miss the companionship and sense of purpose provided at the office? That is why social institutions are part of the strategy for dealing with automation.

POLITICAL DECISIONS

Attitudes towards inequality among politicians changed in the 1980s, reflecting the broader change in public morality following the various economic crises of the 1970s. As a result of this, four sets of decisions by politicians have contributed to inequality: decisions to reduce top tax rates, to 'liberalise' labour market law and restrict trade union activity, to prioritise tackling inflation rather than unemployment and to liberalise capital markets.

The Thatcher government reduced the top tax rate from 83% to 60% in 1980, and to 40% in 1989. This of course increased post-tax pay differentials, but Thomas Piketty and others have suggested that this and similar measures under Reagan led to increases in pre-tax pay.[xv] This could be because it made high pay more worth having and perhaps also by contributing to the social acceptability of very wide differentials. (It may also have led to more open reporting of high pay, exaggerating the apparent increase in differentials.)

Low and falling wages, and increased insecurity, have been concentrated in three sectors—retail, hospitality and care homes—and in manual services such as cleaning, delivery, driving cabs and security.[xvi] These sectors and occupations have two important things in common: they face zero competition from overseas, and have not yet been significantly automated (even if distribution is now via online platforms such as Uber). In other words, while change in the developing world and automation reduced the number of good jobs available, and thus helped depress wages generally, they were not direct drivers of the lowest pay levels. Political decisions to 'liberalise' labour market law, that is reduce employment rights, and to restrict trade union activity have been more important.

These decisions made casual labour more prevalent and reduced the ability of workers to negotiate without fearing they would be fired. No UK government of the left or right has even considered taking steps to help unions counter the decline in membership and weaker bargaining power that the global trends already described brought in their train. It is true that a minimum wage has been introduced and steadily increased—but until recently at a very cautious rate indeed. It was sometimes argued that allowing stronger labour market protections to persist would have damaged the economy, employment prospects and average living standards. Curiously, restricting the rights of workers became accepted by policymakers and Establishment commentators as in the interests of workers themselves: the neoliberal version of paternalism.

The relative market power of labour was also reduced using macroeconomic policy, at least in the 1980s, when it was designed to produce low inflation and a strong exchange rate rather than full employment. This was good for asset values but created downward pressure on wages—and inequality in the UK rose most sharply at this time.

Capital market liberalisation took two forms. Firstly, capital controls were abolished in 1979, resulting in increased capital flows. These, together with rising income inequality and a rising share of national income going to profits, resulted in rising asset prices in the 1980s and to a lesser extent the 1990s. Between 1984 and 1999 the FTSE 100 index trebled in value in real terms (after this it stagnated),[xvii] and between 1982 and 1990 there was also a property boom. Asset owners benefited. After 1997, absence of capital controls and the economic advance of the developing world combined to create a second property boom and therefore increased wealth inequality in the UK. Between 2014 and 2016, 13% of London property purchases were by foreign investors.[xviii] No government did anything to prevent this.

Secondly, regulation of financial markets and of the firms operating in them was relaxed, notably in 1986, resulting in increased opportunities to profit from this asset inflation, opportunities often exploited by American investment banks. Many not especially talented people could make large amounts of money by buying, selling or underwriting assets, or advising others about how best to do so. Financial markets are inherently oligopolistic,[xix] and, after the initial opening up of the market in 1986, high barriers to entry reformed. There has never been any attempt since then to crack down on this oligopoly.

Reversing political decisions that have increased inequality is the most straightforward part of the package. Higher minimum wages, restored trade union rights and fair labour market regulation are part of any solution, and particularly important in the non-traded personal services sector where low wages and insecurity are concentrated. It could also be useful to control capital flows to rein in asset price inflation, especially housing price inflation. Measures of this type are now part of Labour Party policy; and the Conservatives too are raising minimum wages and improving labour market regulation, although to a very limited extent. Such policies are necessary, but as we saw earlier in the chapter, reducing inequality in the future will require governments to go substantially beyond this.

INEQUALITY AND IMMORALITY

Let us now look at the final driver of inequality: business immorality. The structural changes and political decisions already described created opportunities for self-enrichment, but they did not make the levels of inequality we have seen inevitable. Neoclassical economics may assume greed, but that doesn't mean it is unavoidable, let alone good. Intercountry comparisons may point to structural drivers of inequality, as we saw on page 149, but they point to normative drivers as well. Sweden and Finland, for example, are both countries with a lot of investment in intellectual property compared with Spain and Italy, but are relatively equal in comparison with those two countries.[xx] This is the opposite of what you would expect if structure was all that mattered: it looks as if norms matter as well.

In Britain these norms have changed. As John Kay has put it:

> The senior managers of corporations before the 1980s did not pay themselves large salaries because they did not think it appropriate to do so. They would have been insulted by the idea of a bonus or a success fee in much the same way as a doctor or a teacher would still be insulted by a bonus or a success fee.[xxi]

It is now widely considered 'appropriate' to pay oneself a large salary, but this does not make it moral. Three examples of what is widely considered 'normal' or 'appropriate' illustrate the point: it is not the notorious behaviour of a few semi-criminals that creates the problem but the degeneration of more widely held social norms.

First, there is the behaviour of remuneration committees, the non-executive directors that set top pay. We have already heard about these people from Loughlin Hickey in Chapter 6. Typically, these committees aim to pay the executive directors in the top quartile of top managerial salaries at similarly sized firms. There is a weak or non-existent association between executive pay and company performance,[xxii] but it just *could* be rational for an individual company to pay in the top quartile—to ensure the best management. It is also true that pay increases *could* seem more economically rational because of the rising size of firms, and the increased economic importance of intellectual property, since these might make paying for the best seem more worthwhile. However, even if we admit all this—and it is highly contested[4]—consistently aiming to pay in the top quartile *cannot* be rational for the diversified shareholders in whose interests the decisions are avowedly made, and who will generally own shares in companies paying in the top, middle and bottom quartiles. As a matter of logic every company cannot pay in the top quartile and therefore attempts to do so have sent managerial salaries ever higher. This is not a new observation: everyone in the field has known about this for some time—*and that is the point.* It is a fact that everyone knew but chose to ignore. The investment management companies that act for these diversified investors preferred not to rock the boat or to act in their clients' interests to stop this unproductive ratchet. Remuneration committee members and investment managers both acted immorally by acquiescing in a corrupt system, whether or not they themselves benefited from it.[5]

Another example of public immorality has been described by Andrew Smithers, a former leading investment manager and economics consultant, in his book *The Road to Recovery.* As he puts it, many large quoted companies "gouge rents from the rest of the economy and... corporate management is extracting huge benefits from this."[xxiii] The bonus culture that allows this encourages managers to target short-term profits and actually aim for profit volatility; this reduces the value of the company to shareholders holding for the long term. Although managers are the agents of shareholders, they are in effect stealing from them.

A third example has been described in recent research from the International Monetary Fund (IMF). The authors find "strong evidence

---

[4] As long ago as the 1950s, management guru Peter Drucker reported on some J. P. Morgan Research showing that CEO salaries that were very high relative to those of other managers were negatively correlated with company performance.

[5] The remuneration consultants themselves were in some cases incentivised to recommend increased pay levels since some of them also ran headhunting practices which were paid a percentage of the recruit's package.

that lower unionization is associated with an increase in top income shares in advanced economies during the period 1980–2010."[xxiv] Indeed, they estimate that this explains as much as *half* of the top 10%'s rise in share—a truly remarkable finding. Lower levels of unionisation increased the power differential between managers and workers, which managers did not have to, but chose to, exploit. They were in a position to choose how the firm's revenues were divided between themselves and the previously unionised workers. They screwed down the wages of the lowest paid in order to benefit themselves. Market fundamentalists might have expected competitive forces to erode the extra profits that weaker unions permitted, in effect removing managers' freedom of manoeuvre and ensuring that they did not gain personally from weaker unions. They might have expected that any gains would be passed on to consumers. However this is not what actually happened. Oligopoly power trumped market forces.

As we saw in Chapter 6, business people can be very uncomfortable when discussing these issues. There was a tendency among those I spoke with to change the subject when I raised it: typically to the inordinate complexity of remuneration systems, or to the tendency for packages to reward failure rather than performance. One otherwise very enlightened individual felt the topic was largely inspired by envy. It seems likely that business leaders will need some external help if they are to rediscover the professional self-esteem referred to by Kay that made enormous bonuses unattractive. This points to the need for structural change—I will return to this in the next two chapters.

PAYING FOR CLIMATE CHANGE AND PUBLIC SERVICES

Redistribution is not just a matter of increasing income equality: it is also a matter of ensuring good public services, and of addressing climate change. Both are going to be more expensive than in the past, and who pays the costs will be a central political issue.

Renewables may no longer need massive subsidy, and this may create opportunities for some businesses and some countries—one of the reasons green growth has become so popular. However, getting the proportion of fossil fuel-generated energy down from 80% to zero in 30 years (which is the least we are going to have to do), is going to mean writing off existing fossil fuel-based assets and investing in far more new plant than would otherwise have been needed. What we spend on this new plant cannot be spent on consumption. More wind farms means fewer holidays. The same principle applies to cars. To get the proportion of electric cars from 2% to 100% in the time frame needed may require us to scrap industrial plant, or even vehicles that could otherwise remain in use, and invest in new plant and vehicles that might not otherwise have been produced.

The main bearers of the cost will not be consumers paying higher prices for energy or taxpayers providing a subsidy for this energy—renewable energy is, or will be, competitive. Instead, the *direct* bearers will be the owners of stranded assets, for example coal company shares (these have already plunged in value in the United States), and in due course oil company shares. Consumers and taxpayers will not get off free, though. They may well end up compensating the owners of assets that are written off, and so bearing the costs *in*directly. This is because a very high proportion of these assets are in the developing world. For example, Chinese coal-fired power stations generate over 930,000 megawatts of electricity, and power stations generating a further 210,000 are either under construction or planned. The equivalent Indian figures are 215,000 and 130,000. The developed world also makes a major contribution: coal-fired power stations in the United States generate 278,000 megawatts, in Germany 50,000 and in Japan 44,000.[xxv] The biggest political challenge is likely to be deciding who is to bear the cost of writing off these coal-fired power stations and other emission-generating assets, particularly those in China and across the developing world (electricity generation only accounts for about a quarter of greenhouse gas emissions, but the same principle applies in other sectors). How much of it will be down to the countries where the assets are located or owned and how much of it will be down to Western consumers and taxpayers? Technologies may be found to make these power stations carbon neutral (there is absolutely no guarantee), but this simply changes the precise form of the question, not the underlying dilemma: who will bear the cost of the research and of any subsidy needed once these technologies are rolled out?

It is inconceivable that China and the rest of the developing world will do what we would like them to do: write off all their carbon burning power supply, and accept that they are responsible for all the associated costs. As is frequently pointed out, much of the carbon emitted in the developing world is emitted while producing products exported to the West, and in any case, it was production in the West that got us in this mess to start with. So, if we really want the developing world to reduce emissions, then we are going to have to pay. To put the predicament into more concrete terms, some of the money we send to China to buy cheap televisions and clothes will have to be diverted to compensate the owners of coal-fired power stations that we want closed down. Sometimes this will be the state; some of it will have to be diverted to compensate the workers in these and other carbon-intensive industries or to subsidise the investment and training needed to create replacement jobs; some of it will have to be diverted to new technology research and development. Other things being equal, we will end up with fewer televisions and clothes, but at least we will not face climate catastrophe.

Given that consumers vote for governments, we are more likely to tackle climate change successfully if Western growth levels are reasonably buoyant: funds can then be diverted to compensate citizens of the developing world for writing off carbon-emitting assets without actually lowering Western living standards (one of the better-established pieces of well-being evidence is that a reduction in consumption causes a far greater change in well-being than the equivalent increase—see page 232). Of course, if the foreign currency earnings that finance this subsidy were themselves the result of carbon-intensive industrial activity, there would be little net gain. We would be polluting the world in Britain in order to pay for reducing pollution in China. But as it happens, the best prospects for UK export growth are in low-carbon services and high-value, low-weight products where a very small proportion of the value is derived from energy or other 'stuff'. Even now, a lot of thought is going into how UK growth could be completely decarbonised and largely dematerialised.

Proponents of 'degrowth' or a 'steady-state economy' argue that this kind of 'decoupling' of consumption, carbon emissions and raw materials use is unrealistic. Their arguments tend to take the form of extrapolation: if we continue to grow at this rate, and the developing world catches up, we will need to achieve 99% decoupling (reduction in carbon intensity) to reach global emissions targets; given the nature of our economy and society, this percentage will be very difficult to achieve—at any rate, we have never achieved anything like it in the past.[xxvi] This is convincing, until you ask what the alternative is. The standard reply is reduction in consumption, whether the result of individual or collective, i.e. political, choices, but either way given that we live in a democracy, a voluntary reduction in consumption. This is plausible to the extent that well-being does not require ever increasing consumption (see pages 57 and 233–5 for a discussion of this point). The trouble, though, is that the line can be challenged using a form of argument very similar to that used by the degrowthers themselves: your alternative requires a voluntary reduction in consumption. Given the nature of our economy and society this will be very difficult to achieve—at any rate, we have never achieved anything like it in the past. Degrowthers can of course reply 'we have to do something we have never achieved in the past, or we are done for,' but then so can advocates of growth. And proponents of both sides of the argument are right: we do have to do something we have never done before or we are done for. The argument boils down to which is more plausible, radical decoupling or a voluntary reduction in consumption?—or rather, what mix of the two is most plausible?

But conducting the argument in this way—framing the question as about growth—is overly abstract: there is no decision to be made about growth or no-growth as such. The fact is we are going to see massive increases in productivity as a result of automation, and so the questions are: first, can and should we channel some of the gains this will create into increased exports, which we then use to help pay for climate change mitigation, for example writing off assets? Then, can we redistribute what's left (as discussed on pages 150–2 and 156)? And finally, should we encourage people to take their share of the gains in the form of increased leisure rather than in the form of increased consumption, perhaps working a four-day week (as discussed on pages 152–5)? I have already argued that the answers to the second and third questions are 'yes', but if the answer to the first question is also 'yes', then there will be fewer gains to share, meaning it will be tricky to get people to work less until the mitigation bill has been paid. People will have to wait a bit longer for the four-day week that pays a five-day wage—the arithmetic suggests about half a dozen years longer.[6] To put this in terms of the growth/degrowth debate, we will have to grow GDP for a few years to pay for mitigation, but eventually we can stabilise or even reduce it as people choose to work less. Of course, during this interim period we still

---

[6]This is based on an on-going mitigation 'bill' to cover costs in the UK and a UK contribution to developing world costs of around 7% of GDP ('on-going' means GDP is 7% lower than it otherwise would have been), and a business as usual growth rate of 1.5% of GDP. The Potsdam Institute has suggested a smaller cost bill (around 4.5%) in an analysis, but I am envisaging a larger transfer to the developing world. To put this 7% in context, the government's analysis of the on-going cost of Brexit with a free trade agreement is around 5% of GDP.

have to crack down on carbon emissions and raw material use, but that just means we need policies and metrics appropriate to these objectives. We should not use GDP as a loose proxy for these any more than we should use it as a loose proxy for well-being.

So, to return to the question about plausibility, zero consumption growth or even a modest reduction may be plausible in the long term when associated with a shorter working week. However, in the short to medium term this option will not be available. Many of the gains from automation will be needed to pay for Chinese and other developing world write-offs and will not be available to take as a shorter working week. The alternative—asking British voters to agree to cut their living standards so as to pay for these—seems to me, at least, totally implausible.

Even given growth, a politically acceptable mechanism has to be found to actually pay the compensation. On the face of it, a transfer to the developing world to pay for asset write-offs doesn't stand a chance, whatever the growth rate is, certainly if it is structured as overseas aid. An alternative way of packaging it could be a tax-funded subsidy of certain UK exports: not simply green technology, but anything that can help newly industrialised nations restructure their economies and create jobs for those displaced by the write-offs, and, of course, that doesn't itself compete with those countries' industries. The subsidy would also help create jobs in the UK and could be presented as supporting green growth both here and in the developing world. It would require explicit intergovernmental agreement on the international division of labour. A second mechanism would be a system of tariffs and subsidies, designed to tilt developing world exports towards green products, and with at least some of the transition cost in effect paid for by Western consumers. The aim—easier said than done—would be to accelerate transition without increasing too much the disruption it brings about. These are merely illustrative ideas: this is a complex problem and the aim here is just to show that it is possible to think about alternative ways of tackling it.

Similar issues arise when it comes to paying for improved public services: it is easier to say we want good services than to find politically safe ways of raising the money. Most people in the UK still feel they are entitled to the best possible medical attention, that their children are entitled to the best possible education, and that they should be protected by the best possible police force. Indeed, these are necessary conditions for flourishing. The spirit of Aneurin Bevan's National Health Service Act and Lord Robbins's report on higher education remains alive and well. The 2017 British Social Attitudes Survey reports that an increasing proportion of voters believe taxes should rise to pay for better public services.[xxvii] However, as any politician will tell you, this does not mean they will vote for the party promising the biggest tax increases. Cracking this problem is a matter of both mechanisms and morality: designing mechanisms that people feel are fair, or at least don't feel oppressive, and then fostering the sense of responsibility that will sustain support for them.

If increasing general taxation is difficult, an alternative is 'hypothecated' taxes—taxes designated for particular purposes. Gordon Brown raised National Insurance contributions when he was Chancellor, and linked this directly to increased NHS spending. This worked; there were few complaints. Taxpayers accepted that taxes might have to go up to pay for better healthcare, but they did not like paying money to 'Gordon' (as focus group participants sometimes described general taxation). Hypothecation deals with this problem, the OECD recommends it,[xxviii] and John McDonnell is reported to be considering it as well. The principle can extend beyond the NHS. For example, capital and corporation taxes could be hypothecated to education—'an investment in the future'[xxix]—while higher rate income taxes could fund programmes and transfers designed to relieve poverty: if the prosperous who pay these taxes were to complain, they would be complaining about poverty relief.[xxx] Reviving the 'contributory principle' for cash benefits is also often suggested, in reality another form of hypothecation.

This might sound tediously technical, but if implemented in a wholehearted way with a legislative basis, it would amount to a revolution in the way government is conducted and tax and spend is thought about. It would create rigidities and restrict ministers' and officials' freedom of manoeuvre, but that is the point: it is called democracy. The price of a more adult public discussion about tax and spend is a more constrained private one. The approach has traditionally been opposed by Treasury officials, presumably because they do not see the political challenge it addresses as part of their job.

The kind of fund-raising mechanisms described here, whether for climate change mitigation or public services, will only work if voters accept them. The evidence, not surprisingly, is that they are much more likely to do so if they see them as ways of paying for things that they value rather than as impositions by only remotely accountable authority.[xxxi] That is the thinking behind hypothecation, and behind linking developing world transfers to green growth. However, if this, and effective communication, is still not enough to win support, we may need to do more to make the decisions involved more like consumption decisions, albeit collective consumption decisions, and less like traditional top–down exercises of authority. That could involve changing the way the decisions are made, so that individuals feel some sense of responsibility. This is not a call for referendums: experience shows that these do not tend to increase levels of responsibility. It could be that forms of deliberative and local democracy would be more effective. We return to this in Chapter 10.

PLANNING, REDISTRIBUTION AND FLOURISHING

How are the ideas and knowledge about flourishing set out in Chapter 3 relevant to the approach set out in this and the previous chapter?

Above all, they will help us develop a picture of the society and economy we wish to see. This can then provide a guide to the planning described in Chapter 7 and legitimacy to the redistribution described in this chapter—and may help cement the partnership needed between government and business. The ideas can also contribute to the framework and the evidence for any deliberative democracy that may also be needed.

Planning includes taking a broad view of how many jobs of what kind will be needed, and this cannot be done well without understanding the contribution of working, consuming and other activity to meaningful activity and flourishing. The other half of this coin is planning for leisure as well as work, and this also requires an understanding of what encourages flourishing. Planning also includes planning new housing developments and settlements. While the approach to housing policy I have proposed is in some ways similar to that of the 1940s and 1950s, we need to avoid the mistakes of the 1940s and 1950s, and we are more likely to do so if we take into account what we know about how architecture and urban design make flourishing more or less likely. Finally, planning includes planning the investment in technology and infrastructure that will mitigate climate change; this too cannot be done well without an understanding of likely consumption and working patterns of the future. These are not givens: we have some choices, and to make these choices well we need to understand the impact of different patterns on flourishing. We will need to know, for example, which kinds of consumption are most valuable to people, and which could be more readily foregone were we to reduce the influence of advertising and the patterns of production and consumption it tends to encourage.

Redistribution will include bigger cash benefits, that is a UBI, provision of quality public services and paying for climate change mitigation. Devices such as hypothecation, appropriation of copyrights and a sovereign wealth fund may make this more politically acceptable, but it may still be difficult to sustain public and business support if they are framed in traditional social democratic terms, designed to deliver social justice. The collectivist and egalitarian ethic associated with this framing appeals to many people, but perhaps not to enough people, particularly among those in business. This matters because of the importance of the government–business partnership. To argue that the various measures, including compensating developing world owners of coal-fired power stations, should be done on justice grounds is going to be difficult. To argue that the role of business and government is to create the conditions in which people can flourish may be easier. Similarly, if we are relying on deliberative democracy, that is structured discussion between groups of citizens, to help set levels of taxation, we will need to provide the information that people need to make the decisions. The most convincing information will be about what makes people flourish.

If our aim was simply to optimise consumption and redistribute—ensure GDP was maximised and allocated efficiently and fairly—it would all be much easier. We might then rely on neoclassical economics, and not bother with what makes people flourish, or with a more democratic decision-making process. There would be only one big political decision to make—how much redistribution to have—and it would be reasonable to ask the electorate that question every five years. The approach would work were the problems of markets confined to particular, limited market failures, a little pollution, a little monopoly and the other relatively minor inefficiencies that markets are known to produce. These are technical issues and economists can advise.

Neoclassical economics and the idea that democracy consists of first-past-the-post elections every five years fit together well, but neither are sufficient given the scale of our problems. Neoclassical economics is not a theory of organisations or of ethics, or of the "social, cultural and political expectations and institutions" within which markets are "embedded."[xxxii] Such theory is required alongside a theory of markets if officials and politicians are to be equipped to guide the economy in a particular direction, in the way they are currently equipped to make it grow and be efficient. The ideology of flourishing, linked to deliberative democracy, is the foundation for this.

NOTES

i. Jeffrey Sachs, 'America's Deepening Moral Crisis,' *The Guardian* (4 October 2010).

ii. Author's calculations based on Fortune 500 data, http://fortune.com/fortune500.

iii. Jonathan Haskel and Stian Westlake, *Capitalism Without Capital* (2017).

iv. Author's calculations based on Forbes List 2013, https://www.forbes.com/global2000.

v. OECD, *Focus on Top Incomes and Taxation in OECD Countries: Was the Crisis a Game Changer?* (2014).

vi. Nick Srnicek and Alex Williams, *Inventing the Future: Postcapitalism and a World Without Work* (2015).

vii. Martin Sandbu, 'Universal Basic Income: Renaissance for a 500-Year-Old Idea,' *Financial Times* (8 December 2017).

viii. Stefano Bartolini, Ennio Bilancini, and Maurizio Pugno, 'Did the Decline in Social Connections Depress Americans' Happiness?' *Social Indicators Research* (2008, Vol. 110:3, pp. 1033–1059).

ix. Juliet Schor, Speaking at *About Time*, a Seminar Organised by the New Economics Foundation and the LSE Centre for Analysis of Social Exclusion (January 2012), http://b.3cdn.net/nefoundation/bd7cbe3d-0c570fdabe_bfm6i2n8n.pdf.

x. OECD, *Hours Worked Indicator* (2018), https://data.oecd.org/emp/hours-worked.htm.

xi. OECD, *Better Life Index* (2017), http://www.oecdbetterlifeindex.org/topics/work-life-balance.

xii. Saamah Abdallah and Sagar Shah, *Well-being Patterns Uncovered* (NEF, 2012).

xiii. Charles Seaford, 'Happy Planet, Happy Economy, Happy Consumers?' in Miriam Tatzel, *Consumption and Well-being and the Material World* (2013): $r^2 = 0.3904$. Note that there is almost no relation between Gini and GDP and a weak relation between GDP and hours worked with hours worked falling as GDP rises.

xiv. Juliet Schor, *The Overspent American: Why We Want What We Don't Need* (1998), p. 57.

xv. Thomas Piketty, Emmanuel Saez, and Stefanie Stantcheva, *Taxing the 1%: Why the Top Tax Rate Could Be Over 80%* (CEPR December 2011), https://voxeu.org/article/taxing-1-why-top-tax-rate-could-be-over-80.

xvi. Faiza Shaheen and Charles Seaford, *Good Jobs for Non-Graduates* (NEF, 2012).

xvii. Calculation based on raw data, https://markets.ft.com/data/indices/tearsheet/historical?s=FTSE:FSI and RPI figures, https://www.ons.gov.uk/economy/inflationandpriceindices/timeseries/bamq/mm23.

xviii. LSE London (June 2017), http://blogs.lse.ac.uk/politicsandpolicy/what-is-the-role-of-overseas-investors-in-the-london-new-build-residential-market/.

xix. http://www.telegraph.co.uk/finance/financetopics/profiles/8556638/Lord-Myners-I-want-to-do-things-that-are-creative-enterprising-and-closer-to-my-core-values.html.

xx. For levels of investment in intellectual property, see Jonathan Haskel and Stian Westlake, *Capitalism Without Capital: The Rise of the Intangible Economy* (2017). For levels of inequality, see OECD data, https://data.oecd.org/inequality/income-inequality.htm.

xxi. John Kay, 'Understanding and Misunderstanding the Triumph of Capitalism,' in Dominic Barton, Dezsö Horváth, and Matthias Kipping (eds.), *Reimagining Capitalism* (2016), p. 112.

xxii. Alistair Bruce and Trevor Buck, 'Executive Pay and UK Corporate Governance,' in Kevin Keasey, Steve Thompson, and Mike Wright (eds.), *Corporate Governance, Accountability, Enterprise and International Comparisons* (2005).

xxiii. Andrew Smithers, *The Road to Recovery* (2013), p. 230.

xxiv. Florence Jaumotte and Carolina Osorio Buitron (International Monetary Fund Research Department), 'Power from the People,' *Finance and Development* (March 2015).

xxv. https://endcoal.org/global-coal-plant-tracker/summary-statistics/.

xxvi. The first person to develop a rigorous analysis along these lines was Tim Jackson in *Prosperity Without Growth* (Sustainable Development Commission, 2009). Unlike some of his followers, he was not categorical about the implications for the decoupling versus degrowth debate.

xxvii. NatCen Social Research, *British Social Attitudes* (34th ed., 2017).

xxviii. OECD, *What Drives Tax Morale?* (2013), http://www.oecd.org/ctp/tax-global/what-drives-tax-morale.pdf.

xxix. Institute for Fiscal Studies, *Tax Revenues: Where Does the Money Come from and What Are the Next Government's Challenges? Briefing Note 198* (2017); Office for Budget Responsibility, *An OBR Guide to Welfare Spending* (2017). At the moment the amount raised would just about cover the amount spent: about 4% of GDP.

xxx. Ibid.: The top 1% pay 2.3% of GDP in income tax, roughly equal to the amount spent on Income Support and Job Seekers Allowance.

xxxi. OECD, *What Drives Tax Morale?* (2013), http://www.oecd.org/ctp/tax-global/what-drives-tax-morale.pdf.

xxxii. Mariana Mazzucato, 'Innovation, the State and Social Capital,' in Michael Jacobs and Mariana Mazzucato (eds.), *Rethinking Capitalism: Economics and Policy for Sustainable and Inclusive Growth* (2016) following Karl Polyani, *The Great Transformation: The Political and Economic Origins of Our Time* (1944).

CHAPTER 9

The System's Limits

The question we have to ask ourselves is whether ethical capitalism is possible. I believe we have no choice. The public have made their feelings clear. The unethical pursuit of profit at the expense of others is no longer acceptable....A system designed to create wealth for all has been exploited by a few to create unparalleled inequality. The problem doesn't lie with capitalism, but with those capitalists who have put self-interest and short-term gain ahead of the good of the people.

Cut to the speaker's boyfriend Alex, meeting a Russian mafioso at a champagne and caviar reception at Versailles. This speech was not made in real life but in *McMafia*, the BBC drama about money laundering, drug dealing and Russian gangs. The speaker was Rebecca, innocent girlfriend of the Russian-born, English-educated banker who, while she speaks, is being sucked into the criminal underworld.

Not a fair account of business in Britain, but a good example of the cynicism with which most people treat 'ethical' capitalism. A UK poll conducted in January 2015 showed that 78% of the sample believed big business put profits before ethics.[i] Another (global) survey conducted in December 2014 suggested just 20% of the public believe business leaders can be trusted to tell the truth or make ethical decisions,[ii] while a third survey offered slightly better news: 34% of people in Britain trust business leaders to tell the truth.[iii] A survey for the CBI, also in 2014, revealed that only 53% thought that business made a positive

© The Author(s) 2019
C. Seaford, *Why Capitalists Need Communists*,
Wellbeing in Politics and Policy,
https://doi.org/10.1007/978-3-319-98755-2_9

contribution to society.[iv] This scepticism is not entirely surprising. One survey of 34 directors of US Fortune 200 companies reported that 31 of them would cut down a mature forest or release a dangerous unregulated toxin into the environment in order to increase corporate earnings.[v] That is the United States, you might say, but even in the most respectable of British companies, corners are cut for personal gain. When Mike Rake, former Chairman of British Telecom, first arrived there in 2007, he found that small suppliers were made to wait for months for payment. When he insisted that they were paid on time, he was asked 'But what about our bonuses?' (To his credit he did not back down and payment times were reduced).

Business leaders may be concerned about the lack of trust, but they are only beginning to wake up to what putting that right means. As one well-placed observer says, only sometimes do their conversations about trust stretch to what business actually does. Rake accepts the criticism: "people say you live in a bubble—and we do." Many business leaders' initial response to bad news, he said, was 'we need to communicate more effectively'. For those outside the business world, some visible and symbolic change of behaviour might have sent the right signal, but even the verbal communication has lacked force. Business leaders are happy to make speeches like the one made by Rebecca, and express discontent in the way we saw in Chapter 6, but they will not criticise bad behaviour amongst their peers. FTSE 100 chairmen know that there are untrustworthy individuals in the business world, Rake told me. Both Philip Greens (BHS and Carillion), Mike Ashley of Sports Direct and Virgin's Richard Branson spring to mind. These are the 'predators' that Ed Miliband identified when he was leader of the Labour Party. Miliband contrasted them with 'productive' business leaders, but the latter didn't distance themselves from, and criticise, the predators; they preferred to criticise Miliband for drawing attention to them. We could be forgiven for thinking that loyalty to caste trumped loyalty to country.

So perhaps the case made in Chapter 7, for a proactive state working in partnership with business to achieve socially defined ends, is ridiculous or even dangerous. We saw in Chapter 4 how government and business fused in 1950s America. Won't partnership simply cement the relationships needed to bind together a twenty-first century version of the power elite? Since politicians generally "accept the notion that the economic rationality of the capitalist system is synonymous with rationality itself," as Ralph Miliband put it in the 1960s,[vi] then won't this partnership just mean government "helping business in every possible way?" And if this is dismissed as Marxist paranoia, then bear in mind that the right as well as the left is alert to the danger. For example, Liz Truss, Chief Secretary to the Treasury, is wary of industrial strategy, fearing that if government is too close to industry it will reinforce the power of existing big business at the expense of dynamic new entrants. The corporatist experiments of the fascists and Nazis, the appeal Hitler made to big business, also provide warnings of just how regressive a close government relationship or party relationship with business can be. Even Blair's government only formed a partnership with business on business's own terms, according to Ed Miliband. The relationships involved may have looked like partnerships, but in reality they were the results of a negotiation that capital had won. Larry Fink, Chairman of BlackRock, the largest investment management firm in the world, has made this very clear: "the partnership between government and business is going to be imperative," he has said, but "it will require large governmental actions that will satisfy the markets, because ultimately we're going to have to satisfy the markets."[vii]

In short, a 'partnership' between government and business could move us even faster towards the dystopia in which a small minority keeps all the gains from progress. Some members of the business elite may express their concern about the ways things are going, and some businesses may be doing good things, but these alone are not enough to change the direction of travel.

Economist and *Financial Times* columnist Anatole Kaletsky has argued that "many [societal] challenges... can be addressed only if politics creates new economic incentives and new institutions to stimulate the problem-solving, innovative capacities of private enterprise."[viii] However, he concedes that for these incentives and institutions to be effective, "Businesses will have to acknowledge wider definitions of their objectives than maximising their company's share price... they will stop fighting ideological battles against the principle of active government... Managements and investors will need to discover new ways to reconcile financial and political targets." But will they? He asserts that they will go out of business if they don't, and David Blood, Senior Partner at Generation Investment Management, said something similar to me. Good companies will win market share, while bad companies will go into decline. We would all like to think so, but is it true?

One possible sign of hope is the Brexit referendum. Mike Rake reported that it was a real wake-up call for many business leaders.

Liam Byrne, one of Labour's shadow business ministers, confirmed that in his experience business had become more willing to engage with politics since the referendum: they knew they had to do more than they had done, that things wouldn't just get better of their own accord. Colin Mayer, a professor and former Director of the Saïd Business School in Oxford, told me that Jeremy Corbyn's success at the 2017 election had stimulated business leaders to reconsider the way they did business. Simply attacking Labour, in the way that they had done when Miliband was leader, was no longer adequate. Rake agreed: many FTSE chairmen agree that "the future is under threat," that the question "what is the future of our system?" has become live, and that "we have to find a better to way to work... work with government—local and national—and those left behind." He himself feels some frustration and sense of urgency: "how long have we got to change the image of business?" he asked.

As yet, business does not know what it should do, how to respond. It finds itself facing a new challenge: helping build consensus in a society that has become divided. If social divisions are not to be aggravated further and the kind of conflictual politics brought to light by the Brexit referendum is not to continue, it will have to change the way it operates. The question is what it will take to make this happen.

The system as it works at the moment is set out in Fig. 9.1.

The shaded boxes are those who effectively make the decisions: what I have called the incumbent elite. The government and business elite can negotiate or collaborate when making economic decisions. However, whether they negotiate or collaborate, the most effective external pressure on this process comes from the international financial elite (or 'capital' for short). It is true that citizens can also apply pressure, by voting and by joining pressure groups, but citizens generally accept that capital has the stronger hand—it is mobile whereas citizens are not—and so, taking the process as a whole, they don't push things to the wire. No-one wants to lose their job because government is being too tough with foreign investors. This means government is in a weak position when negotiating: at the margin it can impose a sugar tax, but even some on the centre left concede that Macron may have been right to cut wealth taxes. The fate of the Greek Prime Minister Alexis Tsipras during his negotiations (in his case with the foreign governments supplying capital) seems to confirm this judgment. And this is before we even mention capital's influence on citizens through the media.

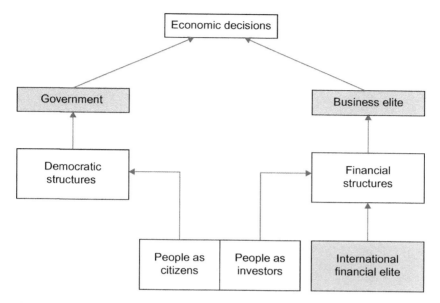

Fig. 9.1   The system as it is

As all progressives know, and as Fig. 9.1 illustrates, the challenge is to balance the power of capital, to create a countervailing pressure on government and business. The nature of this task is summarised in Fig. 9.2. In this new world, people, as citizens and as investors, have more power: the structures that transmit pressure from outside the elite into the elite have been reformed. With these countervailing pressures in place, it will be safer for progressives in government to form partnerships with business. They are less likely to find they are simply "helping business in every possible way." Naturally, structures on their own are insufficient for change. That is why this book is about the *politics* of flourishing and the emergence of a counter-elite rather than just about structural change. However, structures are an essential tool, to be used by individuals who are animated and given cohesion by a new and coherent ideology.

This chapter is about the scope for, and limits to, change given existing structures as set out in Fig. 9.1, that is the limits of negotiation and the limits of the self-restraint sometimes called 'ethical capitalism.' Chapter 10 is about the structural changes as set out in Fig. 9.2 that would expand this scope, and why they are feasible.

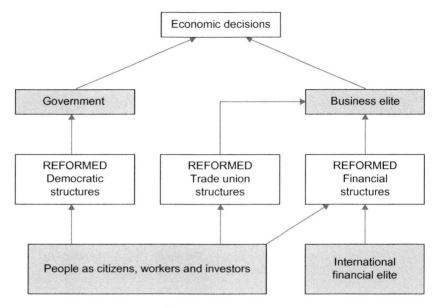

Fig. 9.2   The system after reform

THE LIMITS OF ETHICS

In January 2018 Larry Fink, the investment manager already quoted on the government–business partnership, wrote to the CEOs of all his firm's investee companies, saying:

> Society is demanding that companies, both public and private, serve a social purpose. To prosper over time, every company must not only deliver financial performance, but also show how it makes a positive contribution to society. Companies must benefit all of their stakeholders, including shareholders, employees, customers and the communities in which they operate.
>
> Without a sense of purpose, no company, either public or private, can achieve its full potential. It will ultimately lose the license to operate from key stakeholders. It will succumb to short-term pressures to distribute earnings, and, in the process, sacrifice investments in employee development, innovation and capital expenditures that are necessary for long-term growth. It will remain exposed to [shareholder] activist campaigns that articulate a clearer goal, even if that goal serves only the shortest and

narrowest of objectives. And ultimately, that company will provide sub-par returns to the investors who depend on it to finance their retirement, home purchases, or higher education.

Therefore:

> Companies must ask themselves: What role do we play in the community? How are we managing our impact on the environment? Are we working to create a diverse workforce? Are we adapting to technological change? Are we providing the retraining and opportunities that our employees and our business will need to adjust to an increasingly automated world? Are we using behavioral finance and other tools to prepare workers for retirement, so that they invest in a way that will help them achieve their goals?[ix]

The letter does not reflect how business and investment management are practiced at the moment. It is a prospectus for change and it was needed precisely because most companies are not yet asking themselves these questions. For this reason, they are likely to provide 'subpar returns' to investors. Importantly, the letter implies that there is minimal conflict of interest between shareholders and other stakeholders in the long run, stakeholders being all those with an interest in what the company does, including staff, consumers and those living in the communities in which it operates. It is only by behaving in a responsible way to stakeholders that those companies can deliver good returns to shareholders in the long run. The problems with the government–business relationship and the predatory behaviour referred to at the beginning of this chapter, Fink would argue, reflect the short-term perspective of managers (and some-times their stupidity) and not an underlying conflict of interest. It is true that there is an ambiguity as to whether the 'purpose' Fink refers to is there to serve profit, or the profits are there to serve the purpose, but that is in the nature of any collective enterprise: some people will see it one way and some another.

There is a literature going back at least to the 1980s arguing, broadly, that 'ethics pays'[x] and there is good evidence that companies that take a socially responsible attitude to decision-making do indeed *tend* to per-form better financially over the long term than those that don't. This is because they have better reputations, are subject to less regulatory risk, manage their supply chains better and retain talent more successfully.[xi] For example, a company that takes steps to minimise its carbon footprint is less likely to suffer from future fiscal and regulatory change than one that hasn't. A food company like Unilever which depends on access to commodities needs to ensure that the necessary bio-systems are preserved. Companies like Marks and Spencer or John Lewis, which depend on delivering a certain standard of service, need to pay their staff well. Even Microsoft is adopting a 'softer' approach to business than in the past because its new chief executive recognises the increasing importance of relationships and partnerships to the business. The same principle can extend to nurturing the society on which your business depends. Will Day of PricewaterhouseCoopers (PwC) describes a consultancy assignment for Nedbank, a South African bank. The consultants established that their client's success depended on a thriving economy in South Africa, and that this in turn depended on jobs, housing, education and so on. None of these activities were in Nedbank's loan book, so PwC recommended shifting into these areas by 2030.

The case for ethical capitalism has been made in a popular book by John Mackey, co-founder of Whole Foods Market, a US food retailer with seven branches in up-market parts of London, and Raj Sisodia, a business school professor.[xii] As founder of a business, Mackey is in a position to be less ambiguous than Fink: purpose in business is not just there to serve profit, rather the reverse. Capitalism has a fundamental ethical underpinning and is a great vehicle for enhancing people's lives as workers as well as consumers. Indeed it is "the greatest system for innovation and social cooperation that has ever existed" and business has a 'heroic' spirit. Cynics can dismiss this as "conscience laundering"[xiii] but Mackey and Sisodia really do seem to believe it—the laundering works. Of course, not every capitalist lives up to the heroic ideal—they are happy to admit that—but they suggest that perhaps the model that they have adopted successfully at Whole Foods could be more widely imitated.

The trouble is ethics doesn't always pay. The evidence is only that it *tends* to pay. Whole Foods Market was itself bought by Amazon in 2017—at the time of writing the world's second most valuable company and notorious for the poor pay and conditions in its warehouses. Loughlin Hickey, who as well as being a former partner of KPMG is now a trustee of the Blueprint Trust, promoting purpose and ethics in business, admits that you might want to use a much tougher, command-and-control method if you run these warehouses rather than a wholefoods company. Mike Barry of Marks and Spencer agrees that some retailers sell on price rather than quality service, making decent pay more difficult to justify. Mackey and Sisodia's version of ethical capitalism looks suspiciously like a niche: Whole Foods does not sell on price or ruthless efficiency, but plenty of other businesses, including its new owners, do. For them ethics may not pay, even in the long run.

"Stakeholders make up a company" Mackey, Sisodia and other ethical capitalists say. Indeed the stakeholder versus shareholder is a "false dichotomy," according to one OECD paper on the subject.[xiv] And yet, even Mackey and Sisodia are quite clear that shareholders not stakeholders must control the company: perhaps the stakeholder/shareholder dichotomy is not so false after all. There is a perfectly reasonable case for shareholder control—shareholders have no contractual right to any dividends, so if they didn't control the company they could be exploited by unscrupulous managers and not get any dividends at all (we will return to the limits of this argument in the next chapter). However, if this argument is accepted, it is disingenuous to suggest that shareholders with control are on a par with stakeholders without it. It is reminiscent of those imperialists who insisted that they were acting in the interests of the colonies, but refused to give colonials a vote. In reality, just as with empire, shareholders' interests come first.

Andrew Crane and Dirk Matten are two American business school professors who are slightly more sceptical than Sisodia. They have described how most US companies engage with stakeholders:

> At present companies are far more likely to consult stakeholders in an opportunistic manner in order to build consensus for what they are already doing rather than genuinely engaging stakeholders in a two-way conversation that involves them in meaningful decision-making about what constitutes performance.[xv]

They go on to say that 90% of managers think partnerships with NGOs on sustainability are necessary, but only 30% say their companies are doing it.

Few companies make sustainability a real priority. Only 25% of the 200 largest companies have a goal for carbon reduction in line with the demands of science, which matters because they have revenues equal to 29% of the world's economic output.[xvi] In a downturn, companies are likely to drop sustainability activities and cut staff, at least when it is not integrated into the strategy, and this kind of integration remains unusual.[xvii] Sustainability is not integrated into the operating structure, and sustainability directors lose their jobs in hard times.[xviii] Similarly, corporate social responsibility and business operations staff are for the most part not integrated.[xix] Most companies still avoid the responsibilities associated with outsourcing, although some are imposing minimum wages in the supply chain. Few companies think about their duty to uphold human rights.[xx] Some cheerleaders for ethical capitalism suggest that the need to maintain a good reputation means that even in the short term, the interests of shareholders and other stakeholders are aligned, but analysis by Colin Mayer reveals that this is not true.[xxi] Cutting wages or polluting the neighbourhood can save costs and boost profits despite the damage to reputation these unethical behaviours may create—people may not like Amazon but they buy from it. Advocates of ethical capitalism are going to have to try a bit harder if their model of progress is to be convincing.

Paul Polman, the recently retired Chief Executive of Unilever, does try a bit harder. He admits there is a real problem with capitalism, not just a communication problem. There is a good reason why most people don't trust business: it is amoral; it does not have our best interest at heart; and we only trust those who do.[xxii] His former colleague Thomas Lingard, who is Unilever's Global Director, Climate & Environment, gives an example of how this amorality compromises collaboration with government: some company sustainability departments are not *really* advancing a shift to sustainability; instead they are quietly defending the existing business model while appearing sympathetic to the challenges. This matters, because policymakers can't always tell the difference between the two positions.

Polman believes that if business can get over its amorality, it can play a critical role in addressing social and environmental issues. It brings tremendous resources to the table: trillions in capital and enormous capacity for innovation and fast action. He concludes that "It could serve the needs of citizens and communities with the same vigour with which it has served the needs of shareholders over the years."[xxiii]

An attractive idea, but how is business to get over its amorality? One rather bizarre idea that some otherwise intelligent people suggested to me was that consumer action can drive the change needed. "What would happen if everyone agreed not to buy anything from Amazon for a week?" said one; perhaps Facebook could be brought to its knees by a consumer revolt, said another. Consumer action seems to have a special legitimacy that government action lacks, at least in these commentators' eyes, and perhaps that is why collective action by consumers is particularly attractive to them. It is true that Fairtrade has made a real difference to the lives of many developing world farmers, but after 25 years it occupies 1.7% of the UK food and beverage market[xxiv] (although 17% of shoppers claim to buy Fairtrade products regularly).[xxv] There will always be room for 'ethical' brands serving niche markets, from Patagonia to Whole Foods, but there is zero evidence that ethical brands can dominate the mass market. There is no reason for supposing they will play a major role in the kind of systemic change discussed in the last two chapters, or turn fundamentally amoral organisations into moral ones, prepared to collaborate whole-heartedly with governments and others mandated to pursue the public good.

It is also true that some companies, such as Whole Foods or Unilever, are probably already moral companies. It may well be that over the years, ethical principles have become embedded in the way people think in these organisations, and this will survive any change of leadership—and perhaps of ownership. This can drive real action—Unilever has plenty of public good targets built into its business planning—and by helping build relationships within and beyond the company and helping recruit the best people, it can contribute to financial success as well. But as Polman himself says, one company cannot change capitalism.

It is not that we are aiming for a world without negotiation. There will always be conflicts of interests, and these will always require negotiation to resolve. It is a matter of the limits within which this negotiation takes place. Consider the parallel with political negotiation. This mostly takes place within a democratic framework that everyone accepts (referendums can call into question this framework, which is one reason Brexit has been such a source of anger). Negotiation between government and business also needs to take place within consensual limits. Fink's letter is in effect acknowledging that there is a premium for investors when this happens.

The letter is needed now because the nature of the limits is changing now, and the letter is acknowledging this too. For the past 35 years, these limits were defined by 'the politics of consumption'. A particular social contract—a particular deal between the elite and the masses as described at the beginning of this book—was widely understood, and this framed government–business negotiation. The agenda was maximising GDP, plus dealing with clearly identified market failures and ensuring a reasonably fair distribution of income. Now there is a potential new deal, new limits, and a different role for business. In this new deal, companies' role will be to ensure consumers and workers flourish, and government's role will be to make sure that they do.[xxvi] The problem is that existing structures and the styles of negotiation that they create make these new roles difficult to perform, even if a few exceptional companies have established an ethical tradition that allows them to transcend these structures.

THE LIMITS OF NEGOTIATION

In the normal course of events, government can negotiate effectively with business on behalf of citizens. Almost everyone I spoke to with experience of this process emphasised that government is perfectly capable of taking a tough line—and has to, because business only goes "as far as is required," as one consultant put it. Three former ministers confirmed the need to be tough and exercise leadership. Oliver Letwin put it thus:

> There is no real problem with there being different interests with industry provided everyone understands that there are. If you think business has the same goals as you do, you are mad. But it doesn't help to think they are all villains either—you just need to be open about conflicts of interest. Then you have to be prepared to be tough, to demonstrate you will wield the big stick.

And, he added, if they threaten to run a campaign in the *Daily Mail*, be very clear that you don't care.

There are several things that put government at a disadvantage, though. I have already quoted Lingard on sustainability departments that put on an act for officials, and Letwin agreed that governments often lack the information to negotiate effectively with large companies—you can be dependent on them for information, he explained, and they only give you what they want to give you. Another problem is that the civil servants conducting the negotiations may not be that good at it. They generally lack the commercial experience and in the absence of a very good working relationship with the relevant minister, may end up being unproductively rigid.[xxvii] And they may not know when they can and when they cannot dismiss threats of a *Daily Mail* campaign.

Government's biggest weakness, though, is globalisation: major companies operate in many countries, and can threaten not to invest, or to withdraw operations, if government does not do what they want. James Quincey, Global President of Coca-Cola, told Theresa May in a letter shortly after she became Prime Minister that "The single biggest risk to our ability to maintain our investment in our UK operations is the soft drinks levy"[xxviii]—a rather obvious piece of table thumping, but as Coca-Cola itself said, "no-one should be surprised." The sugar tax went ahead, but May dropped plans to ban pre-watershed advertising of sugary food and drink. In France, the Macron government has explicitly justified cutting taxes for the wealthiest because of the need to attract international business.

Sometimes business overplays its hand and government has to act tough. Sadiq Khan, Mayor of London, had to withdraw Uber's operating licence in Autumn 2017 just to get them to tighten up their safety procedures. Mobile phone networks dragged their feet on roaming charges until the EU forced them to drop them altogether. Hickey pointed out that public affairs advisors often give very bad—aggressive—advice and Mike Barry made much the same point:

> In the 90s the chemicals industry tried to prevent new regulation – and so just ended up with what seemed very draconian regulation at the time. Unless a sector creates a platform for change it will, in the end, suffer. You can stop something for five years – but it is a Pyrrhic victory.

On the sugar tax he says:

> It should have been obvious that the government is going to have to crack this [obesity] so the food and beverage industry should have worked together to propose a range of changes addressing both fats and sugars that will be as genuinely effective as a tax.

Michael Holm Johansen confirms that much of the government–industry discussion of how to tackle obesity descended into an unseemly squabble between sugar-using companies such as Coca-Cola and fat-using companies such as Unilever. Problem-solving was nowhere to be seen, implementation was delayed, and obesity remains one of the UK's top health challenges. As an executive of another company said, it is often difficult when you have a huge investment in a brand not to be defensive.

These are examples of how business finds it difficult to do what Polman suggested it could and should do: serve the "needs of citizens and communities" with the vigour with which it serves shareholders. Sometimes government wins a battle and sometimes it loses, but the two sides rarely work together unless they have to. Indeed, it can be difficult even to get global business to the table. As Johansen, pointed out, an international executive at his level (President of Central and Southern Europe at Coca-Cola) is not *that* interested in what is going on in Austria, while the big US IT companies "fundamentally do not believe they are part of this society." David Pitt-Watson, Executive Fellow of Finance at London Business School, said of BP that it too had "lost its sense that it is part of society." The business consultants I spoke with all agreed that most international executives simply do not see it as their job to engage with government on the kind of broad issues listed in Chapter 2. Consultant Richard Rawlinson said they simply "do not know what should be done about many of the issues" and they only think about them "in terms of what they should do for their own commercial interests." Troy Mortimer of KPMG echoed this: "it is difficult to feel global instability other than when you feel the lack of appetite in the market, or your salary doesn't go up."

This distance can result in a strikingly negative view of politicians and the political process. Larry Fink has said that "only when government is backed against the wall do we see action." Business, he continued, was "looking for a strong message, strong leadership and a little more consistency from government" but was not getting it.[xxix] Gus O'Donnell said that business people tend to blame politicians of both parties. They also believe what the press says about the Labour leadership, which helps to explain their nervousness about a Labour victory. Johansen said they tend to think "politicians are for sale"—not for cash in brown envelopes, but for concessions that they can sell on to their electorate—and which fail to solve the underlying problems. Hickey agreed that many business people claim, absurdly, that they "cannot find a principled politician" and Rawlinson also agreed that many multinationals try to avoid involvement in politics because of the whiff of corruption.

People who have been on the government side of the table tell much the same story. David Willetts, former minister at the Department for Business, Innovation and Skills, believes that there is "room for improvement" in government and business relations. Nick Macpherson told me that in his time as Permanent Secretary at the Treasury, major business engagement with government was far less constructive than it had been in the 1980s: "in 1982 business leaders turned up to discuss important issues. By the time I left HMT, the only people who would turn up were people trying to get contracts—Capita and so on—and quasi-state operations like BT." The reluctance of business to get involved in politics is, he says, "defeatism." A Cabinet Office official thought that it was particularly difficult to get the Googles or Apples of this world to engage with purely national issues. O'Donnell agreed that things have got worse in the last few years. Even on issues where one might have thought there was a shared interest, business often fails to act in a social way. As an official at the Department for Business, Energy and Industrial Strategy put it to me, business has consistently failed to engage in long-term skills planning and persuasion has had no effect.

This failure may be worse in the UK than elsewhere. For example, in Switzerland the apprenticeship system works well and the incentives are not gamed by business in the way they sometimes are in the UK.[xxx] Japanese companies tend to have a nationalistic sense of purpose. In France, a clique of elite Grandes Écoles alumni working in government and business know each other well and—as a consultant advising some of them reflected—they share a belief in their national culture and civilisation in a way that the British elite does not. Forty-seven percent of business leaders have worked in the public sector, whereas only 3% in Britain have.[xxxi] In Scandinavia, business engages more actively with government, and not *just* to protect vested interests. In Denmark, for example, an organisation called the Danish Management Society ('VL') facilitates cross-sector discussion of "managerial, societal and financial issues." Set up in 1965, it has about 4,000 members in the public and private sectors, and is structured into small cells each with 30–40 members.[xxxii]

Business leaders in Britain are also more reluctant to enter into partnership with trade unions than their continental colleagues. Mike Rake favours German style co-determination, but he is in a small minority. There was an almost hysterical reaction to Theresa May's proposal to put workers on boards. Frances O'Grady, General Secretary of the TUC, describes her frustration:

> At a personal level I am incredibly frustrated that even quite modest changes [are opposed]. Even when discussing this with intelligent people, they say privately they agree but then do their utmost to prevent change. They agree we have a company system that isn't fit for purpose, that we need to review the purpose of business. [But] there is irrational and immodest opposition to workers on boards. It is about willingness to share power.

The subject is almost embarrassing in some quarters. Several people changed the subject when I brought it up, or produced the flimsiest arguments against it.

There is some qualification to this negative story about government–business collaboration. The Automotive Council, for example, has helped get the car industry to invest in electric cars and batteries. Mike Barry said that while two or three years ago discussions between government and the retail sector on sustainability were largely irrelevant, there had been some improvement recently. For example, Michael Gove had convened a meeting on the use of plastics, and agreement was achieved in the room on who would do what (although critics say this is not nearly enough). Lingard also thought that there was more collaboration than there had been, an example being the way the UK processed food industry had worked together over several years to reduce the salt content of processed foods, prompted by rising public awareness and action by NGOs such as Action on Salt. As for labour market issues, O'Donnell said "a whole bunch of chief executives" wanted to work constructively with government on minimum wages, skills, apprenticeships and so on. He also said that government can get international businesses to the table on issues where their expertise would be valuable if it makes clear that it is going to tackle the issue anyway. And people from both sides, and from different points on the political spectrum, confirmed that there was more constructive conversation between politicians and business than you might think from reading the papers.

Some businesses also appear to be responding to change more effectively than in the past. Nick Molho, who lobbies for pro-environmental policies on behalf of business, reports that companies are factoring in high carbon prices into their planning, and as we have seen, Volvo and Jaguar Land Rover are phasing out pure petrol cars from 2019 and 2021. The CBI has moved from resistance to environmental regulation to calling for clarity and a level playing field.[xxxiii] Even Exxon, which has tried to slow the pace of change, is waking up to the reality that government intervention is making change happen, according to David Blood. Thomas Lingard of Unilever and Will Day of PwC both cite the United Nations' Sustainable Development Goals as a normative framework for some global businesses. While more progress has been made on environmental than social issues, this is simply because that is what state agencies have focused on—labour protection rules are still being liberalised in some regimes, while environmental rules are being tightened.

The Cabinet Office is currently running a more active, targeted collaboration designed to get business input into social issues, for example, mental health problems in the workforce, poor access to affordable credit, and the difficulties some young people have when starting work for the first time: Polman's model in miniature. The businesses work with the social sector and donate time, expertise and in some cases access to their sales channels and money. They hope the programme will, in a small way, help alleviate the social problems that the referendum result revealed to them, and which they recognise is damaging them as well as society. Officials hope that, as well as addressing specific problems, the programme will contribute to mapping out a post-Brexit agenda, consistent with the values Theresa May articulated in her Downing Street speech on taking office. They are cautious though, and recognise it may not work.

These more positive examples show that in areas where government takes the initiative and sends signals that change is on the way, and where business has learned not to be boneheaded, then collaboration is possible. The Cabinet Office example shows that business is thinking more creatively about corporate social responsibility than it did. But none of these rather small examples shows that a critical mass of business leaders have signed up to Polman's ambitious agenda, or that they think advancing the public good is a central part of their job, or that the divisions that most of those I spoke to described are going away any time soon.

CHANGING BUSINESS

Does this mean there is no hope? No, but it does show that business will need help from those outside business if it is to change. It cannot change on its own.

The economists' view is that people respond to incentives, so change the incentives and you change behaviour. Could we change business by simply changing the incentives? A bit, perhaps, but there are limits to what tinkering in this way can achieve. Money generally fails to incentivise performance against long-term targets,[xxxiv] especially when those targets are broad and ill-defined, as social objectives tend to be. Indeed money can actually weaken rather than reinforce intrinsic motivation, that is motivation inspired by the objective itself rather than the accompanying incentive, although this phenomenon has been overstated.[xxxv] Since intrinsic motivation is more likely to attach to social objectives than to shareholder profits, it follows that money may not be the best way of shifting business objectives. Indeed, it is possible you may have to stop using performance-related pay altogether. This then creates a problem: you will lose some of the clarity provided by profit maximisation and the rewards based on this, and, as I was told by several people, many managers will find this difficult to deal with.

Richard Rawlinson, who has worked with many CEOs, was a little more sanguine. People tend to subscribe to a dominant theory, he said. What they do is then heavily influenced by this theory. If you want to change behaviour, changing incentives is scratching the surface. You really need to change the dominant theory, and this can happen. This implies an underlying flexibility beneath the surface, even if on the face of it business leaders appear stuck with the current system. Frances O'Grady made a similar point. Capital is flexible, she said, and historically has behaved in radically different ways at different times. Even now, big multinationals are hugely adaptable and behave quite differently in different countries (a point Rawlinson agreed on). In Britain, for example, McDonald's does not recognise any trade union, but in the Netherlands there is a union slogan on its place mats.

Rawlinson's 'dominant theory' is part of what I am calling 'ideology'. He is arguing that it is possible to change business ideology—and I agree, largely for the reasons already elaborated in Chapter 6: the prevailing ideology has decayed into an 'ideological fashion', and is no longer a matter of deep-seated beliefs.

Some suggest that younger people have different attitudes that will in due course drive change, but Dominic Houlder, who teaches at the London Business School, and Gay Haskins, another business school teacher I spoke with, are doubtful. Houlder's students in their 20s are if anything more conservative than their equivalents of 30 years ago, although perhaps a little less money-oriented than those studying just before the 2007/2008 crash. Haskins says young people are not rocking the boat in the way they did. There is much talk of using ethics to attract talented millennials, but perhaps these ethics are simply part of a lifestyle offer, comparable to the quality canteens and pool tables that any self-respecting professional business now provides. Young people might adopt a new dominant theory or ideology, but will not shape it.

On the other hand, many of Houlder's older students, those in their 30s and 40s, are adamant that they are motivated by more than money. Lingard said the following about his and his Unilever colleagues' motivation:

> There is the commercial case around building trust in our brands... and about cost savings from eco-efficiency and so on. But there is also a more human motivation: many inside Unilever understand that the world is in a very challenged place, both environmentally and socially. They understand that with power comes responsibility, and governments are simply not able to fix the challenges alone. And so we try harder to find the business cases that help to align financial value and societal value. We cannot run an unprofitable business... that would help no one. But in business there are always choices to make about where to invest time and resources. These choices are increasingly made by individuals who really do understand that ways of doing business have to change... if we want to be in business in 20, 50 or 100 years' time, or indeed if we want to look our grandchildren in the eye when explaining the actions we took when we were at the wheel.

David Blood concurs: "The moral case is important. We are people, and there *are* examples of people doing the right thing." Perhaps Hickey is right when he says that there is a silent majority in business who are willing to be persuaded—who fit into the prevailing norms but who are receptive to change. They are receptive because they do not want to confront sharp trade-offs between different interests, or to face a requirement to behave in an unethical way.

A new 'dominant theory' of business will build on this motivation, but to get anywhere it needs both a broader theory of welfare to replace its current neoclassical foundation, in other words a new ideology, as sketched out in Chapter 3. It also needs changed structures that permit business to develop broader objectives. These structures will also help the counter-elite to coalesce, help give it ordered purpose and unity in the same way that markets have given the current incumbents their purpose and unity. Larry Fink's letter is a step in the right direction, but the theory of ethical capitalism as currently conceived is flawed and cannot deliver either a new set of business objectives, or a counter-elite.

A final point. The four business school teachers I spoke with all believed business schools could and should play a role in moving things on. However, they are not doing so yet. Ethics classes are offered as part of the career guidance offered by business schools, but they are not taught by professional philosophers. The schools would never take a similarly amateur approach to their finance or marketing courses.

NOTES

i. ComRes, *Forum of Private Business Ethics Survey* (January 2015), http://www.comresglobal.com/polls/forum-of-private-business-ethics-survey/.
ii. Susan Adams, 'Trust in Business Isn't Any Better But Trust in Government Gets Worse,' *Forbes* (20 January 2015).
iii. Ipsos MORI, *How to Improve Trust in Business? Look Beyond Profits* (January 2015), www.ipsos.com/ipsos-mori/en-uk/how-improve-trust-business-look-beyond-profits.
iv. YouGov, for the CBI (2014), http://www.cbi.org.uk/news/cbi-launches-campaign-to-boost-public-confidence-in-business/.
v. Jacob Rose, 'Corporate Directors and Social Responsibility: Ethics Versus Shareholder Value,' *Journal of Business Ethics* (2007, Vol. 73, pp. 319–331).
vi. Ralph Miliband, *The State in Capitalist Society* (1965), p. 69.
vii. Bill Javetski, *Leading in the 21st Century: An Interview with Larry Fink* (McKinsey.com, September 2012).
viii. Anatole Kaletsky, *Capitalism 4.0: The Birth of a New Economy in the Aftermath of Crisis* (2010), p. 23.
ix. https://www.blackrock.com/corporate/investor-relations/larry-fink-ceo-letter.
x. For example Douglas Sherwin, 'The Ethical Roots of the Business System,' *Harvard Business Review* (1983); Roger Martin, 'The Virtue Matrix—Calculating the Return on Corporate Social Responsibility,' *Harvard Business Review* (2002).
xi. Robert G. Eccles, Ioannis Ioannou, and George Serafeim, 'The Impact of Corporate Sustainability on Organizational Processes and Performance,' *Management Science* (November 2014, Vol. 60: 11, pp. 2835–2857).
xii. John Mackey and Raj Sisodia, *Conscious Capitalism: Liberating the Heroic Spirit of Business* (2013).
xiii. David Harvey, *Seventeen Contradictions and the End of Capitalism* (2014), p. 284.
xiv. Olivier Frémond (2000), https://www.oecd.org/daf/ca/corporategovernanceprinciples/1930657.pdf.
xv. Andrew Crane and Dirk Matten, 'Engagement Required: The Changing Role of the Corporation in Society,' in Dominic Barton, Dezsö Horváth, and Matthias Kipping (eds.), *Reimagining Capitalism* (2016), p. 126.

xvi. Jeff Gowdy, *The Leaders and Laggards of Sustainability Goals* (2014) quoted by Paul Polman, 'Re-establishing Trust,' in Dominic Barton, Dezsö Horváth, and Matthias Kipping (eds.), *Reimagining Capitalism* (2016).
xvii. Mike Barry, conversation with author.
xviii. Nick Molho, conversation with author.
xix. Andrew Hill, conversation with author.
xx. Alison Tate, conversation with author.
xxi. Colin Mayer, *Firm Commitment: Why the Corporation Is Failing Us and How to Restore Trust in It* (2013).
xxii. Paul Polman, 'Re-Establishing Trust,' in Dominic Barton, Dezsö Horváth, and Matthias Kipping (eds.), *Reimagining Capitalism* (2016).
xxiii. Ibid., p. 21.
xxiv. https://www.fungglobalretailtech.com/research/uk-organic-fair-trade-markets-strong-demand-reflects-buoyant-consumer-spending/.
xxv. https://uk.kantar.com/consumer/green/2018/the-popularity-of-fairtrade-in-the-uk/.
xxvi. I owe this formulation to Gus O'Donnell.
xxvii. Gus O'Donnell, conversation with author.
xxviii. *Sunday Telegraph* (5 November 2017).
xxix. Bill Javetski, *Leading in the 21st Century: An Interview with Larry Fink* (McKinsey.com, September 2012).
xxx. Michael Holm Johansen, conversation with author.
xxxi. Charles Harvey and Mairi Maclean, 'Capital Theory and the Dynamics of Elite Business Networks in Britain and France,' in Mike Savage and Karel Williams (eds.), *Remembering Elites* (2008).
xxxii. The Danish Management Society, https://vl.dk/en/.
xxxiii. Josh Tantram, conversation with author.
xxxiv. John Gibbons, *Employee Engagement: A Review of Current Research and Its Implications* (Conference Board, 2006).
xxxv. The point is contested. It seems that extrinsic incentives may weaken intrinsic motivation but still have a positive net impact in some circumstances. See for example the review by Roland Bénabou and Jean Tirole, 'Intrinsic and Extrinsic Motivation,' *The Review of Economic Studies* (2003, Vol. 70: 3, pp. 489–520).

CHAPTER 10

Structural Change

Let us return again to BlackRock, the firm chaired by Larry Fink, who was extensively quoted in the last chapter. It is the largest investment management company in the world, with $6 trillion of funds under management as of April 2018. However, even it can be put under pressure. One of its clients is Exxon, the largest oil company in the world. BlackRock postponed its plans to launch a 'green' fund for other investors after Exxon threatened to take away its business should it do so.

Fink's letter was not a moral exhortation. It was part of a complex negotiation between governments, company managers and different types of investor. He was conceding that governments have some of the cards, and that as a result businesses ran the risk of losing their 'licence to operate' if they behaved irresponsibly. He was warning them that other stakeholders—more precisely governments operating on behalf of other stakeholders—will act to defend their interests, which means company managers have to respect these to maximise investor returns.

The angels don't always have the cards, though. That was the thrust of the last chapter, and that is what Fink himself found when confronted by Exxon. Given this, the most effective thing we can do is stack the cards, or rather make sure the other side doesn't stack them. Why should we agree to play any hand we are dealt?

While a counter-elite is an essential ingredient of change, its members need to have the right cards. Only when they start to play their hands

© The Author(s) 2019
C. Seaford, *Why Capitalists Need Communists,*
Wellbeing in Politics and Policy,
https://doi.org/10.1007/978-3-319-98755-2_10

will the new elite really cohere, and its ideology start to crystallise into norms of behaviour.

Using Investor Power

We have already met Saker Nusseibeh, Chief Executive of Hermes Investment Management and one of the most prominent investment managers in the City. He has been saying for years what Fink said in his January 2018 letter. To ask the companies you invest in to treat workers well, to respect the environment and local communities, to pay bills on time, is simply to be a good capitalist, that is to say an effective capitalist. This, he says, is why his firm has grown so fast in the last few years and why others are beginning to take notice of what he says.

Fink's letter made waves in the investment community precisely because it represented change: it did not reflect how mainstream investment managers think at the moment. Although a handful of asset managers such as Nusseibeh do put pressure on companies to behave in a 'responsible' way, they have nothing like critical mass. Indeed, according to Mike Barry, "the investor pressure for good tends to be a bit like NGO pressure."

Can the mainstream change and apply pressure more effectively? There are several structural and attitudinal barriers that currently prevent this from happening. The task is to remove these barriers, and this, as we will see, is entirely feasible.[i]

The challenge goes beyond pressing for a responsible form of capitalism that maximises investors' returns over the long term. This is because, as we have already seen, there can be conflicts of interest between shareholders and stakeholders, even in the long run—ethics does not always pay—and these may prevent business and government from forming the kind of partnership I have argued for. The challenge is therefore to get companies to consider the interests of their shareholders in the round, their interests as citizens, workers and consumers as well as their interests as investors.

Nusseibeh makes the point that many companies are now largely owned by, or owned on behalf of, people who are not that wealthy.[1]

---

[1] 'On behalf of' means that they are beneficiaries of pension schemes and other collective investment vehicles rather than direct owners of shares, but for most purposes the distinction is irrelevant and I have tended to ignore it.

Much discussion of capitalism ignores this fact, he says; it is conducted as if companies were still owned by plutocrats. Of course, there *is* enormous concentration of wealth, but this is not the whole story. 'Ordinary' investors now form a substantial bloc, and might even be able to outvote the plutocrats in some companies; certainly they can often exert influence. In Fig. 9.2 on page 174, they are shown as 'People as investors', while the plutocrats are shown as the 'International Financial Elite'. David Pitt-Watson, Nusseibeh's former colleague at Hermes, estimates that 40% of shares in UK companies are owned by UK and overseas pension funds directly and Nusseibeh thinks it could be substantially more globally. We are still talking about a minority—only 44% of working age adults are currently accruing a non-state pension[ii]—but we are not talking about the 1%.

Investment managers and pension fund trustees currently only consider the interests of their clients and beneficiaries *as investors.*[2] Indeed, the law obliges them to limit themselves in this way. They do not consider their interests as citizens, workers or consumers. For a relatively small investor, these other interests may be as or more important than his or her interest as an investor. Nusseibeh uses the example of aggressive tax avoidance to illustrate this: if I am a small investor, it may be that the gains I enjoy as a *shareholder* as a result of aggressive tax avoidance by a company in which I own shares are less than the losses I suffer as a *citizen and taxpayer* as a result of that avoidance (let alone the losses I suffer as a result of avoidance by other companies). So shouldn't the investment manager acting on my behalf put a stop to this? Sometimes they do—one investment manager I spoke to (not Nusseibeh) told me about the pressure his company had put on a very major corporation to pay more tax. However in general, investment managers exert pressure the other way—to maximise short-term post-tax profits and therefore to minimise tax. If they considered all the interests of beneficiaries, their interests in the round, they might behave differently.

[2] In some schemes, pension levels are defined in advance, rather than being dependent on investment performance ('defined benefit schemes'); trustees then have to consider the interests of the employer, which is normally obliged to make up any shortfall caused by poor investment performance. This section is primarily about schemes where the pension level is not defined in advance and does depends on investment performance—a rapidly growing proportion of the total.

It is true that aggressive tax avoidance often *is* in the interests of very large investors (for whom dividends are likely to be more important than their share of the national tax burden).[3] Investment managers, who are looking after all their beneficiaries' interests, have to understand and act on the balance of those interests. On the other hand they also need to understand their investors' ethical stance: some large investors may feel they *should* pay a 'fair' amount of tax, even if it is not in their financial interest (and in any case, whatever investors' stance and interests, Fink's point about responsibility still stands: from a purely financial point of view, companies should negotiate with government within limits).

The same form of argument applies to other decisions that companies make where shareholders have interests as citizens and workers as well as investors: those that affect its carbon footprint, its impact on biodiversity, the influence it has on labour market norms, and—crucially for the argument of this book—the stance it takes when working with (or against) government on public policy issues. This is not just because a failure to behave responsibly will risk the licence to operate, or create regulatory risk, or make it more difficult to recruit the best talent. These things affect profits, shareholders' interests as investors, and are the factors that Fink described. It is also because a failure to behave responsibly may damage the interests of shareholders as citizens, consumers and workers. If companies are acting in the interests of their shareholders 'in the round', they are likely to pollute less, pay better wages, pay more tax and work more cooperatively with government, even if there is no long-term damage to the profits should they fail to do these things.

There is a counter-argument to this which goes roughly as follows. It is true we should remove any barriers to Fink's programme, because if, in the long term, the interests of shareholders and stakeholders are aligned, then of course, companies should pursue those interests. However, we should not go beyond this. To the extent that individuals continue to have different interests as workers, citizens and investors, there are different institutions designed to protect these interests—trade unions, governments, investment managers. It is more efficient, and

---

[3] The international nature of investment is another complication, since, on the face of it, it is in everyone's interest to avoid tax in other countries. To act on this, though, would be classic beggar-my-neighbour activity: it is in all 'small' investors' interest for there to be a norm that all companies pay their taxes wherever they are due, and large international investors managers are well placed to establish this.

indeed more transparent and democratic, if these different institutions retain their distinctive roles and negotiate. The resulting settlement will on the whole represent a better compromise between different interests than something cooked up behind closed doors by a group of powerful City figures.

At first sight this seems convincing. Isn't this how a pluralistic society is meant to work? Different interests compete and a settlement is found that is broadly acceptable to everyone. The problem, as we saw in the last chapter, is that there are limits to what negotiation can achieve. It can indeed produce compromises and trade-offs that are acceptable to all and it can improve the short- to medium-term operation of the economy, but it cannot reset the direction of the economy. Negotiation operates within preset limits. Nor in a global economy can it create the basis for a long-term government–business partnership that isn't simply a victory for business interests, isn't a partnership on business's terms. To create a different kind of partnership, a different kind of conversation, and thus to reset the economy, requires the purpose of business to change. And for the purpose to change, the structural drivers of that purpose have to change.

If this is accepted, then change is needed in capital markets. This has to deliver two things. First, it has to ensure that shareholders' interests as workers and citizens as well as investors are taken into account by those acting on their behalf, that is pension fund trustees and investment managers. Second, it has to reduce the bias to the short term in corporate decision-making that capital markets encourage, and that makes even Fink's programme difficult to achieve, let alone the broader agenda advocated here. This bias is damaging, partly because it encourages decisions that damage economic prosperity over the long term, as for example when the research and development or training budget of a firm is cut to generate profits now, even though this will reduce profits in the future. It is also damaging because the alignment between different stakeholder interests implicit in Fink's letter is much greater over the long term. In other words, the short-term bias increases the pressure on managers to behave in an anti-social way.

Getting shareholders' wider interests taken into account requires a change to the law. This currently obliges pension fund trustees only to consider the interests of beneficiaries as investors, unless specifically instructed otherwise. Change is under active consideration: a European Union Expert Group has recommended that trustees should be obliged to establish how beneficiaries want their "wider interests" to be taken into account, including for example their interest in not suffering from climate change.[iii] A meeting of City professionals I attended in 2017 endorsed this with some enthusiasm. There would be no disadvantage to any firm: the changes would create a new level playing field. The UK could easily adopt the principle, even after leaving the EU. In practice this might mean that default funds—the funds where those saving for a pension and other retail investors' money goes if they do not specify otherwise—could be obliged to include social and environmental criteria in their investment strategies, rather than purely financial criteria as at present. Investors would then be given the option of switching to funds with purely financial criteria should they wish—the reverse of the current arrangement.

Legal changes could also help address the bias to the short term. John Kay, in his report for the government on this subject,[iv] distinguished two kinds of shareholder: long-term 'investors' and short-term 'traders.' For *investors*, the value of a share is the discounted value of future earnings—which can stretch as long as you like into the future. For *traders*, the value of a share is what other people will pay for it in the near future. To be a good investor you have to understand the businesses you are investing in. To be a good trader you have to understand the market. Now 'the market' does not operate in a vacuum. What people will pay for a share depends on information. But the relevant information is precisely prescribed: it is what other people in the market consider to be relevant information. This is circular—but the equation can be solved because there is a norm that it is quarterly earnings figures that are relevant. Everyone knows that these figures are what everyone else will take seriously. For this reason, they drive trading and, because most transactions are the result of trading, they drive share prices.

Corporate managers' incentives are often linked to share prices. Because these prices are driven by quarterly earnings, managers are incentivised to maximise these earnings. Hence the short-term bias. It follows that there are two ways of correcting the bias: you either reduce the influence of traders on the share price, or you reduce the influence of the share price on managers' decisions. The former could be achieved by introducing a transaction tax, designed to make trading uneconomic. It is sometimes suggested that measures of this type would have to be introduced globally to be effective; on the contrary, however, a tax introduced unilaterally, and accompanied by regulations to prevent evasion through off-shore trading, could even be a source of competitive advantage for UK markets. Many businesses would choose to be listed on markets where investors were taking a long-term view, and long-term investors could be attracted to companies which were not being distracted by short-term pressures.[4] Indeed, the whole reformist agenda described here could well get the support of business. Many chief executives dislike the pressure from capital markets for short-term performance and would welcome changes that reduced this pressure. They might even welcome the broader social objectives outlined here if that was part of the package.

As for reducing the influence of the share price on decisions, that could be achieved by regulation of executive pay schemes, plus some restrictions on company takeover activity: maintaining a high share price is often motivated by fear of a takeover, and we have far fewer restrictions on these than other European countries, notably France.[5] Indeed, the Blair government liberalised the regime. However, regulation tends to work best when following the grain of changes in the market, so it would be better if action was taken by investment managers. As representatives of shareholders, they have the right to set management incentives, and could do so if they worked together. They could also ensure that men and women minded to take a long-term approach were appointed to company boards, and then support them in following this approach.

This would require a much more active approach to their investments than they currently adopt, but this is perfectly possible. Again, let us turn to Larry Fink's letter, which promised that BlackRock would start to engage far more actively with companies than it had done in the past:

> Our responsibility to engage and vote is more important than ever.... Just as the responsibilities your company faces have grown, so too have the responsibilities of asset managers. We must be active, engaged agents on behalf of the clients invested with BlackRock, who are the true owners of your company. This responsibility goes beyond casting proxy votes at annual meetings – it means investing the time and resources necessary to foster long-term value.[v]

---

[4]The other standard objection to a transaction tax is that it reduces market liquidity—but that of course is the whole point. Note that it would not be much of a revenue generator; the aim would be to minimise trading and thus the taxes generated by trading.

[5]Managers would still want to avoid a very low share price, which might damage a company's ability to raise debt finance, but they would no longer have a reason to maximise.

This does not mean that BlackRock will change the incentive schemes that encourage short-term performance, nor does it mean that a critical mass of asset managers will imitate their style of active engagement. It does, however, indicate a direction of travel, a different mood, which can be used by those who want to put pressure on asset managers to put pressure on companies in the way just described.

Pressure will definitely be needed, though. "Stewardship [that is engagement of the kind Fink describes] is not seen as the central function of a fund manager" according to David Pitt-Watson. Mark Goyder, an expert on stewardship, concedes that the industry's Stewardship Code is feeble. He and most investment professionals I spoke with thought that the Investors' Forum, designed to facilitate collective engagement with companies by asset managers, had also been feeble. Many in the industry have resolutely resisted pressure from some of the more progressive pension funds for active engagement with companies on issues of concern to those funds.[vi]

You might think that if Fink was right and his approach was going to lead to higher returns for his investors, market pressures would force others to imitate him, but sadly this is not true. First there is a free-rider problem: if you have shares in the same companies as BlackRock you can benefit from its engagement without paying for it. And second, many of the pension fund trustees that employ investment managers are alarmingly ill-informed, both about the law and about economics. They don't know how to exercise such market power as they have over their investment managers, and generally they don't want to. As Peter Michaelis of the Lion Trust put it:

> Trustees don't know how to even begin to give an appropriate mandate to their asset managers. They – and the conventional asset managers – would say 'I think it is impossible to manage two targets'. For the most part [they think] 'as long as it is legal it is fine' because if it is legal you won't be held responsible.

Two absurdities illustrate the problem—and the ignorance and laziness that advocates of change, of a society that puts flourishing centre stage, will have to deal with. The first helps explain capital markets' bias to the short term. Pension fund trustees who hire investment managers on behalf of those saving for or receiving a pension often find it difficult to assess whether those managers are doing a good job. One approach is to monitor the value of the portfolio every three months.

The research evidence (and the Financial Conduct Authority concurs) is conclusive that this is completely useless: you cannot judge performance on this basis.[vii] It is not just useless, it actively encourages investment managers to behave like traders, even when their clients are investing for the long term, behaviour which, as we have seen, may damage long-term returns, and certainly does nothing to encourage the kind of engagement Fink is promising. Despite all this, it remains the most widely used approach to assessing performance. Not all trustees use it—more sophisticated funds use more sophisticated methods and there is evidence that those that can afford these get better long-term results.[viii] But most funds use the useless method.

The second absurdity helps explain why social and environmental objectives are still not widely considered by investors. In 2005, Freshfields, a leading City law firm, established conclusively that trustees could consider these issues when making investment decisions, provided doing so had no damaging impact on financial returns. Even now you hear of trustees who do not understand this and think they are not allowed to consider the issues.

Given these failures, should investment managers be obliged to engage, Fink style, and should the pension fund trustees that employ them be obliged to use more sophisticated methods when assessing their performance? Some guidance may be useful, but regulation on its own is unlikely to be effective. Regulation is generally a tool for enforcing minimum standards, not for driving the innovation and energy needed to improve engagement and assessment. However, what it *can* do is unleash pressures which can then drive trustee and investment manager action. The answer could be a new obligation on trustees, and other investment intermediaries, to consult with pensioners, those saving for a pension and other shareholders in a far more active way than they have done in the past; consult, that is, on the instructions that these end-investors wish to give to the managers of the companies they own. These obligations could be backed up by much tougher enforcement than in the past: not just best practice but 'a stick to drive change,' as one industry professional put it. The process would use modern information technology to create accessible, clear, interactive communication which would make it easy for investors to vote for business policies and to monitor the real-world and financial implications of having done so. Linked to the changes in default funds already referred to, this could create a second form of democratic pressure on company managers, to complement that channelled through government.

Various investment professionals have told me that investment inter-mediaries can and should be asking end-investors how they want to leave the world for their children, that they need to tell these investors the 'whole truth' about their investments and the behaviour of their compa-nies, and that all this can be facilitated by an app that would allow them to see how well their portfolios were performing against social and envi-ronmental, as well as financial, criteria.[ix] At the moment almost no one exercises such rights as they have in the investment process: it is boring, apparently complex, and in any case is unlikely to have any influence. Technology could facilitate participation, and so too, perhaps, could the emergence of the investment equivalent of political parties, that is inter-mediaries which channel opinion and so exercise power.

There are reasons for thinking this is more than a fantasy. Crucially, there are individuals who are in a position to help drive the changes needed: Steve Waygood, for example, whose job is to ensure that Aviva's £500 billion portfolio is invested responsibly, offered the famous Margaret Mead quote when I asked him how change of the kind dis-cussed in this chapter would happen: "Never doubt that a small group of thoughtful, committed citizens can change the world; indeed, it's the only thing that ever has". He reported a real culture change at Aviva, after his Chief Executive spoke at the UN General Assembly at the launch of the Sustainable Development Goals (SDGs) in 2015. In addi-tion, he had almost doubled the size of his responsible investment team in the 18 months before I spoke with him. Perhaps, he said, some of the £3 billion of dormant assets in the UK (and £40 billion globally) could be used to fund work on the systems needed to make systematic change real. Elizabeth Corley, Vice-Chair of Allianz Global Investors, agreed that if you get the right people in the room, you can make real change, and sensed that opinion in the City was swinging towards change. Nusseibeh told me that the reason Hermes was the fastest growing asset manager in the City was its progressive approach, and David Blood described his own company, Generation, as already an impact investor, one designed to create real world change as well as financial returns.[6]

---

[6]A significant number of businesses are owned by private equity funds rather than directly by shareholders or pension funds, and they can be relentless profit maximisers. However, the funds that own these businesses are themselves largely owned by the same institutions that invest in the stock market. So, in principle, the same approach can be used to influence private equity-owned and quoted businesses.

As just noted, business leaders could well be supportive of this agenda, and while the kind of active shareholder democracy described does not exist anywhere, other countries have made more progress than Britain in making responsible investment mainstream. In France, for example, funds such as FRR and IRCANTEL have made social purpose central, with a particular focus on quality employment and labour relations. Major pension funds in the Netherlands are using the UN SDGs to guide their investment criteria.[x] The Nordic and Canadian sovereign wealth funds actively push this agenda and punch above their weight because they are well respected. The fund in Norway for example, would be quite capable of threatening to disinvest if a company proposed using off-shore tax avoidance vehicles.[xi]

Finally, the technical work needed is already taking place: in academic institutions like the Institute for New Economic Thinking, in consultancies like Towers Watson and EY, and in investment management firms. Metrics for assessing impact investment—that is, investment with specific social and environmental objectives—are already in use (for example in the Greater London Authority (GLA) fund described on page 137) and there are numerous initiatives underway that can encourage use by the mainstream.[xii] As yet there are no common standards in the way there are for financial reporting, but an international accounting body, the International Integrated Reporting Council, is working on this and, given some political pressure, common standards will emerge. New user-friendly investment platforms that make sophisticated use of information technology have appeared in the last few years (see, for example, some of the peer-to-peer lending platforms), and the mainstream pensions and investment industries could make good use of some of the techniques involved.

Still, there are limitations to what reform of the investment sector can deliver. Plenty of investors will remain as ruthless and as focused on the short term as ever, and even long-term investors have reason to think short term on occasion. More generally, the changes described here, while entirely feasible, really do require concerted action given the conservatism of the industry. Given the uncertainties this creates and the importance of the outcome, there is also a need to think about how to increase the relative power of stakeholders other than shareholders, in line with practice in many other countries. One of the most important things that broad-minded investors like Fink, Corley, Blood, Waygood and Nusseibeh can do is to support changes of this type.

CORPORATE GOVERNANCE

I have already quoted business school professors Crane and Matten (see page 177). They have this to say about corporate purpose and its relation to governance:

> Changes in the corporate purpose… will have significant implications for how corporations are governed and how concomitant norms of public accountability and transparency of companies will be reshaped. Taken seriously these constitute a systemic change in the nature of corporate form. But in our view, it is this kind of systemic change that is necessary.[xiii]

There are two questions to answer about this systemic change. Who should be entitled to exercise power over the chief executive? And how should this power be exercised?

The short answer to the first question is stakeholders. I have already argued that our big problems require business to adopt a social role, and that ethics, negotiation, and even the mobilisation of small shareholders may not be enough to deliver this. It follows that some additional pressure is needed and fortunately there is a widely used and proven model available. Granting stakeholders power will not guarantee that business adopts a social purpose, but, in combination with the other structural changes proposed in this chapter, it will at least make it more likely. There is a longer answer to this question which specifies *which* stakeholders, and even the relative weight that different classes of stakeholder should have, but I leave that aside for now. I will also pass over the details of how power is to be exercised, but just set out one or two general principles that have to be borne in mind if the agenda is not to get lost in formalistic detail (as discussions of corporate governance often do).

A good chief executive will try to avoid sharp conflicts of interest between different stakeholders. As Thomas Lingard of Unilever points out (page 187), there is always some choice about what to do in business. So he or she will, whenever possible, avoid strategies that require clamping down on wages, or polluting the local environment, or selling shoddy products, or delaying supplier payments. The strategy presented to the board will advance the interests of all stakeholders. This is what Fink says, and it is even more likely when governance is designed to increase the power of stakeholders. Nonetheless, while there may be no conflict between them, while a successful company will advance all of them, the interests of different stakeholders remain different. Workers want decent wages, the local community wants clean air, customers want decent products, suppliers want to be paid on time—and shareholders want dividends. In principle, therefore, the various interests need representatives who are looking out for them, who review the strategy for its likely impact on these interests, and hold the chief executive to account for his or her delivery accordingly. While the same representatives could, in theory, look after all the interests, and perhaps any company needs some directors who take this broader, balanced standpoint, the danger is that if everyone takes it, it will simply reflect the management view. It is much more likely that the various interests will be defended effectively if each one has someone dedicated to doing so.

The legal position is that directors should only be concerned with the interests of the company as such. This is a bit disingenuous (or legalistic): a moment's thought reveals there is no such thing. It is true that any organisation will have a 'core group'—the individuals who identify with it most closely, who have most power, and whose interests tend to be protected by it.[xiv] Very often what people refer to as the interests of an organisation are really the interests of this core group. Company growth, for example, is often primarily in the interests of its management, but may be spoken of as in the interests of the company itself. It is also true that an organisation may have a mission—a real mission, not just a mission statement—and this may trump all other interests, may in a sense be the organisation's interest. NGOs, churches and political parties are sometimes like this. Commercial companies, however, are very rarely like this, because even those with a genuine social purpose tend to balance different objectives and the interests of different groups. Take the Tata group, majority-owned by charitable foundations and often cited as an example of a company with a social purpose. It is indeed such an example, and its social purpose is no doubt genuine. But it is also run in the interests of its family shareholders, as well as a range of other stakeholders. For Tata, and other such companies, its social purpose is in effect an 'interest' and may need a representative to defend it, alongside all the other interests.

A social purpose may also be formalised legally, and in this way further entrenched. In the USA some companies have become so-called Benefit Corporations or B-Corps. The Delaware version of this requires the directors to balance: "the pecuniary interests of the stockholders; the best interests of those materially affected by the corporation's conduct [i.e. stakeholders]; and the specific public benefit(s) identified in its certificate of incorporation."[xv] The directors of such companies are protected from shareholder litigation if they fail to maximise profits.

A popular objection to multi-stakeholder governance structures of the kind just described is that the whole thing is a complex waste of time. It is true that this is a danger: I worked as a consultant for a major German company, and its management routinely tried to outwit the supervisory board, generally succeeding. The problem would have been easy to solve however: management incentives were weighted to profits, and were not aligned with supervisory board priorities. Likewise, the supervisory board at Volkswagen did not prevent seriously damaging, and self-damaging, malpractice in that firm, arguably because it contained too many 'insiders', that is former executives. Michael Holm Johansen, who is now chairman of a Norwegian company's supervisory board, argues that the system can work well provided there are clear rules of engagement that prevent this kind of thing. Indeed, formalising the process of stakeholder engagement might even *save* rather than waste time, particularly if investment managers are going to engage with company managers in a more active way than in the past. There are complications—exactly which stakeholders should be represented? How should representatives be chosen? Should there be a two-tier board? What should the relative power of different stakeholders be? What size of company would these rules apply to? Should different stakeholders have ownership stakes? How should the supervisory board be incentivised? Suffice to say, other countries seem to have managed these complications, and where there is a will there is a way.

Another objection is that this kind of structure will make it more difficult for companies to raise finance. Large companies quoted on public markets do not generally raise finance externally (they use retained earnings), and stakeholder governance rules could be restricted to the kind of large companies quoted on public markets, although this does not deal with the problem. Private equity investors, who *do* supply finance to companies, might be reluctant to invest if they thought that their exit route was via a market requiring stakeholder governance, and that this could result in lower share prices.[7] One investor I spoke to confirmed that he would never invest in a company which was not profit maximising.

---

[7]Another objection sometimes raised is that companies might just list overseas. However, the arrangements would then apply to their UK subsidiaries.

As with the first objection, however, other countries have managed the problem. UK law is unusual in the priority it gives to the interests of shareholders. The Companies Acts, reinforced by a series of reviews of corporate governance in the 1990s, make the shareholder pre-eminent.[xvi] It is true that the 2006 Companies Act does stipulate that directors should take account of the interests of other stakeholders when advancing the interests of shareholders, but this was deliberately made unenforceable by David Sainsbury, the Labour minister responsible, on the grounds that a rule with teeth would have been anti-business.[xvii] In France, by contrast, directors have a duty to advance the "general corporate interest" of the company, as opposed to the interest of shareholders. In Germany directors are required to take the interests of parties other than shareholders—a mix of objectives is accepted so long as financial viability is protected.[xviii] These differences reflect and perhaps explain some quite long-standing differences in behaviour: a 1990s survey, for example, showed that just 17% of middle managers in Germany and 22% of middle managers in France thought that the company they worked for was run for the benefit of shareholders as opposed to all stakeholders. The equivalent figure in the UK was 71%.[xix] They do not, however, mean that French and German companies are starved of capital and invest much less than British ones in plant, research and development and training. Investors recognise that they remain a powerful interest group, in most cases the most powerful interest group, and are prepared to invest accordingly.

Perhaps most important of all, changes of this type are realistic politics. Theresa May, when first appointed Prime Minister, said that she wanted workers on boards, and she had sufficient political capital at the time to make it happen. She backed down in the face of virulent opposition from business, but there is still latent support in some parts of the Conservative Party. Changes of this type are part of Labour policy. If, as a result of such changes, government and business can work together, then the public interest can be advanced in a more bottom–up, pluralist way than is possible when government works on its own. Different firms will pursue different priorities, reflecting their different competitive advantage, different perspectives or the different requirements of their stakeholders, and in some cases contributing an international perspective.

This section has been about mainstream big business, but much of the economy consists of small- and medium-sized enterprises (SMEs). Capital market and corporate governance structures are largely irrelevant to these owner-managed businesses. There is, however, a 'social enterprise' sector, that is SMEs with a social purpose, in effect B-corps. It only forms a small proportion of the economy, perhaps 10% of the SME sector using the broadest definition of 'social',[xx] but it could play a more important role, particularly in sectors where external customers are vulnerable to opportunistic behaviour by businesses: old people's homes and provision of credit to low-income households are two obvious examples. In a world where listed companies are subject to stakeholder governance, such companies could aim to be listed in due course, and to become listed without losing their social purpose. This could make it easier for them to attract external finance, and encourage the kind of entrepreneurs who want to combine social and financial ambitions. In other words, changes to the governance arrangements for large companies could have a positive knock-on effect on small companies.

DEMOCRACY AND TRADE UNIONS

In Fig. 9.2 on page 174 I illustrated a world in which the structures that transmit pressure onto the elite from outside it had been reformed. They included financial structures, just discussed, and democratic structures and trade union structures, which are dealt with briefly in this section.

Democratic structures include international institutions, to the extent that these institutions are controlled by democratic governments, and, in the case of the European Union, directly elected representatives. They are all the more important given globalisation. Harvard economist Dani Rodrik has set out the challenge: you can have two but not three of the sovereign nation state, democracy and a truly integrated global economy. If political decisions are made at the national level but the economy is global, then citizens will be excluded from the economic decisions that matter—they and their governments will be too dependent on international corporations. If democracy triumphs at the national level, then we will retreat from a fully global economy—international corporations will be restricted by national decisions to some extent. And if we want democracy and a global economy, we will have to develop more democratic international institutions that replace some of the functions of the nation state.[xxi] If we take it as read that we do not want to abandon democracy, the choice is between a less global economy and stronger international institutions.

Of all the implausibilities in this book, the idea that the IMF, the World Bank, the UN and the European Union can be 'structures that transmit pressure onto the elite from outside it' may seem the most implausible. But let us hold that idea for a moment. The UN gave us the SDGs, the IMF and the World Bank have highly competent and at times progressive secretariats, and the same can be said of some of the EU directorates. What if we were to agree that maintaining a better balance of power between labour and capital was one of their central functions? What if we were to think about changes to structure and governance that would hardwire this function into the organisations?

At the moment, though, these institutions are in retreat, as the Brexit saga makes painfully obvious. The World Economic Forum 2017 Global Risks Report pointed out that more and more states around the world (not just in Europe) are withdrawing from international cooperation mechanisms and it identified this as one of five "key challenges" facing the world.[xxii] The SDGs may be a success but their impact will depend on their "normative clout"[xxiii]; as there is no system of international governance. In 2010, Anatole Kaletsky, who as we have seen, was rather sanguine about capitalism's ability to adjust, wrote that "at the international level, effective public institutions do not exist, and... probably cannot exist."[xxiv] Nick Macpherson's view is that it will be large companies, not international bodies like the IMF or the UN that will shape change over the next century. He believes inter-governmental cooperation may be successful, but it will be ad hoc: banking regulation here, climate change mitigation there. However, this will not be enough to deal with the big issues: ad hocery is always responsive and does not permit the coordination across issues needed for proactive change. In the 1940s and 50s people recognised that problems were interlinked and international and so they created international institutions. Now, we are seeing the reverse—and the left, the *left*, of the Labour Party is as guilty as anyone.

For hardcore neoliberals, this is a triumph. They continue to celebrate Tom Friedman's 2005 book *The World is Flat*, which proclaimed the irrelevance of the nation state.[xxv] A critic has pointed out that there was "not a single table, chart or footnote" to back up this assertion,[xxvi] and any senior executive of a global firm will tell you that the world is not homogeneous, that local cultures vary and that borders matter.[xxvii] However, this vision of a world fit for corporations became received wisdom very quickly, capturing as it did the spirit of the times. Curiously it echoed Friedrich von Hayek's proposal for a European economic union that preserved nation states. He proposed this, precisely and presciently, because the combination of economic union and national sovereignty would make significant democratically driven intervention in markets difficult.[xxviii]

What then is to be done? Should we simply abandon the global economy, or democracy, or should we attempt to revive these institutions? And if we do, what does that mean? Macron is interested in reform of the EU, and in international institutions more generally, perhaps as the only way to save globalisation; he asked the OECD to organise a ministerial event on the subject in the spring of 2018. But the left should not be leaving the agenda to the right. Progressives in the UK need to be rather more interested in the subject than they are—the TUC is part of an effective international network, but the Labour Party is not. Changing the function of these institutions in the democratic way just described, and in this way reviving them, should be high on the agenda.

What about democratic structures at national and local level? I am not going to rehearse the familiar arguments for proportional representation and devolution of power to regions and city regions, which have been discussed at length by others, but both have the potential to reduce the distance between non-elites and elites and so increase the influence of the former. They are not panaceas—devolution, for example, has to be accompanied by transfers from wealthy to less wealthy regions, which would need to be entrenched in some way. And in any case, it is not clear just how much impact becoming as proportional and devolved as, say, Germany would have. We need at least to think about how other less familiar changes could help.

The visitor from Podemos, whom we met in Chapter 3 and who criticised the British left for lacking a narrative, went on to explain that her party had "one foot in the institutions and one foot in the street."[xxix] The party had emerged from a social movement, the Indignados, and while it was distinct from that movement, it retained its connection. This was valuable, partly because it would help win elections, but it would also help once Podemos had won power. It would provide legitimacy and pressure for the actions the party had promised. The general political lesson for us is that parties need to mobilise opinion, and that this is not just a matter of press management or sophisticated use of social media advertising, valuable though both of these are. For a progressive government, it is also a matter of more active engagement with people, with 'the street'. If this is effective, the government will stay on course and complete its projects, and need not be distracted by fears of losing the next election. What is more, international capitalists will know this, and as a result may be less confrontational.

Podemos's emergence from a social movement is the twenty-first century version of Labour's formation by the trade unions, and plenty of British politicians are attracted to it. George Kerevan of the SNP, for example, has said that Britain's problems need a hybrid of social movement and political process—and of course the 'Yes' campaign before the Scottish referendum was a classic example.[xxx] Successful social movements with specific objectives include the suffragettes, the Brexit Leave campaign, and the Movement for the Ordination of Women, and in all these cases success depended on persistence and focus over many years. Unfocused social movements without specific objectives, such as Occupy, have at least helped to get issues such as inequality onto the agenda, and sometimes very quickly. Sociologist Manuel Castells has suggested that social movements can mobilise opinion in the way that right-wing populists do, that they are "functionally equivalent," and can therefore become sufficiently powerful to negotiate with and shape the agendas of political parties.[xxxi] This is partly because, as he puts it, they bring "the wind of dreams into the sails of [the most progressive parties'] strategies," and partly because less progressive parties are forced to respond to the threat that this creates. It is all the more likely because these movements can grow and communicate effectively using social media.

Can this happen in the UK? The electoral system is against the formation of new parties, so the danger is that social movements that attempt to go beyond a specific issue get bogged down in internal party factionalism. Momentum, the leftist Labour organisation, is a case in point. Some hoped that it could mobilise public opinion behind a left programme, and while it succeeded in getting to base camp, that is a left-wing leader who did reasonably well in a general election, it hasn't even begun on the next stage, building a broad popular movement. Podemos, operating within a social movement culture, runs a sophisticated online process for gathering the views of members. It makes a point of reaching out to sympathetic non-party experts. The Cinque Stelle in Italy runs a similar process, and it too has attracted an array of thinkers, creating a lively, if incoherent, political grouping. The strength of these social movement-based parties is their openness, their ability to mobilise diversity. Momentum, by contrast, has a leadership schooled in 1980s Labour Party factionalism and has become obsessed with internal party battles. It has certainly not reached out to the wider electorate in the way that any movement or party has to in a democratic system if it is to gain power. Perhaps it will in the future: some discussion within the movement, including recognition of the problems to date, would be useful.

Labour under Ed Miliband tried a different approach. He encouraged local Labour parties to engage in community projects and, while he was leader, the party published a guide to 'community organising' which stated that it was "critical to Labour's chances of winning in the next general election."[xxxii] There is evidence that this was effective electorally, and activism of this type is, of course, valuable in itself. This is Monbiot's 'politics of belonging,' referred to in Chapter 1. What is more, sometimes its impact can go beyond the purely local. Fracking, for example, is in decline in the UK because of the costs of dealing with community groups: local action leading to national results.[xxxiii] Similarly, Class War, an activist NGO, has helped tenant groups change the way estate regeneration is conducted by local authorities across the country: they are now much more likely to be engaged in the decision-making than in the past.

Some see community activism as a route to mobilising opinion more broadly, a "school for collective decision-making," as one enthusiast put it to me. If people take responsibility for decisions locally, if people are engaged in democratic processes at this level, then perhaps this will gradually bring about a more constructive political culture at the national level. This will then make it easier to take rational decisions about how to raise taxes and how to deal with climate change (or whether to leave or try to reform the EU). A progressive government will find it easier to sustain support. I hope this is true but am not aware of any evidence for it, and remain sceptical. Most people simply don't want to belong to activist groups. Many do not identify that strongly with a local community, let alone a community group. In any case, small is not always beautiful, as anyone who has taken part in local party politics knows. Even if most people did engage in this kind of thing, there are no structures for creating unity, for creating any consistency of opinion, and the elite's power, as we saw in Chapter 4, rests on the masses' fragmentation. Neal Lawson, a strong advocate of grassroots organising, admits that at the moment the grassroots create "a cacophony not a symphony."

Deliberative democracy could be an alternative, or at any rate something to combine with local activism. It is a process currently run by third-sector organisations, for example Involve, and it really is a "school for collective decision-making." It allows groups of citizens, selected at random, to take decisions, or to express an opinion, once they have been briefed fully on the facts and have then discussed the issue in a structured way. The facts can, of course, include the implications of alternative courses of action for well-being, when this is relevant and known. Small-scale trials in this country and overseas suggest that these facilitated discussions are far more constructive than most popular political debate as shaped by the media, and far more constructive than formulaic public consultation processes.[xxxiv] An interesting range of techniques is available, including participative theatre, which was used by activists to engage housing policymakers and to influence the 2017 Homelessness Reduction Act.

Such techniques cannot replace representative democracy, and only a very small proportion of the population can ever take part. However, if the results of the process were publicised effectively and mandated by legislation, they could acquire democratic legitimacy, in other words provide political cover for politicians in the way that referendum results do. This might in turn strengthen the government's hand in its negotiations with capital, and make it easier to take politically difficult decisions, like raising tax rates. Having said this, it is not a neutral process—any more than the decision to hold a referendum is. The choice of what topics to debate is critical and may be contested.[8] Decisions on this choice will be guided by an ideology, or more precisely by the political projects which have emerged from that ideology and which the ruling party has chosen to pursue. Deliberative democracy may be a useful way of engaging the public, resolving genuine dilemmas and creating electoral support for policies, but it is not a substitute for these projects.

One initiative that could help create such projects, and bring together insiders and outsiders in the way advocated in this book, was launched in January 2019 by Michael Jacobs, a No. 10 policy advisor when Gordon Brown was Prime Minister, and more recently Director of the Commission on Economic Justice at the IPPR. His objective is to improve the communication between 'insiders' and 'outsiders', that is think tanks such as the IPPR and networks of activists, such as NEON, which provide training and advice and help build connections between grassroots groups. The aim is to develop and promote the ideas about economic systems change that this insider–outsider dialogue brings to light. In doing so it will tap into the energies and ideas of local activists

---

[8] There are objective standards of good evidence, but the question of what information to provide may also be contested (as the 'neutral' BBC knows well).

and members of social movements, giving the resulting projects a better chance of adding up to a coherent whole.[xxxv]

The biggest social movement in Britain remains the trade unions. They have been in decline, but there are signs that they are reviving. "When the Pope, the Organisation for Economic Co-operation and Development, the International Monetary Fund and mainstream economic gurus such as Larry Summers all weigh in on the importance of unions, something is afoot" wrote Gavin Kelly, Director of the Resolution Trust at the end of 2017.[xxxvi] He went on to mention a number of promising signs. USDAW, which organises in the retail sector, has increased its membership by 100,000 over the last decade. New, militant unions like the Independent Workers of Great Britain have been surprisingly successful at organising some of the worst-paid workers—cleaners, security guards, couriers and foster carers. It and other unions are using a new mix of techniques, including legal action, threatening reputational damage and lobbying shareholders. Unions are using social media to identify and build support amongst employees for specific workplace campaigns. Plans are also being developed for cooperative agencies, or platforms, for freelance workers, which, if successful could help increase the incomes and reduce the insecurities of those working in the gig economy.[xxxvii]

Unions may also be able to influence business objectives and culture. This might be through collective bargaining, but also through worker representation on boards as already described. This role could also improve unions' own performance, according to Frances O'Grady. Business too has the power to help the movement reform itself, and there is widespread agreement that despite the progress just described, it needs this help. Some business leaders will be reluctant to support unions in this way, but if they are, investors can and should put pressure on them.

There could also be a role for a new generation of tripartite institutions to guide and strengthen the economy. Liam Byrne, a Labour shadow minister, is eloquent on the subject of economic institutions (not specifically tripartite ones). "The secret of capitalism is institutions" he says, and we need to design or reform these institutions in the public interest. "Dick Whittington in the 14th century helped build the institutions that were important to Tudor success: the English bond market, livery companies, the Staple, the City of London Corporation, the

English market charters." Now we need new institutions, new "social technology" to create the "norms, trust and culture" associated with a successful economy and society. Dominic Houlder, at the London Business School, is equally enthusiastic about creating new economic institutions and when I spoke to him was planning a project on the subject involving figures from the public and private sectors. This should not just be a charter for quangos: such institutions can be the vehicle for the kind of government–business partnership argued for here. Trade unions need to take their place alongside business and government to help ensure that the interests of capital don't always trump those of labour.

In short, in addition to the changes within the investment and corporate sectors that I proposed, there is a series of changes to democracy and its institutions that are also feasible and necessary. These include stronger international and tripartite national institutions, regional devolution, a refashioning of Labour's own social movement, more experiments with deliberative democracy, and support by investors for stronger trade unions. The structural changes advocated in this chapter will each help address specific problems, but taken together they will do more than this: they will also catalyse the emergence of the counter-elite that will drive the policies described in Chapters 7 and 8. Just as it is easier for the incumbent elite to retain its unity because it is running the current system, so the structures of a reformed system will help unify the counter-elite: it will coalesce around them. These new structures will be given life by ideas about flourishing—and by making these ideas practical they will make them more prominent.

For these reasons they are key to addressing the big five problems. They should therefore be at the top of any progressive's agenda.

Notes

i. Charles Seaford, *Could the Investment System Contribute to Sustainable Prosperity?* (CUSP 2017), https://www.cusp.ac.uk/themes/aetw/investment-system/.
ii. http://www.pensionspolicyinstitute.org.uk/pension-facts/pension-facts-tables/private-pensions-table-13.
iii. DG FISMA, *Financing a Sustainable European Economy*, Final Report by the High-Level Expert Group on Sustainable Finance (2018).
iv. *The Kay Review of UK Equity Markets and Long-Term Decision Making: Final Report* (2012).

v. https://www.blackrock.com/corporate/investor-relations/larry-fink-ceo-letter.

vi. Notably the Assocation of Member Nominated Trustees's Red Line Initiative. See http://redlinevoting.org/.

vii. Financial Conduct Authority, *Asset Management Market Study: Final Report* (2017).

viii. For example, 'The Top 20 Do Better Than the Next 280', as reported by Willis Towers Watson, https://www.willistowerswatson.com/en/press/2017/09/Assets-at-worlds-largest-pension-funds-return-to-growth.

ix. Troy Mortimer, Steve Waygood, and Saker Nusseibeh, conversations with author.

x. https://www.top1000funds.com/analysis/2017/08/17/dutch-pension-funds-embrace-un-goals/.

xi. Michael Holm Johansen, conversation with author.

xii. Elizabeth Corley (ed.), *Growing a Culture of Social Impact Investing in the UK* (2017). See also, for example: The London Energy Efficiency Fund (http://www.leef.co.uk/about/index.html), Accounting for Sustainability (https://www.accountingforsustainability.org/en/index.html), The Global Reporting Initiative (https://www.globalreporting.org/Pages/default.aspx).

xiii. Andrew Crane and Dirk Matten 'Engagement Required: The Changing Role of the Corporation in Society,' in Dominic Barton, Dezsö Horváth, and Matthias Kipping (eds.), *Reimagining Capitalism* (2016), p. 130.

xiv. Art Kleiner, *Who Really Matters: The Core Group Theory of Power, Privilege, and Success* (2003).

xv. http://www.ethicalcorp.com/stakeholder-engagement/better-governance-think-stakeholders

xvi. Ismail Erturk, Julie Froud, Sukhdev Johal, Adam Leaver, David Shammai, and Karel Williams, CRESC Working Paper Series, Working Paper No. 48, *Corporate Governance and Impossibilism* (2008).

xvii. Private conversation.

xviii. Colin Mayer, conversation with author.

xix. Masaru Yoshimori, 'Whose Company Is It? The Concept of Corporation in Japan and the West,' *Long Range Planning* (1995, 28), pp. 33–44.

xx. According to Fergus Lyon, Professor of Enterprise and Organisations in the Centre for Enterprise and Economic Development Research, Middlesex University.

xxi. Dani Rodrik's weblog (2007), http://rodrik.typepad.com/dani_rodriks_weblog/2007/06/the-inescapable.html.

xxii. The World Economic Forum, *The Global Risks Report 2017*, https://riskcenter.wharton.upenn.edu/publications/global-risks/.

xxiii. Arild Underdal and Rakhyun Kim, 'The Sustainable Development Goals and Multilateral Agreements,' in Norichika Kanie and Frank Biermann (eds.) *Governing Through Goals: Sustainable Development Goals as Governance Innovation* (2017), p. 242.

xxiv. Anatole Kaletsky, *Capitalism 4.0: The Birth of a New Economy* (2010), p. 333.

xxv. Thomas Friedman, *The World Is Flat: A Brief History of the Twenty-First Century* (2005).

xxvi. Pankaj Ghemawat, *World 3.0: Global Prosperity and How to Achieve It* (2011).

xxvii. Richard Rawlinson, conversation with author.

xxviii. Quoted in Wolfgang Streeck, *Buying Time: The Delayed Crisis of Democratic Capitalism* (2014).

xxix. New Economics Foundation (NEF), *Changing Our Economy Today, Not Tomorrow* (Event, 11 October 2016), http://neweconomics.org/2016/09/changing-our-economy-today.

xxx. Ibid.

xxxi. Manuel Castells, *Networks of Outrage and Hope* (2nd ed., 2015), p. 277.

xxxii. The Labour Party, *Real Change to Win—Community Organising: A Labour Party Guide*, p. 4.

xxxiii. Jonathon Porritt, conversation with author.

xxxiv. The think tank Policy Network has reported on deliberative democracy; see for example Sven Gatz, *A Citizens' Cabinet: Experimenting with Deliberative Democracy*, http://www.policy-network.net/pno_detail. aspx?ID=4989&title=A-citizens-cabinet-experimenting-with-deliberative-democracy. See also the Think Tank Democratic Audit, http://www.democraticaudit.com/?s=deliberative.

xxxv. Laurie Laybourn-Langton and Michael Jacobs, *Moving Beyond Neoliberalism: An Assessment of the Economic Systems Change Movement in the UK* (2017), http://www.friendsprovidentfoundation.org/wp-content/uploads/2017/11/Michael-Jacobs-LLL-Moving-Beyond-Neoliberalism-Report-5-Oct-2017.pdf.

xxxvi. Gavin Kelly, 'Rebooting the Rank and File: Why There's Still Hope for the Unions,' *Prospect Magazine* (November 2017).

xxxvii. Stefan Baskerville, *A Driver Owned Alternative to Uber Is Not Wishful Thinking: We Are Building It Right Now* (New Economics Foundation, October 2017), http://neweconomics.org/2017/10/putting-drivers-control/?_sf_s=platform+taxi+drivers.

CHAPTER 11

Epilogue: Where Now?

This chapter is a summary of the argument of the book and a call to capitalists and communists to work together.

PROBLEMS AND SOLUTIONS

I have argued that we face five big problems—rising inequality, rising house prices, automation, public services under pressure, and climate change. I have also argued that we are capable of solving these problems and of creating a society that is better than the one we have now. These big problems are not intellectual puzzles. They make people's lives bad.

Rising inequality means that the gains from growth have been appropriated by those who don't need them, that median hourly wages have stagnated despite continuing economic growth, and that there has been increasing relative poverty, exacerbated by insecurity. Rising house prices means that the least well-off now spend nearly five times as much on housing as the best-off as a proportion of income. It will lead to a massive increase in inheritance-based privilege. Automation is not a problem in itself: it may turn out to be a wonderful enhancement of most people's lives. However, it could lead to mass unemployment or underemployment. Pressure on public services results from natural rises in real costs and our collective failure to decide what quality of service we want and are prepared to pay for. Addressing climate change is a matter of limiting the average temperature rise across the globe to 1.5 °C.

© The Author(s) 2019
C. Seaford, *Why Capitalists Need Communists*,
Wellbeing in Politics and Policy,
https://doi.org/10.1007/978-3-319-98755-2_11

This will take a lot of planning and cost a lot of money and we haven't decided who is going to pay.

To solve these problems we will need to plan and redistribute. For example, we will need to plan in order to create more well-paid, fulfilling jobs that cannot be automated. To do this we will have to influence what people buy: if all people like me ever buy is beautifully designed but automatically produced objects, music downloads, dry-cleaning and pizza, then the number of good jobs will be limited. This should be possible—business influences taste all the time—and business and government will need to work together on this. They will also need to make sure people have the skills needed for these jobs. And they can start now.

We also need to plan to reduce working hours. If we do this automation is less likely to create unemployment and more likely to help people flourish, and we will be better placed to address climate change. This is partly a matter of making it easier to work fewer hours if people wish to—a matter of labour market regulation and a universal basic income, perhaps financed by royalties on the software that makes automation possible. It is also a matter of making extra leisure more attractive than extra income. This involves strengthening those social institutions which help people engage in disciplined, purposive and sociable activities outside work.

Reducing inequality, apart from being good in itself, will also increase the relative appeal of leisure over income: there is statistical evidence linking equality and a shorter working week, and there are two good reasons why this is the case: firstly, the need the worst paid have to work very long hours just to survive, and secondly, the importance of relative income and status symbols in unequal societies.

How are we to reduce inequality? It is partly a matter of creating jobs as just described, but it is also a matter of redistribution. The universal basic income will play a part, particularly if it is funded by a software royalty, but higher minimum wages, restored trade union rights and fair labour market regulation are more immediate tasks. We will also need to tackle the immorality in the business world that made powerful people feel it was ok either to exploit others, or to tolerate exploitation that they could prevent. Exhortation won't do the trick: we will need to change the financial and governance structures which shape business norms.

Solving the housing shortage will also make a significant impact on inequality. This requires the state to act as the entrepreneur, to side-step the market and plan output. This approach would mean granting planning permissions in the absence of applications from developers and then forcing them to build. This is similar to the approach adopted by the new town development corporations of the 1940s and 50s.

Ensuring public services meet most people's expectations will require more public spending and taxation, and the challenge will be to get this accepted by voters. 'Hypothecated' taxes—taxes designated for particular purposes—will help, and so will use of deliberative democracy. These two tools combined would amount to a revolution in the way government is conducted.

I described three barriers to tackling climate change effectively—not the only barriers, but sufficient I hope to illustrate the nature of the challenge. First, there is no obvious substitute for oil when it comes to powering lorries and planes, or for many petro-chemical products. This requires government investment in research and development and partnership with business. Second, some governments—certainly the UK government—haven't got a grip on the infrastructure investment and planning needed. This too is going to require partnership with business on a scale we have not yet seen. Third, mitigating climate change is going to be expensive, not least because we must write off assets and make jobs redundant across the globe. Paying for this—like paying for public services—has to be accepted by voters, and again deliberative democracy may be useful. It will be easier if it doesn't require a fall in living standards, in other words if accompanied by some growth.

Planning of this kind is needed because we cannot rely on tax, subsidy and regulation, or, more generally, on modifying price signals. For price signals are generally about what is happening now. They becomes less relevant over time and cannot mobilise the very significant action needed to address major structural problems with the economy. When government does plan, it is only imitating what any well-run company does.

Government cannot plan on its own. Take adult education: we need business input to ensure we don't end up with a supply of skills for which there is no demand, or demand for skills for which there is no supply. However, government cannot just take its orders from business: companies have no interest in training large numbers of people for the kind of well-paid, fulfilling jobs that can survive automation. Government and business can and should work together to set a direction for the economy and reduce uncertainty, rather as French government and business did after the war. The objective, though, will be different: not just economic growth, but solutions to the five problems with a view to increasing flourishing. The process will be different too: more democratic and with much more local participation than the 1940s version.

THE CONDITIONS FOR CHANGE

Making all this happen requires more than the capture of power by the leaders of a radical political party—ask Mitterrand or Hollande. It requires more than protest. And it requires more than a few victories at grassroots level. For the most part, though, the left lacks an adequate theory of change, or perhaps of power. That is one reason for this book.

Why does change *not* happen most of the time? What is it that cements elites' power? It is not enough to say they command resources—by definition they command resources. The question is why some command and others don't. To answer this, it helps to think of power as a form of social capital—that is, the "norms and networks that facilitate collective action."[i] C. Wright Mills's account of the mid-twentieth-century "power elite" in the USA is an example of this approach. The power elite shared values and codes, and they did so because they ran the system, and performed a single, generally understood set of roles. Their codes—or ideology—reflected this. Those outside the elite didn't run the system or perform a single generally understood set of roles. That meant the elite were united while those outside the system were disunited. Hence the elite's power.

But sometimes things change: the elite loses its morale and its ideology decays, typically because it has been unsuccessful in ruling the country, perhaps leading to debt crises and arguments over tax. This creates an opportunity for a counter-elite to emerge, a group typically made up of educated professionals excluded from the existing power structure, together with some dissident members of the incumbent elite. This counter-elite is unified by a strong new ideology and forms an alliance with the population at large.

We saw how this pattern was repeated during the English, French and Russian revolutions, and in slightly different form in Eastern Europe in 1989. We have seen something like it happening twice in post-war Britain. In the late 1950s the dukes, bankers and Conservative MPs of the old elite seemed to be in a state of decay, failing and seen to be failing to run the country effectively. There had been a modernising surge in the 1940s, but the incumbent elite of the 1930s had not been entirely displaced by the Labour counter-elite and was back in power—in politics and many parts of business and finance. They appeared backward-looking, in contrast with the group of 'new' men (and a few women) who had fought together in the war. This latter group—mandarin planners, Labour politicians, founders of new universities and new towns—had attitudes and behaviour that became consciously 'counter' to those of the old elite. They formed a 'counter-elite' and in due course came to form a new Establishment.

Twenty-five years later they too seemed to have lost impetus, failing to deal with the big challenges, and they too were dismissed as 'the Establishment' in exactly the same way as the dukes and bankers had been. The baton was passed to a third group associated with business who shared a belief in the market, and perhaps a business school education. By the time Owen Jones wrote about them in 2014, they too could be called the 'Establishment.'

So can the baton now be passed to yet another group, a new counter-elite? The existing incumbents promised they would deliver ever better lives, above all better lives for the next generation. But the promise is not being delivered and their orthodoxy, market liberalism, is under assault. Free trade in particular has become a flashpoint. Those who lose their jobs don't get jobs that are as good as the ones they have lost, and self-esteem and communities suffer. It is hardly surprising that Donald Trump and others have abandoned the old liberal free-trade rhetoric and replaced it with the politics of fear and its offer to provide protection from enemies. In a low-growth economy this may be a more credible promise.

At the same time, market liberalism remains the official doctrine, even if few people genuinely believe in it. It has become a little like communism in 1980s Eastern Europe, or the theory of absolute monarchy in France in the 1780s. It is an ideology in decay, an ideological fashion, that survives mainly because everyone expects everyone else to operate according to it. But it does not have answers to the big challenges: it either denies they exist (automation, worsening inequality), or comes up with solutions that violate widely shared principles (abolishing planning controls, charges for the NHS), or seem inconsequential when compared to the scale of the problem (climate change). It has been the thinking behind industrial strategy as practised by all parties, designed to make the successful more successful in the vain hope that prosperity would trickle down. This didn't work and left large parts of England feeling 'left behind'; the result was the Brexit vote and the agonies both main British political parties have suffered over it.

Given this, it is hardly surprising that many of those I met while writing this book felt that Britain was once again stuck, just as it had been in the late 50s and late 70s. Once again, the elite seems to have run out of steam, seems to have lost its grip, does not know how to deal with the problems. And it is not just outsiders and leftists who think this. These are the feelings of insiders: business leaders, former permanent secretaries, management consultants, investment managers. At least some of the elite are ready for change, and many may be ready to abandon their 'dominant theory,' as one of those I spoke with put it, to throw it off like an old suit of clothes. They have not done so yet—talk without action is widespread—but resistance to change is likely to be half-hearted. More positively, some of the disaffected are thinking about what to do about their disaffection.

Hence there *is* an opportunity for a counter-elite, and for the kind of radical change such elites have brought about in the past. On the two occasions since the War that a counter-elite emerged in Britain, it was associated with a new type of organisation: in the 1950s with public institutions, in the 1980s with international businesses. Elites in general, I have argued, only achieve their cohesion because they are running a system, have a single set of roles, and these new types of organisation, and the networks they formed, have provided cohesion in just the same way. If a third counter-elite is to emerge—and it has not emerged yet—it too will be associated with a new type of organisation.

This will not be 'ethical business', for while sometimes the ethical approach pays off, all too often it does not. It therefore fails to provide a secure basis for the committed government–business partnership needed to address the big five problems. Nor does it provide the basis for business's social purpose as advocated by Paul Polman, or help ensure that business really does try to make consumers and workers flourish. For it is structures that drive purpose, and ethical business does not involve a change in structure. To put the point a different way, a counter-elite with a new dominant theory or ideology cannot emerge while these structures predominate; it cannot achieve the cohesion and shared norms needed for collective action. So we and they need new structures, a quite different type of organisation—just as the previous emergent counter-elites did.

We have also seen that neither counter-elites nor the masses effect significant change on their own. In combination, though, they can do a lot, whether through revolution or the kind of incremental change Britain enjoyed between 1860 and 1950. In modern democracies this means getting the support of the electorate, in other words securing political alliances. But while opportunities to vote against the Establishment have mobilised voters in Britain and elsewhere recently, the challenge is broader than this. As I suggested in Chapter 9, the opportunity is to balance the power of the international financial elite, to create a countervailing pressure from outside the elite. This also requires reform to the structures that transmit this external pressure.

One set of such structures is the investment system. The good news is many public companies are now largely owned by, or owned on behalf of, people who are not that wealthy. This means the system can be reformed in relatively minor ways to create external pressure, and in doing so help form the counter-elite and its alliance with public at large.

Investment managers and pension fund trustees could act in the interests of their clients and beneficiaries in the round, their interests as citizens, workers and consumers as well as their interests as investors, and in doing so drive very substantial change in the companies that they control. They could ensure that these companies do adopt a social purpose, do form an effective partnership with government, do try to make consumers and workers flourish. For this to happen there will have to be changes in the law, to oblige intermediaries to act in this way, and to ensure that they are held to account effectively by end-investors and beneficiaries, but these are perfectly achievable. Indeed the European Commission is considering changes along these lines and there are individuals in the City who are pushing for others; many business leaders would welcome reform of this kind if it reduced investor pressure for short-term profit maximisation at all costs. Still, it won't be easy: the investment industry is riddled with complex structures, ignorance and laziness and some tougher legal changes could be needed as well, for example a transaction tax, regulation of executive incentive schemes and restrictions on takeovers. Reform of the investment system will need to be complemented by reform of corporate governance, including a bigger role for trade unions.

These changes should be complemented by more democratic public structures—at local and global levels. Why shouldn't maintaining a better balance of power between labour and capital be one of the central functions of the IMF, the World Bank, the UN and the European Union? Shouldn't we also think about domestic institutions, that will cement the partnership between government and business, and involve trade unions and academics as well? Why shouldn't Momentum abandon its internal Labour Party factionalism and mobilise public opinion behind a left programme? Why not use deliberative democracy to resolve difficult problems?

As well as structures and alliances, the counter-elite has to have an ideology of its own, something that gives it the unity that the incumbents are losing and that allows it to take over. In revolutionary situations, according to Crane Brinton, this creates "a flaming sense of the immediacy of the ideal,"[ii] a belief in an "abstract, all-powerful force." In 1945, politicians and people alike believed in something like this: not a set of detailed prescriptions so much as an attitude and approach. Even now, the strength of the Chinese Communist Party is underpinned in this way.

I have argued that this ideology cannot be the revived social democracy encapsulated in the Labour manifesto in 2017, nor the radical localism that is the principal left alternative to it. The former lacks a vision of the better life—"the ideal"—or indeed any real analysis of our biggest problems, any account of how the contemporary world works and what is needed to change it. There is no sense of an "abstract, all-powerful force." Social democracy was a triumph in its day, correcting as it did the defects of mid-twentieth-century capitalism. However, life has moved on and we need a new story. Radical localism, a system in which economic and political power is passed down to the lowest possible level, cannot provide this, for all its merits (which are real). Most of our problems are caused by macro-trends and global capitalism, so it is hardly surprising that localism fails to provide an effective response to automation, rising inequality, the housing shortage, rising pressure on public services or climate change.

Fortunately, however, there is an emerging and coherent set of ideas and ideals that can form the counter-elite's ideology, and that can replace market liberalism, Corbynite social democracy and localism. It could provide a large purpose for a left-of-centre government, like that of 1945, but it could also provide a large purpose for a right-of-centre government, albeit one that was more concerned with traditional social institutions than with free markets.

The core of this set of ideas is the notion of flourishing, that is to say having a good relationship with the world in which you find yourself, and as a result feeling happy and in control of your life. I argued in Chapter 3 that this was a better account of the good life than Benthamite utilitarianism, and that it reflected long-standing religious and secular traditions. It presents humans as fundamentally social: this is better philosophy than individualist utilitarianism, since human consciousness is the result of language and language is by its nature social. It is better self-help than utilitarianism too, because relationships, being part of something bigger than oneself, having a sense of meaning and purpose, make mortality less catastrophic.

I also argued that maximising the number of those who flourish should be the ultimate objective of public policy. For much of the time policymakers work towards intermediate objectives, stepping stones to this ultimate objective, but sometimes these intermediate objectives are called into question. It can then be important to know the extent to which achieving this or that intermediate objective advances flourishing, and what the trade-offs between them are. The difficulties we are having addressing the big five problems set out in Chapter 2 suggest that conventional wisdom about intermediate objectives, such as GDP growth, is no longer adequate.

The existence of survey evidence about what makes flourishing more likely also allows us to escape market liberalism's theoretical grip on policy. Neoclassical welfare economists rely on *that which is chosen* as a guide to the good life, and this justifies the market as a social institution. Well-being survey evidence means we can call into question market outcomes and sometimes markets themselves. This means we can take into account the impact of policy on workers and communities, and escape the bias in favour of consumer interests which this elevation of markets encourages, and which Nick Macpherson, the former Permanent Secretary to the Treasury was happy to admit to. It also means we have the basis for the kind of planning that I have advocated—it will not be random, or simply reflect the preference of the planners.

And there is plenty of this evidence. For example, it tells us that stability and security—especially stable and secure employment—is often more important than increases in income; that we should not rely on population movements and long commutes to deal with regional or local underdevelopment; that the quality of work is important; that employees should have more control over the number of hours they work. It tells us that if we want people to flourish, then reducing inequality should often be a higher priority than increasing GDP. It gives us some clues about how to design homes and the developments of which they are part. It makes clear that not all consumption is the same: there are products that enhance well-being—for example those that save time and reduce hassle, those that reinforce a strong sense of identity or of being part of a meaningful world, those that act as a vehicle for relations with others, those used in activities requiring focus or effort. But it also tells us there are also products which fail to enhance well-being, or even damage it, that only sell because of addiction, stress, ignorance and laziness.

When we start to plan, when we start to address the problems, we can ask what mix of increased free time and increased consumption people are most likely to want, what the contribution of working, consuming and other activity is to flourishing, what kind of work is most valuable, what kind of consumption is most valuable (and what we might sacrifice should climate change require it), what level of inequality to tolerate, what kind of social institutions are needed to develop discipline and leisure-related skills for young people and for adults, how we should design new developments. We will not tell people how to live. But if we are going to make collective decisions, we will do so more effectively if we understand what helps people flourish.

Evidence is not always clear-cut, and there may not be quantitative answers of the kind neoclassical economists like to provide. In such cases evidence may be no more than raw material for forms of deliberative democracy, a vital complement to representative democracy, and particularly important if we are going to finance decent public services and climate change mitigation. The idea that democracy consists of first-past-the-post elections every five years fits neoclassical economics well: both imply there is really only one big political decision to make—how much redistribution to have. But this is no longer true, if it ever was.

The ideology of flourishing may also help legitimise redistribution, whether this means a universal basic income, decent healthcare or helping developing countries reduce emissions. It may be more effective at attracting public support and particularly business support than the language of social justice and state provision associated with social democracy. Given the importance of a government–business partnership, this matters.

WHAT SHALL WE DO?

This final section is addressed more directly to the reader. If you have got this far, you probably want the world to change for the better. You are probably also either an insider or outsider (a 'capitalist' or a 'communist'), at least to some extent. Or you may be both, an insider in one world, an outsider in another. The argument of the book has been that we will only make the kind of changes that we would like to see if insiders and outsiders work together, form a counter-elite and then form an alliance with the people at large. This is the lesson from past episodes of change—and it is the lesson from the stasis of the last 11 years and the Brexit crisis.

What, though, does this mean? Perhaps this is one of those half-interesting ideas that makes no difference, certainly no difference when the stream of events is as turbulent as it is now. Is there anything that we can do that *will* make a difference?

First of all, there is an uncomfortable ethical point, which it would be pleasanter to avoid, and which the writer of a book like this has no status to make, but which is inescapable. Whether we are in business or politics, or are public servants or academics, or work in the third sector, we have to decide whether or not we accept the fundamental assumption set out on page 52, that is that "we can shape the future." This assumption underpins almost everything in this book, but those who don't accept it are perfectly entitled to retire to the country and cultivate their gardens. I don't agree with them, and I don't think the historical evidence is on their side; however, their opinion is not in itself immoral. By contrast, those who do accept the assumption have to confront its implications. For if we can shape the future and we don't, it will be because we have chosen not to. Moreover, if 'we' do not shape the future, it is certain that other people will, and we may not like what they do. Nothing in society happens by itself.

I have argued that flourishing is the core concept for a new ideology. I would, of course, like people to discuss this, think about whether they agree, and if they don't come up with alternative ideas. It seems like a good idea to me, and I hope I have shown that it is useful, that it can provide a guide and legitimacy for the actions we need to address the big five problems identified in this book. However, I have not claimed that history tells us it is inevitable, that it is the only possible basis for an ideology at this point. On the other hand, I *am* claiming that *some* ideology that incorporates a vision of the good life is a pre-condition for radical change, and that history does indeed show this. So, one of the first steps is to develop such an ideology, not simply as an exercise in fantasy, but as a guide to action.

Insiders and outsiders will need to work with each other on this: the insiders on their own will be too comfortable with the status quo, too cautious about what is or is not possible; the outsiders on their own will not know enough about how the world works to translate idealism into action. An ideology, remember, is not just an ideal, is it also a set of ideas about how the world works. The point about flourishing is not just that it is agreeable—that is obvious—but that thinking about how to increase it is a useful guide to action, and can help us address the big five problems. We need either to expand and develop this idea, or to come up with an alternative. Simply to be against the system is not enough, and simply to be in favour of the system and incrementally improving it is not enough. Above all, it not enough to say 'one day we will'. To abandon ideology *now* is to choose not to shape the future, and to leave the field to those who will.

I have also argued that planning and redistribution are the twin pillars of future policy. The approach I have set out is an outline—this is a book, not a manifesto or a think tank report. Whether or not the categories I have used turn out to be helpful, long-term policy planning of the kind described certainly needs to happen if we are to shape the future, whether this takes place in government, political parties, think tanks or academia. To some extent it does already, but the connections between the different kinds of organisation need to be strengthened, and in particular insiders and outsiders need to challenge each other: the insiders will need to ask 'what will we need to do to make this work?' and the outsiders will need to ask 'how will what you do make any difference to us?' (forming these connections is one of the things that the new organisation referred to on page 211 promises to do).

The third area of action I have covered is structural change, principally in the investment system, although I also touched on corporate governance, international institutions, public engagement of different types and trade unions. Changes to the investment system are, not surprisingly, critical to changing capitalism, and, fortunately, it is the area where change seems most likely to happen. The conditions are ripe, but progressive politicians need to pay more attention than they have done hitherto. They need to conduct detailed and challenging discussions with those in the financial world who are either proposing change, or are at least supportive. It is shocking that the politicians who are most critical of capitalism allow the Jacob Rees-Moggs of this world (Rees-Mogg is a right-wing Conservative who is also an investment manager) to be seen as the investment experts amongst politicians. This is where outsiders can help insiders most obviously: radicals can put pressure on politicians to take this part of the agenda seriously. They can also ensure that the agenda does not end up confined to tedious and marginal regulatory change of a kind that no-one outside the industry cares about.

In all three areas—ideology, policy and structure—insiders and outsiders need to work together. It is this dynamic that will give the dissident insiders the confidence and power to effect change. In due course they will join forces with some outsiders to form the kind of counter-elite that can drive change. Those at the centre of things can do the most, but it is not necessary to be at the centre of things. Individuals can say what they think and take part in debate in a whole range of fora, more so now than ever before, and in this way influence those who *are* at the centre of things. And sometimes they can do things for themselves as well.

NOTES

i. Michael Woolcock, 'Social Capital and Economic Development: Toward a Theoretical Synthesis and Policy Framework,' *Theory and Society* (1998, Vol. 27, pp. 151–208).

ii. Crane Brinton, *The Anatomy of Revolution* (1938, revised edition 1965), p. 46.

Appendix: Well-being Evidence Relevant to Economic Policy

The World Database of Happiness (https://worlddatabaseofhappiness.eur. nl/) now has almost 15,000 findings about the conditions which tend to be associated with more or less well-being. This Appendix is not even remotely a summary of this database. Instead, it gives a little more detail about the findings about the relative importance of growth set out in Chapter 3. It is intended to give the reader a flavour of the evidence, no more.

Stability and Security

The importance of stability and security, as opposed to growth, is evident in several sets of facts:-

Unemployment

- Unemployment is very bad for well-being, much worse than the associated loss of income.[i] Furthermore, the unemployed do not adapt to their circumstances in the way that those who gain or suffer income changes generally do—the impacts just described are long lasting (or, if they do adapt, the long-term unemployed suffer additional harms over time).[ii]

© The Editor(s) (if applicable) and The Author(s) 2019
C. Seaford, *Why Capitalists Need Communists,*
Wellbeing in Politics and Policy,
https://doi.org/10.1007/978-3-319-98755-2

- High levels of unemployment are associated with loss of well-being amongst the employed, presumably because they create fear of unemployment.[iii]

Insecure Employment

- Insecure employment is very bad for well-being. Indeed, the average impact on life satisfaction when measured on a scale of 1–10 of moving from secure to insecure employment is one half of the impact of moving from secure employment to unemployment.[iv]
- Job security is the job feature most commonly cited by employees as desirable.[v]
- Casual workers enjoy lower levels of well-being than full-time workers.[vi]
- Casual work is damaging to men's mental health and women's life satisfaction.[vii]

Personal Finances

- Loss of income damages well-being significantly more than a comparable gain enhances it.[viii]
- Levels of wealth, and the security associated with wealth, are more strongly associated with levels of well-being than are levels of income.[ix]
- Short-term debt, such as credit card debt or payday loan debt, has a negative effect on well-being over and above the associated poverty. However, longer-term debt, such as mortgages or debts taken out to invest in assets, does not have a negative impact on life satisfaction.[x]

The Economy as a Whole

- Well-being is negatively associated with very high growth rates, presumably because of the disruption that almost always accompanies very high growth.[xi]
- Inflation is also negatively associated with well-being, although the overall impact of inflation is significantly less than the impact of unemployment; volatile inflation rates are worse than steady inflation rates.[xii]

EQUALITY AND GROWTH

The extent to which *£1 is worth more to a poor person than a rich person* varies with the measure of well-being used and the country.[xiii] At the time of writing, the study based on the largest data set was conducted in 2010 in the US, with over 450,000 respondents.[xiv] This showed that when well-being is defined in terms of affect (positive feelings and a relative absence of negative feelings), increases in household income have no impact on well-being above $75,000 (this is an average across households). In addition there is a clear inflection point in the curve at around $50,000 where the marginal impact of an extra dollar falls sharply, suggesting that income may be relatively unimportant above this level (relatively as compared with, say, quality of personal relationships, social capital or the local environment). However, when the well-being score is defined as an assessment of one's life as compared with the best possible life, the study picked up no real limits to the impact of more money (at least up to its top income category of above $150,000) although there are still, as one would expect, declining marginal returns.

This kind of result does not in itself show that addressing inequality is always more important than raising average or median incomes: if the affect measure is used, there is quite a long way to go, even in the US, before the median income reaches $75,000 and growth *could* be an easier way of reaching this target than redistribution (it seems unlikely, but you would have to present additional arguments to show that this was not the case). The result does, however, reinforce the traditional diminishing returns argument for at least considering more redistribution, showing as it does just how much the returns diminish—that is to zero.

The importance of *relative income* is one explanation of the 'Easterlin paradox,' named after the academic who identified it,[xv] and is supported by a large number of studies.[xvi] This contrasts the positive, albeit declining, relationship between income and well-being, evident in the study just cited, and time series data which suggest that in the UK, the USA and some other developed countries, well-being[1] has not risen at all, or risen very weakly over the last 30–50 years despite substantial increases in average disposable incomes and despite the fact that most incomes in

---

[1] Measured in terms of life satisfaction or self-assessment of overall happiness.

these countries are below the point at which further increases have no or little impact when measured at a given point in time. The paradox is sometimes misstated, even by experts in the field, and the assertion made that rising GDP per capita, as opposed to rising average incomes, has had no positive impact on well-being. However, generally this finding only holds after controlling for variables such as health that are themselves influenced by GDP. The USA is an exception in this case—the finding holds without controlling for these variables, perhaps because the health-care system has been so dysfunctional that rising GDP has not been associated with improved health levels in the way that it has in other countries, with similar considerations applying to factors such as crime, leisure time and so on. In most countries, though, GDP matters but not because of its impact on disposable income.

To the extent that this explanation is true, rising average disposable income does not increase the well-being of anyone other than those right at the bottom of the income distribution (assuming, contrary to the facts, that they get their share of the proceeds). This weakens the argument for inequality on the grounds that it is needed to increase the size of the cake. It does not eliminate the argument though, first because the relative income effect is probably only part of the Easterlin paradox story, and in any case incentives are needed to avoid reductions in living standards, economic instability and unemployment, all of which, as we have seen, are damaging to well-being.

The relative income explanation of the Easterlin paradox is in some ways counter-intuitive. It seems to run against the common-sense feeling that having a bit more money, in absolute as well as relative terms, may increase opportunities for the kinds of activities that encourage fulfilment and happiness (pursuing a hobby, having friends to stay, going on holiday, etc.) or remove some of the obstacles (poor childcare facilities, poor medical care, poor transport, the daily struggle for survival). In fact, when analysed it turns out that many of these increased opportunities result from increased relative income, because the kinds of goods and services they depend on don't get more plentiful or cheaper as a result of productivity increases and general rises in disposable incomes. Since reducing inequality tends to increase most people's relative income, it turns out that the way to make lives better is often to reduce inequality after all, not to stimulate growth.

The Easterlin paradox is sometimes put down to measurement error, peculiarities of the way life satisfaction is measured in surveys. People judge their lives using a frame of reference which moves with time: as life gets better they judge it against a higher standard, and so it never scores higher; in any case the scale is bounded (1–10) and therefore the score cannot get that much higher. This might be convincing if all time series showed static average scores, but they don't: in some countries there have been very sharp increases in life satisfaction as average incomes have increased. Measurement error does not explain the variations that exist between different countries.

GROWTH AND OTHER OBJECTIVES

A second explanation of the Easterlin paradox is the possibility that in the societies studied there have been negative influences on life satisfaction that have counteracted the positive impact of higher incomes. There is evidence that some of the most likely candidates for these influences, such as the sharply increased social isolation in the USA[xvii] or increased workplace stress, are associated with rising incomes. This would suggest not that rising absolute incomes are valueless (which simply relying on the relative income explanation would do), but that the value of rising incomes delivered in the way that they have been may be reduced or cancelled out by side effects. This is a strong candidate, because the time series data vary between developed countries: the paradox does not appear to apply to Italy, for example, to the extent that it applies to the UK, and perhaps Italy has not suffered the negative side-effects of growth to the extent that the UK has. The lesson in this case is not that reducing inequality is a better way of increasing well-being than growth, but that growth should never be an objective unless its damaging side effects can be monitored and managed. It is also, as argued in Chapter 3, that human relations rather than consumption should be the primary focus of economic policy.

NOTES

i. Paul Dolan, Tessa Peasgood and Mathew White, *Review of Research on the Influences on Personal Well-being and Application to Policy Making. Final Report for Defra* (2006), pp. 49, 51; Andrew Clark, 'Work, Jobs and Well-being Across the Millennium,' in Ed Diener, John Helliwell, and Daniel Kahneman (eds.), *International Differences in Well-being* (2010).
ii. Ibid.
iii. Andrew Clark, 'Work, Jobs and Well-being Across the Millennium,' in Ed Diener, John Helliwell, and Daniel Kahneman (eds.), *International Differences in Well-being* (2010).

iv. Saamah Abdallah, Laura Stoll, Franz Eiffe, *Quality of Life in Europe: Subjective Well-being* (Eurofound, 2013).

v. Andrew Clark, 'Work, Jobs and Well-being Across the Millennium,' in Ed Diener, John Helliwell, and Daniel Kahneman (eds.), *International Differences in Well-being* (2010).

vi. Paul Dolan, Tessa Peasgood and Mathew White, *Review of Research on the Influences on Personal Well-being and Application to Policy Making. Final Report for Defra* (2006), p. 50.

vii. Ibid., p. 49; Andrew Clark, 'Work, Jobs and Well-being Across the Millennium,' in Ed Diener, John Helliwell, and Daniel Kahneman (eds.), *International Differences in Well-being* (2010).

viii. For example see Daniel Kahneman and Amos Tversky (eds.), *Choices, Values and Frames* (2000).

ix. Paul Dolan, Tessa Peasgood and Mathew White, *Review of Research on the Influences on Personal Well-being and Application to Policy Making. Final Report for Defra* (2006), p. 42.

x. Ibid., p. 42.

xi. Eduardo Lora and Juan Camilo Chaparro, *Understanding Quality of Life in Latin America and the Caribbean* (2009).

xii. Paul Dolan, Tessa Peasgood and Mathew White, *Review of Research on the Influences on Personal Well-being and Application to Policy Making. Final Report for Defra* (2006), p. 60.

xiii. Laura Stoll, Juliet Michaelson and Charles Seaford, *Well-being Evidence for Policy: A Review* (NEF 2012), section 1.1. Evidence cited there includes R. Layard, G. Mayraz and S. Nickell, 'The Marginal Utility of Income,' *Journal of Public Economics* (2008, Vol. 92, pp. 1846–1857).

xiv. Daniel Kahneman and Angus Deaton (2010), 'High Income Improves Evaluation of Life but Not Emotional Well-being,' *Proceedings of the National Academy of Sciences of the United States of America* (2010, Vol. 107: 38, pp. 16489–16493).

xv. Richard Easterlin, 'Will Raising the Incomes of All Increase the Happiness of All?' *Journal of Economic Behavior and Organization* (1995, Vol. 27: 1, pp. 35–47).

xvi. For a review of some of this evidence, see Laura Stoll, Juliet Michaelson and Charles Seaford, *Well-Being Evidence for Policy: A Review* (NEF, 2012), section 1.1, Paragraph 6.

xvii. Stefano Bartolini and Ennio Bilancini, 'If Not only GDP, What Else? Using Relational Goods to Predict the Trends of Subjective Well-being,' *International Review of Economics* (2010, Vol. 57, pp. 199–213). Between 1984 and 2004 the number of Americans with 'no one to talk to' rose from 8% to 24%.

INDEX

240   INDEX

Printed by Printforce, the Netherlands